Queering the Shakespeare Film

Queering the Shakespeare Film

Gender Trouble, Gay Spectatorship and Male Homoeroticism

Anthony Guy Patricia

THE ARDEN SHAKESPEARE
LONDON • NEW YORK • OXFORD • NEW DELHI • SYDNEY

THE ARDEN SHAKESPEARE
Bloomsbury Publishing Plc
50 Bedford Square, London, WC1B 3DP, UK
1385 Broadway, New York, NY 10018, USA

BLOOMSBURY, THE ARDEN SHAKESPEARE and the Arden Shakespeare logo are trademarks of Bloomsbury Publishing Plc

First published in Great Britain 2017
This paperback edition first published 2019

Copyright © Anthony Guy Patricia, 2017, 2019

Anthony Guy Patricia has asserted his right under the Copyright, Designs and Patents Act, 1988, to be identified as the author of this work.

For legal purposes the Acknowledgements on pp. xiii–xv constitute an extension of this copyright page.

Cover design: Irene Martinez Costa
Cover image: Imogen Stubbs as Viola and Toby Stephens as Orsino, *Twelfth Night: or What You Will* (1996) directed by Trevor Nunn
© Renaissance Films / AF archive / Alamy Stock Photo

All rights reserved. No part of this publication may be reproduced or transmitted in any form or by any means, electronic or mechanical, including photocopying, recording, or any information storage or retrieval system, without prior permission in writing from the publishers.

Bloomsbury Publishing Plc does not have any control over, or responsibility for, any third-party websites referred to or in this book. All internet addresses given in this book were correct at the time of going to press. The author and publisher regret any inconvenience caused if addresses have changed or sites have ceased to exist, but can accept no responsibility for any such changes.

A catalogue record for this book is available from the British Library.

A catalog record for this book is available from the Library of Congress.

ISBN: HB: 978-1-4742-3703-1
PB: 978-1-350-08446-9
ePDF: 978-1-4742-3705-5
ePub: 978-1-4742-3704-8

Typeset by Fakenham Prepress Solutions, Fakenham, Norfolk NR21 8NN

To find out more about our authors and books visit www.bloomsbury.com and sign up for our newsletters.

For my parents, Richard and Margaret Patricia; my cousin, Savannah Hall; and my mentor and friend, Evelyn Gajowski

CONTENTS

List of Illustrations ix
Acknowledgements xiii
Introduction: The presence of the queer in the Shakespeare film xvii

1. Max Reinhardt and William Dieterle's *A Midsummer Night's Dream* and the queer problematics of gender, sodomy, marriage and masculinity 1
2. The queer director, gay spectatorship and three cinematic productions of Shakespeare's 'straightest' play – *Romeo and Juliet* 41
3. The visual poetics of gender trouble in Trevor Nunn's *Twelfth Night*, Baz Luhrmann's *Romeo + Juliet* and Michael Hoffman's *William Shakespeare's A Midsummer Night's Dream* 89

4 Screening the male homoerotics of Shakespearean romantic comedy on film in Michael Radford's *The Merchant of Venice* and Trevor Nunn's *Twelfth Night* 135

5 'I am your own forever': Iago, queer self-fashioning and the cinematic *Othello*s of Orson Welles and Oliver Parker 181

Conclusion: Queering the Shakespeare film in the early twenty-first century 213
Notes 221
Bibliography 249
Index 259

LIST OF ILLUSTRATIONS

Figure 1   A downcast Hippolyta (Verree Teasdale) with a black snake wrapped around her bosom, shoulders and arms. *A Midsummer Night's Dream*, dir. Max Reinhardt and William Dieterle, 1935. 5

Figure 2   Demetrius (Ross Alexander) and Lysander (Dick Powell) falling into each other's arms. *A Midsummer Night's Dream*, dir. Max Reinhardt and William Dieterle, 1935. 34

Figure 3   From left to right, Mercutio (John Barrymore), Benvolio (Reginald Denny) with strategically placed sporran at his waist, Romeo (Leslie Howard) and Tybalt (Basil Rathbone) brawling in the streets of Verona. *Romeo and Juliet,* dir. George Cukor, 1936. 48

Figure 4   Mercutio (John Barrymore), centre, with a large gold hoop earring clearly visible in his left ear. *Romeo and Juliet*, dir. George Cukor, 1936. 50

Figure 5   Romeo (Leonard Whiting), in tights, attempting to reason with Tybalt (Michael York), in tights and with his back to the audience/camera. Both are surrounded by a cadre of Montagues and Capulets in *Romeo and Juliet*, dir. Franco Zeffirelli, 1968. 57

Figure 6   Romeo (Leonard Whiting) and Juliet (Olivia Hussey) in bed after consummating their marriage in *Romeo and Juliet*, dir. Franco Zeffirelli, 1968. 67

Figure 7   Left to right: Juliet/Glenn (Matt Doyle) and Romeo/Sam (Seth Numrich) sharing their first kiss. *Private Romeo*, dir. Alan Brown, 2011. 80

Figure 8	Glenn (Matt Doyle) on the top, and Sam (Seth Numrich) on the bottom, alive, smiling and very much in love after their performance of Romeo and Juliet's death scene (5.3). *Private Romeo*, dir. Alan Brown, 2011.	83
Figure 9	Imogen Stubbs as Viola before her transformation into the boy Cesario in *Twelfth Night*, dir. Trevor Nunn, 1996.	93
Figure 10	Imogen Stubbs as Viola after her transformation into the boy Cesario in *Twelfth Night*, dir. Trevor Nunn, 1996.	94
Figure 11	Duke Orsino (Toby Stephens) and his servant, the young man known by one and all as Cesario (Imogen Stubbs), about to kiss one another in *Twelfth Night*, dir. Trevor Nunn, 1996.	102
Figure 12	Romeo's best friend Mercutio's (Harold Perrineau) title card. *William Shakespeare's Romeo + Juliet*, dir. Baz Luhrmann, 1996.	108
Figure 13	Romeo (Leonardo DiCaprio) cradling his dead best friend Mercutio (Harrold Perrineau) in his arms. *Romeo + Juliet*, dir. Baz Luhrmann, 1996.	118
Figure 14	Francis Flute (Sam Rockwell), with a genuinely innocent smile on his face, moments before being cast by Peter Quince (Roger Rees) as Thisbe. *William Shakespeare's A Midsummer Night's Dream*, dir. Michael Hoffman, 1999.	121
Figure 15	Flute as Thisbe (Sam Rockwell), sans wig, preparing to die so that he/she can be with his/her beloved Pyramus (Kevin Kline) in *William Shakespeare's A Midsummer Night's Dream*, dir. Michael Hoffman, 1999.	128
Figure 16	Bassanio (Joseph Fiennes) kissing Antonio (Jeremy Irons) in Antonio's bedroom in *William Shakespeare's The Merchant of Venice*, dir. Michael Radford, 2004.	148

LIST OF ILLUSTRATIONS

Figure 17   Antonio (Jeremy Irons) 'catching' Bassanio's (Joseph Fiennes) kiss and holding it to his lips in *William Shakespeare's The Merchant of Venice*, dir. Michael Radford, 2004. 150

Figure 18   A compassionate and adoring Antonio (Nicholas Farrell) attempting to comfort an extremely distraught Sebastian (Stephen Mackintosh) in *Twelfth Night*, dir. Trevor Nunn, 1996. 164

Figure 19   A thrilled Sebastian (Stephen Mackintosh) and an equally happy Antonio (Nicholas Farrell) reunited in Illyria in *Twelfth Night*, dir. Trevor Nunn, 1996. 168

Figure 20   Iago (Micheál MacLiammóir) effeminately cloaked and hooded in *Othello*, dir. Orson Welles, 1952. 194

Figure 21   Inside the Cypriot sauna where, a short while later, Iago (Micheál MacLiammóir) will stab Roderigo (Robert Coote) to death in *Othello*, dir. Orson Welles, 1952. 200

Figure 22   Othello (Laurence Fishburne) and Iago (Kenneth Branagh) kneeling, swearing their vows to one another and embracing in 3.3 of *Othello*, dir. Oliver Parker, 1995. 206

Figure 23   Iago (Kenneth Branagh) lying in the crook of Othello's (Laurence Fishburne) leg at the conclusion of *Othello*, dir. Oliver Parker, 1995. 208

ACKNOWLEDGEMENTS

As would be expected in relation to a project that has taken the better part of a decade to complete, I have incurred a great many debts along the way. My most humble thanks go to Evelyn Gajowski for her belief in me and my ideas, for her unflagging support, for her careful nurturing and, above all, for her friendship. I am just as thankful to my parents, Richard and Margaret Patricia; without them, I would never have been able to pursue my education through to a PhD or, ultimately, to write this book.

At the University of Nevada, Las Vegas, I am grateful to Vince Pérez, Ed Nagelhout, Ralph Buechler, K. C. Davis and Philip Rusche, all of whom served as members of my master's thesis and doctoral dissertation committees, the research projects from which this book derives. In addition, Arthur L. Little, Jr, from the University of California, Los Angeles, graciously served as an outside reader of my dissertation; I very much appreciate his generosity and his insights. Ruby Fowler, former Assistant Director of Composition in the English Department at UNLV, has helped me in more ways than I can count over the years, and I cannot thank her enough. All of the staff members at UNLV's Lied Library – especially Priscilla Finley – also deserve recognition for everything they did to provide me with the myriad resources I needed to complete my research and writing. I am, furthermore, particularly grateful to UNLV's Graduate and Professional Student Association (GPSA) – especially to its manager extraordinaire, Becky Boulton – and to the English Department's Research Resources Committee (headed during my tenure at UNLV by John Bowers and Kelly Mays, respectively), both of which funded numerous research and professional conference trips in the years between 2006 and 2014. This book would not exist without either the pastoral or the tangible financial support of both the GPSA and the RRC.

At Concord University, I would like to thank the faculty and staff in the Division of Humanities and the Department of Languages and Literature for making me feel welcome at my new institutional home from the very beginning in August 2014. I am particularly grateful to my colleague Amberyl Malkovich, who kindly read various chapter drafts of this book and provided me with generous feedback mixed with her unique brand of droll, Victorian humour. In addition, Connie Shumate, Evan Painter, Donna Musick, Seth Caudell and Doug Moore of the Marsh Library at Concord, all of whom went above and beyond the call of duty to source the materials I needed to complete this book, are deserving of my thanks as well. Nothing was beyond their reach and their collegiality is second to none. I thank Carolyn Worley, the Division of Humanities and Department of Languages and Literature Program Assistant II, too, for all of her assistance.

Over the years, portions of this book have been presented at professional conferences. In particular, these include: the International Shakespeare Association's (ISA) World Shakespeare Congress (WSC) in Prague, Czech Republic, in August 2011; the 11th Biennial Conference of the Australian and New Zealand Shakespeare Association (ANZSA) on Shakespeare and Emotions, in collaboration with the ARC Centre of Excellence for the History of Emotions (Europe 1100–1800), at the University of Western Australia, Perth, in November 2012; the Fifteenth Annual British Graduate Shakespeare Conference, held at The Shakespeare Institute (The University of Birmingham), in Stratford-upon-Avon, Warwickshire, England, in June 2013; and, finally, the 42nd Annual Meeting of the Shakespeare Association of America, in St Louis, Missouri, in April 2014. I am thankful to the ISA, the ANZSA and the SAA for holding these conferences in which I was able to present on some of the ideas and arguments that are central to this book.

Parts of Chapter 4 appeared in an earlier version as Chapter 11, '"Say how I loved you": Queering the emotion of male same-sex love in *The Merchant of Venice*', in R. S. White, Mark Houlahan and Katrina O'Loughlin, eds, *Shakespeare and Emotions: Inheritances, Enactments, Legacies* (Basingstoke and New York: Palgrave Macmillan, 2015), 116–23, and is reproduced with permission of Palgrave Macmillan. Parts of Chapters 3, 4 and 5 appeared in earlier versions as portions of Chapter 8, '"Through the eyes of the present": Screening the male homoerotics of Shakespearean drama', in Evelyn Gajowski, ed., *Presentism, Gender, and Sexuality in Shakespeare* (Basingstoke and New York: Palgrave Macmillan, 2009), 157–78, and are reproduced with permission of Palgrave Macmillan.

Many thanks to Margaret Bartley at Bloomsbury Arden Shakespeare, who believed in this project from the moment I first pitched it to her at the 42nd Annual Meeting of the Shakespeare Association of America in St Louis, and to her assistant editor, Emily Hockley who, with boundless good cheer, helped me in numerous ways to make sure the manuscript was ready for production. The press's anonymous readers offered insightful feedback that greatly helped me to bring this book to fruition. I am also grateful to the Bloomsbury Arden Shakespeare designer who crafted the perfect cover for the book. The design suits the material herein to a 'T', and I could not be more pleased with the striking image *Queering the Shakespeare Film* presents to the world.

Finally, I am beyond grateful to Mackenzie Hight (Concord University Senior Graphics Design Major, Class of Fall 2016) and to Kevin Bennington, Assistant Professor of Art at Concord University, for their incomparable expertise in preparing the screen capture images included herein that are crucial to this book's argument.

INTRODUCTION: THE PRESENCE OF THE QUEER IN THE SHAKESPEARE FILM

It seems fitting that the Shakespeare film was born not in Hollywood but, rather, in England, albeit in London as opposed to Stratford-upon-Avon. As Judith Buchanan details, the perhaps inevitable development of Shakespearean drama moving from the stage to the screen came about in 1899 when the British Mutoscope and Biograph Company (BMBC) – a subsidiary of its American counterpart, a leading innovator in the earliest days of the film industry – produced a very short, silent cinematic rendering of excerpts from *King John*, starring Herbert Beerbohm Tree. This 'constituted the first film ever made on a Shakespearean subject'.[1] At the time the hope was 'that the mere fact of a Shakespeare film would function as a sanitising and legitimising influence on the questionable reputation of the industry as a whole and the BMBC in particular'.[2] In other words, it was Shakespeare to the rescue of the BMBC and the then fledgling movie business as a whole, which, not unlike the early modern theatre of which Shakespeare was such an integral part, was not very highly regarded by the moral, ethical, cultural, philosophical, governmental and religious authorities of the day. It was also not the first time, nor would it be the last, that Shakespeare was called on to play such a redemptive role in an artistic and commercial medium other than the theatre given the fact that his cultural capital was writ so large in the human consciousness.

Russell Jackson adds to this necessarily brief history of the genesis of the Shakespeare film by pointing out that 'Shakespeare's plays played an honourable but hardly dominant role in the development of the medium.'[3] He proceeds to note that '[s]ome fifty sound films have been made of Shakespearean plays to date [the years 2000–4], but it has been estimated that during the "silent" era ... there were more than 400 films on Shakespearean subjects.'[4] While *in toto* 450 may seem like a large number, Jackson provides the sobering reminder that 'Shakespearean films and other "classics" were hardly a staple of the new and burgeoning cinema business: it was comedy, melodrama, the Western and the exotic historical romance that were regarded as bankable' marketplace commodities.[5] In addition, as the case of the 1899 silent film of *King John* suggests, '[i]t was their prestige value or the power of a particular personality that recommended Shakespearean projects to film companies, or at least overcame their reluctance' to produce what was, and still is for the most part, considered esoteric material for the moviegoing masses.[6] Alas, even with taking into account the valiant efforts of directors and actors like Laurence Olivier, Franco Zeffirelli, Kenneth Branagh, Baz Luhrmann, Julie Taymor and many others, producing the Shakespeare film remains a likely money-losing, albeit an esteem-enhancing, venture for all concerned well over century after the works of Shakespeare first made their debut on the silver screen.

With the strong links between the cinema and Shakespearean drama, studies of Shakespeare's plays on film have not been lacking. These works can be broken down, roughly, into four main categories: guides and encyclopaedias, histories and surveys, topical collections of essays, and more idiosyncratic monographs with a particular analytical thrust. There is a fair amount of overlap between these generic groupings, but they remain useful for delineating the larger trends in this extensive field of study. However, considering the plethora of texts that comment on the Shakespeare film, it is striking that, comparatively speaking, there seems to be a dearth of scholarship on

Shakespearean cinema that addresses the subject from a queer perspective. Whereas volumes of the former number in the dozens, the latter has been limited (with one exception) to only book chapters and journal articles, and those critique only a few Shakespeare films as opposed to a more comprehensive array of examples. This set of circumstances is even more conspicuous when, taking into account that, starting with Joseph Pequigney's *Such Is My Love: A Study of Shakespeare's Sonnets* and Eve Kosofsky Sedgwick's *Between Men: English Literature and Male Homosocial Desire*, both of which were published in 1985, and continuing all the way to the appearance of Madhavi Menon's 2011 collection, *Shakesqueer: A Queer Companion to the Complete Works of Shakespeare* and beyond, queer studies, in the form of monographs and anthologies of essays, of Shakespeare's plays and poetry as written texts have seemingly proliferated.

In any case, since the early 1990s, a cluster of discrete articles, book chapters and a single monograph – all focused on only a pair of Shakespeare films: Derek Jarman's *The Tempest* (1979) and Gus Van Sant's appropriation of Shakespeare's *Henry IV* and *Henry V* plays, *My Own Private Idaho* (1991) – have made it into print and qualify as queer critical interventions on these cinematic texts. These include: Kate Chedgzoy's '"The Past is Our Mirror": Marlowe, Shakespeare, Jarman', Chapter 5 from her book *Shakespeare's Queer Children: Sexual Politics and Contemporary Culture*; Jim Ellis's 'Conjuring *The Tempest*: Derek Jarman and the Spectacle of Redemption'; Joon-Taek Jun's 'Thus Comes a Black Queer Shakespeare: The Postmodern Confrontation of Zeffirelli, Jarman, and Luhrmann'; and Chantal Zabus's 'Against the Straightgeist: Queer Artists, "Shakespeare's England", and "Today's London"'; as well as David Román's 'Shakespeare Out in Portland: Gus Van Sant's *My Own Private Idaho*, Homoneurotics, and Boy Actors'; Richard Burt's 'Baroque Down: The Trauma of Censorship in Psychoanalysis and Queer Film Re-Visions of Shakespeare and Marlowe'; Jonathan Goldberg's 'Hal's Desire, Shakespeare's Idaho'; Matt

Bergbusch's 'Additional Dialogue: William Shakespeare, Queer Allegory, and *My Own Private Idaho*'; and Vincent Lobrutto's *Gus Van Sant: His Own Private Cinema*. Each of these studies offers an idiosyncratic look at Jarman's and Van Sant's films from outside the straightjacket of compulsory heterosexuality. Chedgzoy, for example, analyses *The Tempest* as emblematic of Jarman's 'search for the cultural traces of a queer past' in Shakespeare,[7] while Lubrotto examines the tropes of, among others, hustlers, gay sex and loneliness as they are represented in Van Sant's *My Own Private Idaho* in ways that may well resonate on a queer level with audiences.

Meanwhile, Richard Loncraine and Ian McKellen's 1995 adaptation of *Richard III* has garnered similar critical attention to that generated by Jarman's *The Tempest* and Van Sant's *My Own Private Idaho*. In 'Camp *Richard III* and the Burdens of (Stage/Film) History', Stephen M. Buhler's contribution to Mark Thornton Burnett's edited collection, *Shakespeare, Film, and Fin de Siècle*, the decidedly queer notion of camp is used as a lens through which Loncraine and McKellen's *Richard III* is interrogated as a work that plays subversively with historiography and calls attention to the homoeroticism attendant upon fascism. Michael D. Friedman's 'Horror, Homosexuality, and Homiciphilia in McKellen's *Richard III* and Jarman's *Edward II*', on the other hand, claims that both films depict rather grotesque male characters who derive sexual pleasure through the act of murder (hence Friedman's coinage of the term 'homociphilia'). And Robert McRuer's 'Fuck the Disabled: The Prequel', which appears in Menon's *Shakesqueer* collection, reads Loncraine and McKellen's Richard III as a sexy, queer, disabled figure that manages to give the cinematic equivalent of the middle finger to all things heterosexual and able-bodied.

Other articles or book chapters that warrant mention here include: Peter S. Donaldson's '"Let Lips Do What Hands Do": Male Bonding, Eros and Loss in Zeffirelli's *Romeo and Juliet*', Chapter 6 of his book *Shakespearean Films/Shakespearean Directors*; William Van Watson's 'Shakespeare, Zeffirelli, and the Homosexual Gaze'; Maria F. Magro and Mark Douglas's 'Reflections on Sex, Shakespeare, and Nostalgia in Trevor Nunn's *Twelfth Night*';" Daniel Juan Gil's 'Avantgarde Technique and the Visual Grammar of Sexuality in Orson Welles's Shakespeare Films'; Laury Magnus's 'Michael Radford's *The Merchant of Venice* and the Vexed Question of Performance'; and Anthony Guy Patricia's '"Through the Eyes of the Present": Screening the Male Homoerotics of Shakespearean Drama'. Each of these pieces is concerned in some way with the poetics of representations of queerness in films ranging from Franco Zeffirelli's 1968 *Romeo and Juliet* to Michael Radford's 2004 *The Merchant of Venice*. In addition, Richard Burt, in 'The Love That Dare Not Speak Shakespeare's Name: New Shakesqueer Cinema', Chapter 1 of his eclectic *Unspeakable ShaXXXspeares: Queer Theory and American Kiddie Culture*, glances at the queer moments in a wide range of Shakespeare film adaptations and appropriations (including pornographic versions) to make his case that they are emblematic of Shakespeare's texts having become, by the late 1980s and early 1990s, 'signifier[s] of queer sex *and* of popular culture'[8] in ways that do and do not succeed at, in accord with one of the guiding paradigms of queer theory, posing a sustained challenge to proscriptive heteronormativity. Finally, Madhavi Menon's *Unhistorical Shakespeare: Queer Theory in Shakespearean Literature and Film* directs queer attention to Bollywood film appropriations of *Much Ado About Nothing* and to the smash worldwide hit *Shakespeare in Love* (1998).

In terms of numbers, then, the selective review above catalogues only twenty titles that consider the Shakespeare film from a queer perspective as having been published in the last three decades, and twelve – more than half – of those are concerned with just three movies: Jarman's *The Tempest*, Van Sant's *My Own Private Idaho* and Loncraine/McKellen's *Richard III*. Given the fact that these films have been so thoroughly critiqued from a queer perspective elsewhere, they will not be considered in *Queering the Shakespeare*

Film. Furthermore, space limitations prevent an encyclopaedic approach to the topic at hand; as such, no slight is intended to those who champion particular productions that are not covered in the analyses that follow. However, even with its necessarily limited breadth and depth, this book does attempt to extend the discussion of queer Shakespeare film that has thus far taken place. It does so through close readings of ten mainstream and independent Anglophone movie productions from the sound era of *A Midsummer Night's Dream, Romeo and Juliet, Twelfth Night, The Merchant of Venice* and *Othello*. The films used as exemplars in this book have been chosen specifically because they correspond with the Shakespeare plays that, as written texts, have been subjected to a great deal of productive interpretation from a queer perspective since the instantiation of queer theory at the outset of the 1990s. Hence secondarily this study seeks to link the currently ongoing queer conversation about these playtexts with the burgeoning queer conversation involving their counterpart cinematic texts. Overall, this study critiques the various representations of the queer – broadly understood as that which is at odds with what has been deemed to be the normal, the legitimate and the dominant – particularly (but not exclusively) as regards sexual matters in the Shakespeare film. It is concerned with such concepts as gender and gender trouble, compulsory heterosexuality, the discourses of sodomy, marriage and masculinity, male homoeroticism, gay spectatorship and queer self-fashioning. As such, it embraces the insights, ideologies and explicative strategies authorized by feminism, gay and lesbian studies, queer theory and the 'new kid on the Shakespeare block',[9] presentism.

Chapter 1 of the book begins with the premise that, as opposed to being only a recent development, the queer has always been a presence in the Shakespeare film. This overarching idea is explored using Max Reinhardt and William Dieterle's 1935 production of *A Midsummer Night's Dream*, a movie that, ironically, seems to have no queer content whatsoever. However, when the definition of queer is expanded to encompass things aside from either the homoerotic or the homosexual, the queerness of Reinhardt and Dieterle's *Midsummer* becomes legible. It can be discerned, for example, in the directors' representation of Hippolyta early in the film, who is led into Athens by a triumphant Theseus and appears every bit the unhappy but chaste, silent and obedient woman she must be in a well-ordered patriarchal society. As in Shakespeare's original playtext, the discord evident in the relationship between Theseus and Hippolyta is mirrored in that which exists between Oberon and Titania in the fairy kingdom. For her recalcitrance in bending to his will, Titania is punished in queer fashion by Oberon when she is made to fall in love with the ass-headed Bottom, thereby raising the spectre of bestiality, a crime indelibly linked with sodomy – an act equated almost exclusively with male homosexuality today – in early modern England. The queer also manifests in Reinhardt and Dieterle's *Midsummer* through its subtle but unmistakable intimations of parent–child eroticism as well as in the questionable masculinities of the quarrelling suitors, Lysander and Demetrius.

Exploring the presence of the queer in early Shakespeare film continues in the first part of Chapter 2. Here attention turns to George Cukor's 1936 production of *Romeo and Juliet*, a movie that, like Reinhardt and Dieterle's *Midsummer*, seems to have no obvious queer content. Once again, however, under the pressure of interpretation the queerness of Cukor's film reveals itself in its treatment of age (all of the principal roles are played not by teenagers, but by middle-aged actors) in relation to love; its exaggeratedly effeminate Mercutio; and the fact that its director, writer, set designer and at least one of its music composers were all gay or bisexual – something that, even if only on a subliminal level, impacted the picture that resulted. Jumping forward thirty-two years, the chapter takes up Franco Zeffirelli's *Romeo and Juliet* (1968), a film that from the first was recognized as being avowedly homoerotic even as it told the most well-known, if not the greatest, heterosexual love story in all of literature. One particular instance of this explicit homoeroticism is readily apparent in the camera's treatment of star Leonard Whiting as Romeo, who is made into an object of voyeuristic attention that is queerly and never less than tastefully provocative that invites gay spectatorship. Following up on the considerations of Cukor's and Zeffirelli's *Romeo and Juliet*s, the chapter goes on to study *Private Romeo*, director Alan Brown's 2011 independent appropriation of Shakespeare's play. Though not by any means Shakespeare's *Romeo and Juliet*, *Private Romeo* nevertheless earnestly tells the story of two young male military cadets who, despite society's heteronormative imperatives, fall in love with one another as they act out the lead roles of the tragedy. Aside from the fact that the film, in a way that is somewhat analogous to the conventions of early modern English theatre (there is no male to female cross-dressing), features an all-male cast, the queerest aspect of *Private Romeo* may well be that it ends with a happy ending for the gay couple.

The queer concept of gender trouble – the fact that gender is not an immutable biological characteristic but, rather, a continuously changing performance that all human beings engage in – is the focus of Chapter 3. Gender trouble appears in Trevor Nunn's *Twelfth Night* (1996) the moment Viola transforms herself into the eunuch/male youth Cesario. Indeed, Viola's acting the part of a young man, a performance facilitated by the cutting of her long hair and her donning masculine clothing, is so successful that both the Countess Olivia and Count Orsino find themselves completely infatuated with him/her. Thus Nunn, like Shakespeare before him, explores the queer consequences of what happens when gender is not rigidly policed in accord with normative paradigms. Baz Lurhmann, meanwhile, embraces gender trouble in *Romeo + Juliet* (1996) by representing Mercutio as an 'in-your-face' drag queen. Reflecting the advances made in gay and lesbian and queer criticism in relation to Shakespeare, Lurhmann's Mercutio is also clearly in love with a Romeo who is unable to return Mercutio's love in kind. Arguably, this is why, no matter how progressive it may seem, Lurhmann's depiction of a transvestite Mercutio ultimately fails because it ends up doing nothing more than serving an ideology that demands male same-sex relationships must always give way to opposite-sex relationships, even if that means death to the queer. The last instance of gender trouble discussed in this chapter occurs in Michael Hoffman's *William Shakespeare's A Midsummer Night's Dream* (1999). Here, when Francis Flute is cast by Peter Quince in the role of Thisbe – 'the lady that Pyramus must love' – all of his fellow mechanicals burst into laughter at Flute's expense. In fact, for his fellow players, there seems to be something inordinately funny in the fact that Flute will have to play a woman while wearing a dress. However, since Hoffman chooses not to depict the Pyramus and Thisbe play-within-a-film as a complete farce, as is usually done in cinematic productions, the homophobia that lies at the heart of the mechanicals' laughter at Flute's plight vanishes when Flute, as Thisbe, suddenly and queerly transforms the performance before the Athenian court into one of true pathos.

Chapter 4 engages with the queer topic of male homoeroticism and how it is represented in Michael Radford's *William Shakespeare's The Merchant of Venice* (2004) and Nunn's *Twelfth Night*. These productions were chosen for analysis here because both are highly attentive to the fact that, as groundbreaking textual criticism of Shakespeare's original playtexts pointed out in the early 1990s, the Antonio characters in both of them are in love with their male friends, Bassanio and Sebastian respectively. The male homoeroticism that lies at the heart of the Antonio/Bassanio and Antonio/Sebastian relationships is represented in Radford's and Nunn's productions mainly through their physical interactions – for example, both Antonios choose to put themselves in physical danger on behalf of their beloveds; the couples are often shown hugging and, in one instance at least, kissing each other – and in the passionate ways that each character speaks to or about the other. Hearing and watching such utterances performed by actors on screen, rather than merely reading them in a text, makes their queer inflections all the more apparent. However, Radford falters in his treatment of the male homoerotic at the end of his *Merchant* when Antonio is shown alone and once again descending into melancholy as Bassanio and Portia walk away from him, presumably to consummate their marriage. Nunn (in a sense precipitating Radford, since *Twelfth Night* appeared eight years earlier) also chooses to end his *Twelfth Night* on a heteronormative note. This occurs when Antonio is shown as if he has been cast out of the Countess Olivia's home and into the dreary cold, then walking away from the estate with a grim, melancholic expression on his face. It is reinforced when, as the credits roll, Nunn interjects scenes that show Olivia and Sebastian – as well as Orsino and Viola, the latter garbed in her 'woman's weeds' – in the celebration following their double wedding. The montage is punctuated with a host of images of the two happy heterosexual couples smiling, dancing and kissing passionately. From a queer perspective, it is argued that, for viewers who have invested time watching Radford's *Merchant* and Nunn's *Twelfth Night*, these conclusions are disturbing, especially since, as textual critics have explained, there are other – queer inclusive – ways of ending these works.

In the films of *Othello* by Orson Welles (1952) and Oliver Parker (1995) discussed in Chapter 5, Iago is understood to be a figure of queer self-fashioning. Indeed, he fashions that queer self out of the crucible of forces he is enmeshed in throughout the tragedy in which he plays such a central part. However, the two most prominent forces Iago is subject to are an overpowering feeling of betrayal and an equally overpowering feeling of love, both of which centre on Othello. Welles's *Othello* explores the dynamics that arise from the opposition of these forces through a film noir – a genre that is notorious for its derogatory treatment of homosexuals and homosexuality – *mise-en-scène* that is, in turn, informed by the Freudian idea that male homosexuals are little more than beings filled with utter hatred for others (but particularly for women) because of the fact of their sexuality itself and because they know intuitively that they will never be able to manifest their queer desires for other men in any kind of a fulfilling way given that the norm for most people in the world is heterosexuality. Parker's *Othello*, in contrast to Welles's, eschews both film noir and Freud in favour of a naturalistic treatment of the tragedy. This representational strategy allows for the queer idea that Iago is not acting out because he is a frustrated homosexual but, rather, that he is acting out simply because it is in human nature to do so when people feel they have been wronged by others.

After reiterating the fact that this book covers a necessarily limited time period in the history of the Shakespeare film – the seventy-six years spanning 1935 and 2011 – and an equally limited selection of cinematic adaptations and appropriations of just five plays from the canon, its collective findings are summarized in the conclusion. The study then ends with an expression of hope that it may inspire more critical work of a similar nature, particularly in those areas that had to be elided from the discussion provided herein.

1

Max Reinhardt and William Dieterle's *A Midsummer Night's Dream* and the queer problematics of gender, sodomy, marriage and masculinity

I

Before helming Warner Brothers' 1935 film of *A Midsummer Night's Dream*, co-director Max Reinhardt had staged the play many times in live-theatre venues in Germany and Austria and on the east and west coasts of America.[1] Thus, even though cinema provided a new medium in which to work, he was no neophyte to Shakespeare in performance. The movie Reinhardt and his colleague William Dieterle made offers audiences as much spectacle as Shakespearean comedy: sumptuous sets and intriguing special effects; remarkably innovative cinematography for the time of its making and a *mise-en-scène* that reward careful attention; a range of ebullient music and dancing; and finally, acting that varies from the downright annoying (a young but woefully miscast Mickey Rooney overplays Puck as little more than a screeching primate)[2] to the surprisingly good (James Cagney – a then enigmatic young actor well known and well liked for playing hyper-masculine gangster characters – as Bottom makes the role of the hammy weaver who wants to act every part in 'The Most Lamentable Comedy and Cruel Death of Pyramus and Thisbe' uniquely his own).[3] But for much of its eighty-year existence Reinhardt and Dieterle's *Midsummer* has been both celebrated and disparaged by critics and movie audiences alike. To that point, Russell Jackson provides a solid overview of the film's mixed reception in the popular and the trade press following its premier in the US and UK in 1935. In these outlets the picture was in equal measure heralded as a great success, thought to appeal to only a very limited audience of Shakespeare specialists and aficionados, and dismissed outright as nothing but the most ridiculous nonsense.[4] More contemporary critical assessments of the movie are just as contentious. Jack J. Jorgens describes it as a 'bold effort to interpret and translate Shakespeare in cinematic terms' that makes 'an important contribution to the interpretation of Shakespeare in performance'[5] while Scott MacQueen claims that 'the modern viewer raises an eyebrow as high art collides with high camp' in a production that 'is absolutely bereft of taste, starved for respectability'.[6] There is, as these examples reveal, no single, widely shared consensus on the merits, or lack thereof, of Reinhardt and Dieterle's *Midsummer*. Nevertheless, as only the second Shakespeare play to reach the screen in full-length feature form after the introduction of sound technology to the industry, the production is a significant one in the overall history of Shakespearean cinema. Indeed, given its particular place in the historical continuum, Reinhardt and Dieterle's *Midsummer* proves the ideal adaptation with which to start the larger project of queering the Shakespeare film.

It must be acknowledged at the outset, however, that Reinhardt and Dieterle's *Midsummer*, like most of Shakespeare's original play itself, seems to present an immediate problem as far as the overarching aims of this book are concerned because it is a cinematic text that lacks any obvious gay or homosexual representation. How, then, can it be queered? The work of Madhavi Menon provides a way of navigating through this interpretive crux. She writes that 'if no homosexuals existed in the Renaissance, then did queerness? Thus formulated, the query collapses homosexuality and queerness so that the queer is grounded in specific bodies and acts', such as men who have sex with other men.[7] The result is that '[h]omosexuality and its historical placement [as a discovery/invention of the nineteenth century] become synonymous with the queer' in a way that automatically precludes queerness as a possibility in the early modern period by virtue of appeal to the strictures of teleology.[8] For Menon the solution is one that 'takes queerness away from its primary affiliation with the body and expands the reach of queerness beyond and through the body to a host of other possible and disturbing configurations.'[9] Thus situated, it shall be shown in this chapter that the queer obtains in Reinhardt and Dieterle's *Midsummer* in four signifying registers: those of gender, sodomy, marriage and masculinity, all of which, in this instance at least, have nothing to do with genital homosexuality *per se* in any form.

II

Though grounded in Shakespeare's original playtext, the opening scenes of Reinhardt and Dieterle's *Midsummer* are inflected with a certain kind of queerness, particularly as far as the characters of Theseus and Hippolyta are concerned. This queerness manifests first of all in the style of Hippolyta's costuming and more especially in the disdainful way the former queen of the Amazons acts toward Theseus. Explication of this assertion begins with noting that as the film proper starts to unfold, the trumpets roar, announcing the return of Theseus (Ian Hunter) to Athens with the conquered Hippolyta (Verree Teasdale). The couple walks separately but side-by-side as the throng of Athenian citizens that surrounds them cheers in order to make their joy known to one and all. Hippolyta wears a silver dress with a matching stylized head covering, both of which gleam as the light catches their respective surfaces. At the same time these garments manage to conceal almost the whole of Hippolyta's body, effectively robbing her of the individuality of her gender. It is almost as if she has been unsexed. And that unsexing, contra the fondest wishes of Lady Macbeth, has left Hippolyta powerless.[10] Indeed, she does little more in these moments than stare at the ground with her lips pursed in what comes across as the most severe manner possible. Her defensive posture is only heightened since she keeps her chest covered with her right arm, making it seem like she expects to be assaulted at any moment. But by far the most striking feature of Hippolyta's appearance is the ornamental black snake she wears draped around her arms, shoulders and bosom (see Figure 1). The snake resonates not unlike Hester Prynne's 'A' in Hawthorne's celebrated 1850 Romance *The Scarlet Letter*. Given the rather unsubtle Christian allusion, it brands Hippolyta as a transgressive creature – a serpent, specifically – that has been defanged and compelled to occupy the proper chaste, obedient and silent[11] position all women are 'supposed' to inhabit in Western patriarchal society whether they will or no.

Meanwhile, C. W. Griffin explains that, in four representative twentieth-century film adaptations of *Midsummer*,[12] 'it is often Hippolyta's costume that serves as a potent signifier of her relationship to Theseus, suggesting degrees of compliance with his wishes in concordant versions and degrees of resistance in discordant ones'.[13] The Hippolyta of Reinhardt and Dieterle's *Midsummer* is an example of the latter. According to Griffin, this discordance in costume is complemented by Hippolyta's

FIGURE 1 *A downcast Hippolyta (Verree Teasdale) with a black snake wrapped around her bosom, shoulders and arms.* A Midsummer Night's Dream, *dir. Max Reinhardt and William Dieterle, 1935.*

'looking disgusted with the whole operation' that has brought her to Athens under Theseus's control.[14] The observation is an accurate one. Hippolyta is, for instance, unable to bring herself to look at Theseus when he insists with a condescending laugh that chills rather than humours that he 'woo'd' her with his 'sword' and by doing her 'injuries', and then goes on to proclaim that he will 'wed' her 'in another key, / With pomp, with triumph and revelling' (1.1.16–19).[15] According to A. B. Taylor, these words and

> lines would have met with the approval of an Elizabethan audience imbued with patriarchal values: rebellious and disruptive womanhood, in the person of a warrior queen

who had tried to overthrow one of the oldest civilisations, has been forced to submit to the 'natural' order and is in the process of being returned to the civilised fold through marriage.[16]

Still, only moments later, Hippolyta merely smirks as Theseus is crowned with laurels in recognition of his success in conquering the Amazons and the crowd sings an anthem of praise to the duke's greatness. The specificity of this acrimonious gesture on Hippolyta's part makes it plain that she has little if any respect or admiration for Theseus, much less love for him. In feminist critical terms, the film thus participates, albeit *ex post facto*, in the long-standing interpretive tradition whereby, in the words of Tom Clayton, 'Hippolyta has been aggrandized, Theseus demonized'.[17] As all of the evidence suggests, this approach to the interpretation of these characters is not unmerited, despite Clayton's scepticism of its validity.

Though Clayton goes on to claim that Theseus and Hippolyta's is 'on the showing, a civil(ized) relationship of "mutual love and good liking"' because they are 'social and personal – and military – equals of partly shared background: mythic nobility from different countries of the classical and post-classical mind [about to be] joined in late-Renaissance (or Early Modern) English-poetical matrimony',[18] things are no better between Theseus and Hippolyta not long thereafter when, at the ducal palace, he comes up behind her without alerting her to his presence. Now wearing a black dress with a high collar and a white snake framing her bosom, she is startled out of a reverie in which Griffin claims she is 'recalling her Amazonian past', presumably in all its glory and with its attendant freedoms for women, rather than dreaming of the future, such as it may be, that lies before her in Athens with Theseus.[19] The duke is rather taken aback by Hippolyta's frightened reaction to his unexpected appearance at her backside. But he covers his dismay by launching into his poetic complaint about the interminable passage of the time:

> Now, fair Hippolyta, our nuptial hour
> Draws on apace; four happy days bring in
> Another moon: but O, methinks, how slow
> This old moon wanes! She lingers my desires ... (1.1.1–4)

Viewers cannot fail to note that these lines have everything to do with only Theseus's desires and not those of Hippolyta. It seems in fact that Theseus assumes his desires are exactly the same as hers. As such, Hippolyta responds in a way that, albeit subtly, makes it clear that she can wait for the fulfilment of his desires:

> Four days will quickly steep themselves in night;
> Four nights will quickly dream away the time;
> And then the moon, like to a silver bow
> New bent in heaven, shall behold the night
> Of our solemnities. (1.1.6–11)

In addition, as Theseus speaks to Hippolyta, he can barely refrain from pressing his body against hers and from bestowing kisses on her person.

More than once during this curious exchange Hippolyta makes a show of trying to push Theseus away with her hand even as she also seems to welcome his attentions; this is, contra Clayton, another unmistakable sign of her general discomfort with her husband-to-be. And to confirm the point, though she invests the first three-and-a-half lines of her answer to Theseus with more than a hint of excitement, when Hippolyta mentions how the moon 'shall behold the night / Of our solemnities' she turns her eyes away from Theseus, drops her chin to her chest, and once again stares at the ground in defeat. It is as if she is confronting, inwardly and one last time, the certain knowledge that she cannot escape the fate of becoming the wife, the possession, of the man who destroyed completely her previous, supposedly idyllic, way of life among the race of Amazon women.

Since it refers to what David Halperin describes as '*whatever* is at odds with the normal, the legitimate, the dominant',[20] another word for the discord Griffin explores in various cinematic versions of *Midsummer* like the one directed by Reinhardt and Dieterle under consideration here is queerness. In accord with the dictates of the regimes of the normal – with the normal understood, in this instance, as the heterocentric – Hippolyta should be far less equivocal about her forthcoming marriage to Theseus. Indeed, she ought to be downright ecstatic that Theseus saved her from an 'abnormal' life in a female-ruled society in which the need for men was at the utmost minimum; she ought to be grateful for her deliverance. As such Hippolyta's actions and words in this early part of Reinhardt and Dieterle's *Midsummer* are queer in the sense that they are 'at odds with the normal, the legitimate, the dominant'. She is resisting, insofar as she can, the straightjacket of what Adrienne Rich very aptly labelled 'compulsory heterosexuality'.[21] In this instance, compulsory heterosexuality takes the form of an enforced marriage – and all of its attendant responsibilities, such as house-running and childbearing – for Hippolyta to a man who violently abused her and her people (and then attempted to make a joke out of such misogynistic cruelties by using 'woo'd', 'sword' and 'injuries' as crude innuendos designed, presumably, to both seduce her and excuse his prior behaviour toward her), a man she does not seem to like, much less love, and a man she has not chosen to couple with of her own accord just because the proscriptions of an arbitrary normality demand that she do so. Given their individual and collective resistance to the dictates of compulsory heterosexuality it is not overstating the point to suggest that some queer audience members can possibly recognize at least something of a kindred spirit in Reinhardt and Dieterle's conformity-resisting Hippolyta.

It should be noted, too, that Reinhardt and Dieterle's representation of Hippolyta in their *Midsummer* is an interpellation that, if it exists at all, exists only in the subtext of Shakespeare's play. Griffin points out that a 'major problem attends any discordant performance of the Theseus–Hippolyta opening scene: because Shakespeare's script doesn't show us the process by which Hippolyta is changed, her transformation by the last act [of the play] into a willing bride seems unmotivated'.[22] Griffin claims, however, that Reinhardt and Dieterle grapple with this problem 'squarely – by presenting at least a portion of Hippolyta's transformation, partly through reorganizing the script and partly through a costume change'.[23] By the time Hippolyta and Theseus discuss their impending marriage in Reinhardt and Dieterle's *Midsummer* – something that happens in the very first lines of Shakespeare's *Midsummer* – Griffin discerns this transformed Hippolyta in the queenly style of her dress and in the fact that 'although she seems to take a good deal more pleasure in the thought of the approach of the new moon than she does in that of their (hers and Theseus's) solemnities, she nevertheless does seem quietly resigned to her fate'.[24] In contrast, Shakespeare's Hippolyta seems to have accepted her plight from the initial moments of his *Midsummer*. In fact, she seems to be just as eager as Theseus is for their wedding to take place. That being the case, her transformation into a willing bride, as Griffin characterizes it in relation to Reinhardt and Dieterle's film, needs no motivation; she is that willing bride from the outset of Shakespeare's play. There is no small amount of irony then in the fact that, though designed to provide viewers with the background deemed necessary for them to understand the dynamics at work in Theseus and Hippolyta's relationship, the discordant interpretation of these characters that Reinhardt and Dieterle make central to the opening moments of their cinematic production of the play also brings to the foreground the queerness – as measured, at least in part, by the force of Hippolyta's resistance to the imperatives of compulsory heterosexuality – inherent in such a representation. Arguably, that queerness would have remained more or less unintelligible had Reinhardt and Dieterle chosen not to employ such a specific expositional strategy in their adaptation of *Midsummer*.[25]

The repeated depictions of Hippolyta's resistance to compulsory heterosexuality apparent in the first third of Reinhardt and Dieterle's *Midsummer* come to seem even more queer in light of what occurs in the last third of the film, the part that corresponds with Shakespeare's fifth act in which 'The Most Lamentable Comedy and Cruel Death of Pyramus and Thisbe' is performed before the newly married duke and duchess and their court. Gone completely by this point in the movie is the angry, resisting woman warrior Hippolyta that had to be forced to walk through the streets of Athens led by the one that conquered her and her people. In her place is a relaxed and content Hippolyta who is 'entirely at home in the Athenian court'[26] and wears a genuine smile while walking hand in hand with Theseus through the ducal palace to the places of honour where they will sit as their nuptials are celebrated with mirth and revelling. She now wears a bright, elaborate and heavily bejewelled gown devoid of any accessory resembling a serpent. After questioning Theseus about the strangeness of the tales Hermia, Lysander, Helena and Demetrius have related regarding their experiences in the forest outside Athens, Hippolyta listens intently to her husband's speech about the similarities in the natures of lovers, madmen and poets (5.1.1–22). Though she responds with 'But all the story of the night told over, / And all their minds transfigur'd so together, / Tells more to us [More witnesseth] than fancy's images' (5.1.23–5), suggesting that she is convinced there is actual substance to the young lovers' stories, she also accepts Theseus's explanation without argument, as would be expected of the dutiful and subservient wife of a powerful man. Furthermore, it should be noted that Hippolyta's newfound equanimity toward her husband does not dissipate as the film concludes.

All of this accords with Shakespeare's text. Nevertheless, audiences might well wonder what happened to the irate and defiant Hippolyta that was presented to them earlier in the film and mourn her loss. In New Historicist terms, any subversive qualities she once had have been contained and she has been rendered docile by the dominant patriarchal forces from which she is unable to escape. Yet the queer reading being performed here must register suspicion with the presumed happily-ever-after ending Reinhardt and Dieterle, following the original play, as it were, depict as the ultimate conclusion to Theseus and Hippolyta's story in their *Midsummer*. Even in its cinematic form, that happily-ever-after is easily disrupted given that, in the words of Louis Adrian Montrose, the 'play ends upon the threshold of another generational cycle, in which the procreation of new children will also produce new mothers and new fathers. Within this ending is a potential for renewing the forms of strife exhibited at the opening of the play.'[27] Peter Holland makes a similar point when he writes that *Midsummer* 'leaves entirely open the question of what the issue or outcome of this marriage of Athenian and Amazon will be, describing and blessing the future without directly stating what might or rather *will* happen (*will* because it is already accomplished, already fixed unalterably in the Theseus mythography)'.[28] Holland adds that in 'any version of the Theseus story Theseus does not stay with his Amazon bride ... and the next person on the Theseus list of seduced, raped and abandoned women seems usually to have been Phaedra', whose lust for Hippolytus, Theseus and Hippolyta's only child, will lead to death and destruction.[29] Marriage, in this case between a man and a woman, Theseus and Hippolyta, does not lead to the kind of stability and bliss many believe is the inevitable, ordained and final result of such unions. As Montrose and Holland both make clear by their references to classical Greek mythology, Hippolytus, the son of Theseus and Hippolyta, will engender all sorts of additional strife in his own life and in the lives of his father and mother.[30] Queer interpretation does not shy away from recognizing and accepting the fact that the notion of a relational happily-ever-after like that suggested by Shakespeare's and Reinhardt and Dieterle's *Midsummer*s is, at times, a simplistic, if not an outright dangerous, fiction.

III

Exactly what Oberon wants to do with the young boy Titania is keeping from him is a subject that has exercised critics of Shakespeare's *Midsummer* for some time. Richard Rambuss describes the circumstances as follows: 'What has really set Titania and Oberon at odds is the changeling boy. Titania holds on to the Indian prince, fetish-like, as a keepsake of his dead mother, pampering him in a precious, feminized world of flowers, sweets, and serenades, while Oberon wants to masculinize him' instead.[31] Beyond the issue of custody, though, this is a particularly queer matter where Reinhardt and Dieterle's *Midsummer* is concerned, in large part because the directors opted to feature the child as a character that actually appears on-screen rather than leaving him as a figure that is only spoken about by Oberon, Titania and Puck, but never 'seen', as in the original playtext. This queerness reveals itself when eroticism and sexuality are factored in to the interpretative milieu that surrounds both the play and the film. As Shirley Nelson Garner points out, the playwright provides two related but distinct reasons that explain the fairy king's and queen's respective obsessions with the changeling boy. On Oberon's side the reason is that Titania has stolen the boy from an Indian king and therefore does not deserve to keep him since she obtained him by nefarious means. On Titania's side the reason is that she is rearing the boy because she feels an overwhelming responsibility to the deceased votaress of the fairy queen's order, who was the boy's mother and Titania's bosom confidant.[32] Clayton, trying to rehabilitate Oberon's misogynistic reputation, claims that:

> while Oberon begs Titania to give him the boy, she withholds him, not for *his* [the boy's] sake but for the sake of his deceased mother, her late votary. The loyalty part of the sentiment is creditable but the rest and the effects are not: withholding the boy is made a willful refusal to yield

responsibly and sympathetically to Oberon's begging: it has no evident benefits for the boy, the boy's deceased mother, herself [Titania], or Oberon, now or hereafter.[33]

More problematically however, Garner goes on to insist that both Oberon's and Titania's emotional investments in the changeling boy are charged with eroticism. Of the latter she writes, 'Titania's attachment to the boy is clearly erotic'; of the former she explains, 'Oberon's passionate determination to have the child for himself suggests that he is both attracted to and jealous of him' in equally erotic terms.[34] Though informed by the best insights generated by psychoanalytic theory as applied to the study of literature, this is dangerous territory – this is queer territory – given the prevalence of modern and postmodern anxieties associated with children, adults and sexuality.

Garner's repeated use of the term erotic in her essay is troublesome because it lacks definitional specificity. Drawing on its Greek etymology, the *OED* equates the erotic with the sexual as far as meaning is concerned.[35] But if there is in fact any kind of a sexual component to Oberon's and Titania's respective 'attractions' to the Indian boy, Garner does not make that clear in the course of her analysis; her readers are left to fend for themselves on the interpretation of this point. In either case both erotic and sexual are words that can be further divided into subcategories. These include, among others, the physical and the non-physical, the genital and the non-genital, and the romantic and the platonic. It can be inferred of course that Garner means only for erotic to be understood in its non-physical, non-genital and wholly platonic sense. In that case what she seems to be attempting to describe in relation to Oberon, Titania and the changeling boy is the idea of desire sans either the erotic or the sexual. To be sure, conceding that the possibility exists that Oberon's and Titania's interests in the youth may cross the line between the appropriately parental and the disturbingly criminal forces an entirely discomfiting confrontation with one of the darkest sides of humanity – the abuse of children perpetrated by adults who are afflicted with a deformity in mind, character and spirit as devastating as it is repulsive.

Nevertheless it is one thing to contemplate such disturbing ideas in the comparatively safe realm of textual criticism; it is quite another to do so when concrete visual representations of Oberon's and Titania's erotic desires for the changeling boy are available as in Reinhardt and Dieterle's *Midsummer*. The changeling boy (Sheila Brown)[36] first appears in the film as Puck (Mickey Rooney) regales the fairy in Titania's service (Nina Theilade) with the story that the child was stolen by Titania from an Indian king and that Oberon wants the youngster for himself so that he can be a '[k]night of his [Oberon's] train' (2.1.1–42). Dressed in shiny silver clothing, the boy looks very much like a miniature turbaned raja. Bruce Babbington claims that the boy is 'doubly contradictory; clearly masculine, yet highly feminised; and speechless, which makes him a literal infant, yet a perfectly coordinated child' who 'provides identification for both male (Oberon) and female (Titania) oedipal trajectories within his masculinity'.[37] For the most part, the boy seems to be at home in the forest just outside Athens: he attempts to catch a firefly or two, he is entranced by a group of fairy musicians performing in the tree branches above, and he longs to fly like the fairy children who come to frolic with him in the wood. Clearly there is something very special about this changeling boy; he is at the centre of all the attention and the adoration. He is the object of everyone's desire within and without the film.

When Titania (Anita Louise) finally appears, the fairy queen and the boy run into one another's arms as if they have been parted for an interminable period of time. Babbington describes this portion of the scene in the following way: the changeling 'is ecstatically reunited with the mother [Titania] in a sequence of breathtaking consummation, with the two running towards each other and the camera, so that the audience is alternately positioned with the points of view of mother and child'.[38] The overdetermined effect here is a highly emotional one despite the obviously manipulative qualities that bring the effect to life. As the entire company proceeds to dance its way around the forest Titania takes every opportunity to shower light, feathery kisses on the face of her beloved little boy, the child of her devoted votaress. Before long the fairy queen and the changeling boy are led by the dancing company of her subjects to her bower where she and the child will rest. After placing a wreath of flowers on the boy's head Titania kisses him again four times in a row, once on the nose, once on the cheek and twice on the lips. Then mother and child lie down to sleep in a state of perfect contentment right next to one another. While singing as requested, a few of the fairy queen's subjects cover their monarch and her boy in a blanket woven of fresh flowers, leaves and vines. And for the briefest of moments at least, all seems right in the fairy world. But these interactions between a mother and a child, depicted on-screen as they are in Reinhardt and Dieterle's *Midsummer*, call particular attention to the fraught erotic component inherent in such relationships. It was Freud who claimed that 'sexual love and what appears to be non-sexual love for parents are fed from the same sources; the latter, that is to say, merely corresponds to an infantile fixation of the libido'.[39] In other words, a child's erotic desire for a parent is merely another manifestation of the child's innate desire for a parent's care and nurturing that is part and parcel of the human developmental experience. Drawing on the work of Freud and Julia Kristeva, Aranye Fradenburg describes the dynamics in operation here as follows:

> when we are young, we are in love with people a lot older than we are, and they with us, and we all 'know' it, if not consciously. We cannot become a human subject without taking in how our parents feel about us; the adult's passionate love for the child is also in the child and in the adult she [or he] will become. This love is readily eroticized on both sides. It is not just 'tenderness' but 'in-loveness'; it has a passional quality and is manifested through extraordinary bodily intimacy.[40]

From the initial embrace of Titania and the Indian boy, to the kisses they share, and to the fairy bed they slumber so closely together in, the eroticized 'in-loveness' Fradenburg details in her work is made plain in the images of the fairy queen and her charge that Reinhardt and Dieterle present in this section of their film. Individually and collectively these interactions between Titania and her votaress's son make the passional quality of their relationship readily apparent. And it is a queer imperative to interpret them as such.

Though represented quite differently, Oberon's (Victor Jory) erotic attachment to the changeling boy in Reinhardt and Dieterle's *Midsummer* is no less intense than Titania's. Upon their initial confrontation under the moonlight in the forest a menacing Oberon reiterates to Titania that she alone has the power to bring their quarrel to an end. To this he adds: 'I do but beg a little changeling boy / To be my henchman' (2.1.120–1); then he makes a sudden grab for the boy that is unsuccessful because the child is so well protected by the queen and her coterie of fairies. Once Titania has explained to the fairy king why she will not give the boy up to him, Oberon inquires as to how long she intends to stay in the woods. In a rather sly, taunting, high-pitched voice, she answers:

> Perchance till after Theseus' wedding-day.
> If you will patiently dance in our round,
> And see our moonlight revels, go with us;
> If not, shun me, and I will spare your haunts. (2.1.139–42)

Oberon's not unexpected response is: 'Give me that boy, and I will go with thee' (2.1.143), which causes Titania to flee with the child wrapped firmly in her arms so that Oberon cannot take him from her by force. But when Titania later abandons the changeling boy in favour of the ass-headed Bottom, Oberon rushes into the clearing where the child lies on the ground in tears, and utters a primal scream of triumph as he sweeps the boy into his embrace. With a deep-throated laugh he proclaims 'This falls out better than I could devise'

(3.2.35); then he retreats, with the changeling finally in his sole possession as he wanted all along, back into the forest. Thus what Montrose describes as 'Oberon's attempt to take the boy from an infantilizing mother and to make a man of him' proves successful and, not incidentally, simultaneously ensures the continuation of his vision of the patriarchy.

It should be noted however, that Montrose's summation of the circumstances involving Oberon's acquisition of the changeling and what it means – that Oberon will be able 'to make a man of him' now that the boy has been wrested away from Titania's overwhelmingly feminine influence – is only unproblematic from a traditional patriarchal perspective. Clayton provides the reminder that

> it is not very common for critics to discuss the *boy's* interest ... According to the social norms implicit in the relations between the principals, it must be about the time that the boy would be fairy barmitzvahed and join the men – or elder fairies – if he is ready to be a 'henchman.' So, in the patriarchal fairy culture, *his* interests are best served by joining Oberon.[41]

And indeed, throughout much of Western history, male children were separated from women, particularly their mothers, as a matter of course once they had reached a certain age. This was done so that these youths could be schooled properly in the ways of masculinity as they grew from boys into the men who, among other important tasks, would govern, fight for and produce the foodstuffs and goods that would ensure the survival of their respective societies. The assumption behind this separation of boys from women was built on the ideology that women were incapable of raising true men; only men who had themselves been through the transition from boy to man could bring about such an important metamorphosis successfully. There can be no doubt too that the curriculum for boys on their way to becoming the men they needed to be encompassed formal and informal instruction in sex in its procreative and non-procreative forms. These conventional associations are not at all unexpected as far as Montrose's 'to make a man of him' statement is concerned. But significant complications arise here anyway because of the unavoidable fact that Oberon is perhaps the queer figure of all queer figures in Reinhardt and Dieterle's *Midsummer*.

Christy Desmet notes that the changeling boy 'comes equipped with a maternal lineage [by virtue of being the offspring of Titania's votaress] as ward to the fairy queen that prevents him from being absorbed easily into another Ovidian plot, playing Ganymede to Oberon's Jove'.[42] The myth of Jove's sudden, intense passion for the mortal youth Ganymede – a desire so strong it led Jove to transform Ganymede into the immortal cup-bearer of the gods – is well known. It is also a myth that gay men in particular have claimed as one of their own foundational identitarian stories. Hence Oberon's queer desire for the Indian boy in Shakespeare's and Reinhardt and Dieterle's *Midsummer*s is alluded to intertextually. But Oberon's queerness also reveals itself through the character's potential bisexuality. Following the tumultuous night-time events in the forest outside Athens the fairy king tells Puck as a new day begins: 'But we are spirits of another sort / I with the Morning's love have oft made sport' (3.2.388–9). Most glosses on this passage note that the 'Morning's love' is a reference to Aurora, the mythological goddess of the dawn that makes way for the sun to shine every morning, while 'sport' is a long-standing euphemism for sex. The logical assumption then is that Oberon and Aurora have enjoyed multiple erotic romps together and will quite likely continue to do so in the future. Interestingly, Stephen Greenblatt, editor of *Midsummer* for *The Norton Shakespeare*, adds in a parenthetical aside in the footnote to the lines cited here the following information: 'or Cephalus, a brave hunter, Aurora's lover'.[43] Considering the fact that the 'love' in question is linked grammatically by possession to the 'Morning', Greenblatt's gloss makes a great deal of interpretive sense. More to the point it suggests that

Aurora may not have been Oberon's only object of desire; the fairy king's 'oft made [sex] sport[s]' could have involved the brave male hunter Cephalus exclusively, alternately, or perhaps even simultaneously. It is clear from this evidence then that Shakespeare did not box the character of Oberon into a conventional heterosexual role; his sexual object choices among Aurora and Cephalus are enough to make him queer in a very basic if not exactly revolutionary sense.

Thus a rather heady situation now emerges in relation to Oberon and the changeling boy the fairy king has taken possession of from Titania in Reinhardt and Dieterle's *Midsummer* so that Oberon can make him a 'Knight of his train' (2.1.25), his 'henchman' (2.1.121) and, as Montrose puts it, 'to make a man out of him'. The idea that presumptively heterosexual men inevitably take over the upbringing of boys from women in Western society once they are of a certain age underlies Montrose's thinking. But the fact that Oberon is a queer man assuming charge of the Indian boy's development complicates this normative trajectory in intriguing ways. For some the idea of a queer man being in charge of a young boy's transition to manhood might be anathema of the worst sort. Such individuals may think that the Indian boy's upbringing ought to be left to one like the unmistakably masculine, martial and heterosexual Theseus rather than the to-be-feared queer Oberon who would most certainly damage the child beyond all repair. There is something remarkable then in the fact that Reinhardt and Dieterle – following Shakespeare but punctuating him with specific visual clarity – leave their audiences with the certainty that the changeling boy is going to be raised by the queer Oberon. From a presentist perspective rather than a strictly historical one tied to the mid-1930s or the late sixteenth century, this representation pulses with resonance because Western society has evolved to the point where – as proven by the increasing empirical evidence produced by scientific, sociological, psychological and educational studies – it recognizes and accepts, in most quarters at least, that queer people of all kinds are just as capable of and successful at raising children as their straight counterparts. Like many things associated with queer people, their ability to be decent parents has been hidden from history for far too long. That is no longer the case.

It should be noted too that the eroticism Garner identifies as a constituent part of Oberon's and Titania's individual relationships with the changeling boy is also, as detailed here, presented in stereotypically gendered terms. Titania's interest in the boy comes across as at once intimate and nurturing; Oberon's, on the other hand, seems intimate and aggressive. The words motherly and fatherly could also be used as adverbial descriptors in these particular circumstances with only some pause. However, what ultimately disturbs the rigid male/female binary Reinhardt and Dieterle construct in their interpretation of the Oberon/Titania conflict over the changeling boy is the fact that the king's and the queen's respective desires are in the end displaced from the child and on to another, age-appropriate, though certainly no less problematic, figure: Bottom, the hapless weaver and amateur actor compelled by naïve, but no less sincere, dreams of grandeur.

After Titania spurns him yet again over the changeling boy and disappears into the forest with the child folded tightly against her chest, Oberon vows revenge: 'Well, go thy way; thou shalt not from this grove / Till I torment thee for this injury' (2.1.146–7). He then sends his gentle Puck off in search of the 'love-in-idleness' (2.1.168) flower, the liquid of which he plans to use to bring Titania to heel. The fairy king envisions his vengeance taking the following form:

And with the juice of this I'll streak her eyes,
And make her full of hateful fantasies.
. . . .
The next thing then she waking looks upon
. . . .
She shall pursue it with the soul of love.
And [before] I take this charm [off from] her sight
. . . .

I'll make her render up [this boy] to me. (2.1.257–8, 179, 182–3, 185)

Though not technically needed to understand what is going on and why in this part of the film, it is nevertheless rather strange that Reinhardt and Dieterle chose to leave out Oberon's list of the various kinds of creatures he imagines Titania experiencing an immediate erotic attraction to. In Shakespeare's *Midsummer* this roster includes lions, bears, wolves, bulls, monkeys and apes, as well as lynxes, cats, leopards and boars (2.1.180–1; 2.2.29–30). According to Jan Kott, '[a]ll these animals represent abundant sexual potency, and some of them play an important part in sexual demonology'.[44] Bottom of course is transformed by Puck into an ass, a beast that, Kott explains, '[f]rom antiquity up to the Renaissance ... was credited with the strongest sexual potency and among all quadrupeds was supposed to have the longest and hardest phallus'.[45] Beneath the comedy of this plotline then there lies something altogether darker and more troubling. Taylor points out that 'it is not lust of which Oberon is curing his wife: he is exploiting her sensual nature to cure her of the most fundamental fault of all in marriage, the fault from which all others spring, a wife's disobedience of her husband'.[46] But in order to make Titania pay for her transgressions against him, Oberon is doing everything within his power to create the circumstances in which he will have the 'pleasure' of seeing his wife coupling romantically and, presumably sexually, with an animal rather than another anthropomorphic fairy of her own kind. From this perspective Oberon is unable to escape the charge of being little more than a sadistic panderer of bestiality – a practice so far beyond the pale of 'the normal, the legitimate, [and] the dominant' that it cannot be anything other than queer as well.

Due largely to the efforts of Thomas Cromwell, 'An Acte for the punysshement of the vice of Buggerie', also known in its short though unofficial form as the Buggery Act, was passed into law by the English Parliament in 1533, well into the nearly forty-year reign of King Henry VIII. The act criminalized the 'detestable and abominable Vice of Buggery committed with mankind or beast'[47] in the civil and ecclesiastical juridical realms. This was a legal proscription that curiously enough had never been effected in Europe prior to the early sixteenth century. According to the act, those who committed the crime of buggery and 'being herof convict by verdict confession or outlawry shall suffer such pains of death and losses and penalties of their goods chattels debts lands tenements and hereditaments as felons do according to the Common Laws of this Realme'.[48] Put another way, those found guilty of buggery forfeited all of their worldly goods to the crown and their lives to, it is a safe assumption, the vengeful Christian God of the Old Testament. Where semantics are concerned, it is clear from the text of the act itself that buggery and bestiality are for all intents equated as one and the same within the linguistic confines of the new law Cromwell shepherded through Parliament and that, a generation later, Queen Elizabeth I reinstated (it having been repealed in 1553 under the reign of her half-sister, the staunch Catholic Queen Mary), in perpetuity this time, in 1563.

Although the legal framework for prosecuting those suspected of committing buggery was in place in England by 1533, Bruce Thomas Boehrer reveals that '[d]ocumented cases of bestiality are rare in early English records'.[49] He adds that:

> This is not to deny that real people were tried, punished, and even executed for bestial buggery; they most certainly were. Yet the miniscule numbers of such trials; the extreme inconsistencies of sentencing, which could range from a virtual handslap from the church courts to hanging under the common law; the massive contrast between the heated language of Renaissance moralists and legal theorists and the trickle of prosecutions for buggery of any kind; and the occasional way in which bestiality charges were tacked on to other, more serious accusations as a kind of judicially

unnecessary lily-gilding – all these suggest that the rhetoric of bestiality was in some basic ways more important than the crime itself.[50]

In other words, merely discoursing about bestiality took more prominence in 1530s England than the commission of the actual acts associated with bestiality.[51] Even so, with his representation of the sudden love affair between Titania and the ass-headed Bottom in *Midsummer*, Shakespeare seems to be flirting recklessly with the spectre of out-and-out criminality, albeit theatrical criminality, whether viewed from a sixteenth- or an early twenty-first-century perspective. Regardless, there can be no doubt that Titania and Bottom's relationship in the play, and Reinhardt and Dieterle's film version of it, violates both the word and the spirit of Cromwell's Buggery Act. But if the rhetoric of bestiality – the words, the treatises, the laws, the arguments, the literary treatments, in short, the overall discourse, of bestiality – was, as Boehrer explains, of more interest than the actual crime itself to the authorities in early modern England, then Shakespeare was likely on safe ground where this particular dramatic fiction of bestiality was concerned since it was, apparently, just another cog in the larger discursive nexus associated with these transgressive types of behaviour.

Still, the very real slipperiness of terminology – the tension between the signifier and the signified – is only magnified when modern words for sexual acts and identities are placed into conversation with their early modern English counterparts. As Alan Bray explains, it

> [...] was not until the 1890s that the term homosexual first began to be used in English, and none of its predecessors now survive in common speech: ganymede, pathic, cinaedus, catamite, bugger, ingle, sodomite – such words survive if at all in legal forms or deliberate obscenity, or in the classical and theological contexts from which they were drawn.[52]

That being the case, Bray goes on to question whether a more historically accurate term for homosexual existed during the fifteenth and sixteenth centuries. He writes that '[o]nly two of the possible candidates, bugger and sodomite, were in general use and neither was synonymous with homosexuality alone. "Buggery" could be used with equal ease to mean bestiality as homosexuality', and so could sodomy.[53] So not only were buggery and bestiality synonymous in early modern England, but sodomy was equal to both, and all three could be used to signify what individuals in the late twentieth/early twenty-first centuries conceive of as homosexuality.

But layered on top of this impreciseness is even more impreciseness. Bray reveals that the 'Elizabethan "sodomy" differed from our contemporary idea of "homosexuality"' in a number of other ways also. It 'covered more hazily a whole range of sexual acts, of which sexual acts between two people of the same sex were only a part.'[54] Elizabethan sodomy was 'closer, rather, to an idea like debauchery. But it differed more fundamentally also in that it was not only a sexual crime. It was also a political and a religious crime and it was this that explains most clearly why it was regarded with such dread.'[55] Elizabethan sodomy was also a crime that anyone could commit at any time in their lives; it did not carry the monolithic identitarian force that the concept of the homosexual does today. No one in early modern England would have referred to him- or herself as a sodomite, whereas millions of people the world over have, do and will continue to refer to themselves as homosexual (or gay, queer, bisexual and so forth) in the present and the future. Given this morass of definitional problems, it is not at all surprising that Foucault described sodomy as 'that utterly confused category' in his groundbreaking three-volume history of sexuality.[56] It is an utterly confused category indeed.

So what from a queer perspective can be inferred from this utter confusion about sodomy in relation to Reinhardt and Dieterle's *Midsummer*? The answer is, a great deal. In his work on bestial buggery in the playtext Boehrer asserts from the outset that Shakespeare's comedy 'is patently about bestiality'.[57] He adds that, '[o]n the most immediate level, Titania's animal passion for the asinine Bottom climaxes the play's fairy subplot. In the process, this passion tests the bounds of Elizabethan theatrical decorum'.[58] The same two points can be made about Reinhardt and Dieterle's film, with the latter morphing into something like: Titania's drug-induced desire for Bottom the ass pushes the envelope of twentieth-/twenty-first-century cinematic appropriateness. Movie depictions of simulated bestiality – like the allusive performances of simulated bestiality must have been on the theatre stages of early modern England – make it difficult if not impossible to ignore or to dismiss the literal fact that such activities between humans and other species do occur in the material world and have likely done so since the beginning of time. In Reinhardt and Dieterle's adaptation the representation of the simulated bestiality between Titania and ass-headed Bottom is very subtly done but nonetheless troubling considering what it conveys in its specificity and immediacy: that is the physical manifestation of bestiality itself, a set of sexual acts and behaviours that the vast majority in Western society find abhorrent.

As Bottom sings in order to hold fear at bay after his fellow amateur thespians have left him alone in the forest audiences of Reinhardt and Dieterle's *Midsummer* are provided with a lingering shot that features Titania sleeping in her bower with the changeling boy by her side. When she stirs, her thoughts are focused on the source of the singing: 'What angel wakes me from my flowery bed?' she asks (3.1.124). Her votaress's son is, it seems, no longer of interest to her. Having left the child behind, Titania approaches Bottom; when she is near enough to his ass/person, she cannot keep her hands, or much of the rest of her body, for that matter, off his.[59] Before long the fairy queen swears in Bottom's ear 'I love thee' in a voice infused with breathless passion (3.1.136). Moments later Titania repeats the fact that she loves Bottom and, while doing so, she strokes and kisses his muzzle before embracing the creature fully and then curling up against his chest (3.1.147–50). Thus, in the words of Michael P. Jensen, a certain kind of strangeness is made apparent in the film, and that 'mostly because of its implied perversity', given the all-too-obvious fact that Titania and Bottom are two different species on the verge of coupling.[60] Titania clearly wants for physical and emotional intimacy with the ass-headed Bottom. Indeed Kott claims, bluntly, that the 'slender, tender, and lyrical Titania *longs* for animal love ... This [Bottom the ass] is the lover she wanted and dreamed of; only she never wanted to admit it, even to herself.'[61] She instructs her fairies to fashion 'night-candles [tapers]' out of the 'waxen-thighs' of 'humble-bees' so that there will be enough light for her '[t]o have my love to bed' where she proceeds to 'dote' on him in a pronounced state of ecstasy (3.1.164, 162, 161; 4.1.44). That 'dote' is little more than a euphemism for sexual activity is made clear by Gail Kern Paster, who writes:

> Bottom's languor at his appearance with Titania in act 4, scene 1, his passivity and apparent bodily contentment at being scratched, petted, and adorned, may well suggest the postcoital. We are free to assume that in the interval since their first encounter in act 3, scene 1, the monstrous [i.e., bestial] mating has occurred – an action manifestly unstageable but not unimaginable.[62]

A monstrous mating of this kind is also unfilmable but not unimaginable. But the implication of its occurrence is unmistakable and impossible to ignore in the film. Jensen explains that '[w]hile the scene is handled chastely, they *are* embracing in Titania's bower. Freud would have loved this scene', he adds,

> especially when Titania winds him [Bottom] in her arms and sings to him of their physical contact, then encourages him to sleep. Reinhardt and [music composer] Korngold took a song that is in Shakespeare, but repeated the lines

about their physical contact ['I will wind thee in my arms' (4.1.39)] again and again, cutting most of the others. Adding to the perversity, Oberon and Puck look on approvingly.[63]

It ought not to go unnoticed that the Indian boy, following the lead of Oberon and Puck, is also looking on at the intimacies taking place between Titania and Bottom, increasing the perversity of the moment Jensen remarks on exponentially by invocation of a decidedly queer primal scene.

While the dialogue cited above is spoken in Reinhardt and Dieterle's production, the visuals that accompany them also make it very clear that Titania and Bottom are, both before and as they slowly make their way to her bower for what remains of the night, being united in the state of holy matrimony. Titania's fairy attendants craft the queen a veil and train from the silky webs of the forest's spiders while they also spiff Bottom up and provide him with an oversized sunflower boutonniere for the impromptu ceremony. Even the soundtrack is made to participate in the signifying equation of this particular matrimonial performance, especially when the triumphant, celebratory strains of Mendelssohn's ubiquitous 'Wedding March' can be heard. Given the fact that these circumstances involve respectively a fairy and an ass/man rather than the traditional human man and woman, they demonstrate the fact, as Arthur L. Little, Jr. insists, that 'no Shakespeare play succeeds more than *A Midsummer Night's Dream* in trafficking in the possibility of queer marriage'.[64] Indeed, *Midsummer*'s participation in the multiple possibilities of queer marriage is on full display in Reinhardt and Dieterle's film; this is most evident in the directors' depiction of the very queer, quasi-marital relationship between Titania and Bottom.

The wedding of Titania and Bottom in Reinhardt and Dieterle's *Midsummer* is also queer because it is an event that does not actually occur in Shakespeare's playtext. For Shakespeare, it is enough that Titania and Bottom love each other; in the playwright's view, nothing else is required to authorize their sexual relationship. So then what is the significance of the fact that Reinhardt and Dieterle chose to show Titania and Bottom marrying immediately prior to the commencement of their physical intimacies? The specificity of such a representation makes it seem like the marriage between Titania and Bottom is effected in one example of early twentieth-century Anglophone Shakespearean cinema for the sole reason of serving heteronormative and patriarchal ideological ends. Although Titania and Bottom are not real personages, they are fictional approximations of real personages. They can be considered then as figures that were part of the Elizabethan fascination with what Boehrer describes as the rhetoric of bestiality as opposed to the actual manifest reality of the crime of bestiality. In addition the statistics Boehrer provides in his work suggest that, had they been living, breathing beings, Titania and Bottom likely would not have been prosecuted or convicted for participating in acts of bestial buggery in early modern England. Since it was, as Bray writes, a social, a political and a religious offence rather than merely a sexual offence, it does not seem at all likely either that Titania and Bottom would even be suspected of committing sodomy in the circumstances Shakespeare and Reinhardt and Dieterle present them in where their respective versions of *Midsummer* are concerned. It seems that because they are presumptively heterosexual, they get a pass as far as their other (adulterous, bigamous and, potentially, child abusive) behaviours are concerned.

By cloaking the queerness of bestiality in the banal respectability of heterosexual marriage, even one that transforms Titania into a bigamist because she is also still married to Oberon, Reinhardt and Dieterle almost succeed at rendering the bestial buggery enacted by Titania and Bottom in their production of *Midsummer* unnoticeable, or at least easier to dismiss as unimportant. Elision of this exact kind has been put forth in studies of Shakespeare's playtext. For instance, Deborah Wyrick claims that 'the dalliance between the ass and the Fairy Queen is one of amusement' and nothing more.[65]

In this reading, comedy trumps the bestial so decisively that the bestial disappears. Similarly, Joseph H. Summers insists that: 'As almost every audience recognizes, the scenes between Bottom and Titania do not descend to nightmarish bestiality.'[66] Thus without taking the historical record into account like Boehrer and other scholars have done, Wyrick and Summers seem to attempt to eradicate any hint of the bestial in Shakespeare's *Midsummer* by rhetorical fiat alone. Although Shakespearean film critics have to this point in time not commented explicitly on the subject of bestiality in relation to the characters of Titania and Bottom in Reinhardt and Dieterle's *Midsummer*, it is not at all impossible to surmise that some of them might be inclined to engage in the same kind of disavowals that Wyrick and Summers do in their respective studies. Still, given the fact that the vengeance Oberon takes on Titania serves the needs of patriarchal and heteronormative ends, presumably no real harm is done in these circumstances and, in fact, the 'natural' order of things with the man once again in control of the woman is restored by the time all is said and done between the fairy king and queen. On this point Garner writes that '[s]ince he cannot persuade Titania to turn the [Indian] boy over to him, he humiliates her and torments her until she does so. He uses the love potion not simply to divert her attention from the child, so that he can have him, but to punish her as well' for her transgression against him and his superior, masculine authority.[67] Oberon's actions toward Titania function as a sharp reminder that as her husband Oberon is also her lord and master and that she must submit to all of his whims, desires, demands, orders and so forth – no matter how unfair, demeaning, disrespectful, outrageous or degrading.

With the work of Boehrer and Garner being two on a shortlist of notable exceptions, traditional criticism of *Midsummer* – as a play and in its Reinhardt and Dieterle cinematic incarnation – has remained largely silent on the issues of bestiality and adult/child eroticism, not to mention male and female homoeroticism, that the comedy wrestles with. Indeed, Rambuss notes that the forest in which the bulk of the action of the play (and the film) takes place is a 'dreamscape lush with sexual possibilities: not only the homoeroticism that sometimes encumbers, sometimes oils the marriage machine of Shakespearean comedy, but also child-love, anality, and bestiality'.[68] Still, as far as Reinhardt and Dieterle's treatment of the fairy king, the fairy queen, the changeling boy and the ass-headed man is concerned, a queer reading like the one carried out here discerns a rather striking hypocrisy. Oberon and Titania, the straight couple, are the transgressors *par excellence* when it comes to bestiality and adult/child eroticism. Regarding the former, Boehrer, with pithy bluntness, describes Oberon as a 'king and semideity who acts like a peeping Tom with a taste for animal fornication'.[69] Because of Oberon's spiteful machinations, Titania indulges in the pleasures of bestiality and becomes technically speaking a bigamist in the process. Furthermore, both Oberon and Titania are adulterers and both harbour barely repressed, quasi-inappropriate erotic desires for an underage boy. Yet in previous criticism of Shakespeare's play and Reinhardt and Dieterle's cinematic adaptation of it, neither Oberon nor Titania is held accountable for their individual and collective violations of propriety and/or outright law-breaking. It is as if the fact of their heterosexuality alone absolves them of any wrongdoing. They are certainly not made to suffer like their queer brethren are and have been for centuries for their supposed emotional, psychological and spiritual deformities, and their resulting behavioural, emotional and physical 'lapses' outside of the realm of the 'normal'.

IV

The treatment of masculinity in Reinhardt and Dieterle's *Midsummer* is also demonstrably queer in at least one sense because it does not offer a unified representation of what it means to be a man nor of how men should ideally comport themselves in the world of Athens and its environs. Take, for instance, Theseus, a character that first appears in the film dressed in the manner of an ancient Greek warrior. His uniform includes the traditional short soldier's tunic of the period with a fan of metal strips to shield his waist, as well as a gleaming silver breastplate designed to protect his upper body from harm and which accentuates his muscular chest. An armoured helmet with martial feathers both crowns his head and frames his handsome face, a face that is marked by large, lively eyes, a well-shaped nose and a neatly trimmed beard. The tights Theseus wears only highlight and draw attention to his long, well-developed and shapely legs. Though it may very well push against the boundaries of critical decorum to say so, some audience members might find this Theseus an attractive figure, including those whose desires are queer and encompass members of the same sex as themselves. However, it must be remembered, too, that at this early point in the movie, Theseus is leading Hippolyta – as the prisoner of war he conquered by force rather than consent – through the centre of the city like he might lead a dog on a leash. The talk of his desire to marry Hippolyta in another key, '[w]ith pomp, with triumph, and with revelling' (1.1.19), rings hollow considering the fact that, in light of Theseus's success in defeating Hippolyta through violent means, he has managed to restore the 'natural' patriarchal order to the Western world in which men rule over women given the former's assumed innate superiority, wisdom and prowess.

Following Shakespeare, Oberon and Egeus are shown in the film acting similarly to how Theseus acts toward Hippolyta as regards 'their' women. When Titania steadfastly refuses to part with the Indian boy her votaress gave birth to, Oberon moves decisively and vindictively to humiliate Titania into submission so that he can take the child for himself. And Egeus is so determined to marry his daughter Helena off to Demetrius, even though she loves Lysander, that he is willing to see her dead and buried or relegated to a convent for the rest of her life just because she is choosing to deny him his paternal right to 'dispose of her' (1.1.42) as he sees fit and without consideration of her feelings, wishes or desires in the matter. The actions of Theseus, Oberon and Egeus thus confirm the fact that the world they inhabit is one in which men are the masters and women no more than their subordinate subjects. Their deeds reflect their understanding of the normative when it comes to how relations between men and women are supposed to work in a well-ordered, properly functioning, male-dominated society.

Yet there is another significant representation of masculinity in Reinhardt and Dieterle's *Midsummer* that warrants comment in the present context; it is to be found in the film's depiction of Lysander (Dick Powell) and Demetrius (Ross Alexander). Whether they were directed to do so or chose to do so of their own accord, Powell and Alexander play Lysander and Demetrius, respectively, as foppish, effete buffoons. Often their exaggerated mannerisms border on the effeminate with Powell's Lysander the more egregious of the two as far as such acts are concerned. Early in the film, for instance, as Theseus is being feted by the citizens of Athens for his victory over the Amazons, Demetrius rolls his eyes around in his head when he catches sight of Helena (Jean Muir) waving at him from across the square and then dissolving into tears because of Demetrius's cruel disdain for her. Seconds later, however, Demetrius is nothing but smiles when his attention falls on Hermia (Olivia de Havilland) who, ironically (and not unjustifiably), turns her back on him. When Lysander and Demetrius spar over which one of them should be allowed to take possession of Hermia from her father, Lysander speaks with a pronounced falsetto, waggles his head on his shoulders, and puckers his lips in a disdainful – and decidedly unmanly – fashion. This is particularly evident when Lysander tells Demetrius, 'You have her father's love ... Let me have Hermia's; do you marry him' (1.1.93–4). Indeed, Lysander seems to have no shame whatsoever when it comes to his treatment of Demetrius here; it is as if Lysander is deliberately trying to provoke the other young man into some kind of reaction regardless of what consequences may issue from such foolhardiness.

Lysander is also presented as fond of skipping and hopping as opposed to merely walking or even running like a man might be expected to do when he needs to move about. He is shown gambolling in such a manner twice in Reinhardt and Dieterle's *Midsummer*. The first occurrence happens when he follows after Hermia as she flees from the presence of her father and the duke upon hearing the latter's pronouncement that she must do as Egeus demands and marry Demetrius rather than Lysander. 'The course of true love never did run smooth' (1.1.134), Lysander coos into Hermia's ear once he has skipped and hopped up behind her and has taken her into his arms. Later, transformed by Oberon's magic love juice because of Puck's having 'mistaken quite, / And laid the love-juice on some true love's sight' (3.2.88–9), Lysander is seen prancing through the forest wide as he pursues Helena, with whom he is now completely enamoured because of the fairy king's and his sprite's inadvertent machinations. Toward the end of the forest madness section of the film, and once Oberon and Puck have sorted out the convoluted business that has taken place between the two couples and night has given way to day, Hermia and Lysander and Helena and Demetrius individually, then collectively, pantomime their reactions to all that befell them in the preceding hours. Soon Hermia and Helena and Lysander and Demetrius are paired in this impromptu dumb show. What is significant about the male couple's interaction here is that it includes the spectacle of Lysander falling repeatedly into Demetrius's arms along (see Figure 2) with Demetrius catching Lysander before Lysander can fall to the forest ground. It is striking that Lysander seems to have no qualms about being held by another man and, conversely, that Demetrius has no qualms about holding another man so closely to his own person. Lysander's penchant for skipping, hopping and seeking out the embrace of other men as he does in Reinhardt and Dieterle's film is problematic because such

FIGURE 2 *Demetrius (Ross Alexander) and Lysander (Dick Powell) falling into each other's arms*. A Midsummer Night's Dream, dir. Max Reinhardt and William Dieterle, 1935.

actions fall into the same classification of effeminate gestures as limp wrists, sashaying with hands poised on hips, speaking with a lisp and assuming a falsetto instead of a normal voice in speech, among others – all of which have been linked negatively, in the West in particular, with specifically male homosexual behaviour and identity since at least the mid- to late nineteenth century.[78]

Though innocent in and of themselves, the effeminate behaviour and actions of Lysander and Demetrius remarked on here resonate on a queer level precisely because of the boundless heterosexist zeal, operative from the moment the homosexual was according to Foucault discovered some 145 years ago, to categorize such behaviour and actions as deviant, as non-normative and as unacceptable for 'real' men to engage in if they were intent on maintaining the unquestioned status of their masculinity. At the same time, it must be conceded that Reinhardt and Dieterle's representation of Lysander and Demetrius is anachronistic, although only partly ahistorical. To that end, Stephen Orgel reveals that in early modern England 'the most persistent line of medical and anatomical thought from the time of Galen had cited homologies in the genital structure of the sexes to show that male and female were versions of the same unitary species'.[70] That being the case, the 'female genitals were simply the male genitals inverted, and carried internally instead of externally'.[71] Because both men and women were thought to bring about the genesis of life via ejaculation, the logical extension of this idea was that 'male and female seeds are present in every fetus', while 'a fetus becomes male rather than female if the male seed is dominant, and generates enough heat to press the genital organs outward'.[72] Given such an understanding of 'anatomical history, we all begin as female, and masculinity is a development out of and away from femininity'.[73] Orgel goes on to point out though that the 'frightening part of the teleology [of gender] for the Renaissance mind' was its possible reversal.[74] This very real fear was fuelled by the 'conviction that men can turn into – or be turned into – women, or perhaps more exactly can be turned *back* into women, losing the strength that enabled the male potential to be realized in the first place' in the womb by the formation of outward-facing genitals.[75]

The way early moderns attempted to circumvent this, to them, horrific possibility had much to do with the child-rearing philosophies of the era. As was customary at this time in history, male children were, by the age of seven, removed from the care and nurture of their mothers and placed in circumstances intended to encourage the development of their masculinity to its fullest realization. Indeed, once he had reached that critical age, 'for a [growing] man to associate with women was felt to be increasingly dangerous – not only for the woman, but even more for the man: lust effeminates, makes men incapable of manly pursuits' like hunting, war and so forth.[76] In slightly different terms, what made a man effeminate in early modern England were his affection, desire and love for a woman and nothing but his affection, desire and love for a woman.[77] Some 500 years or so later almost the exact opposite is true: a man's affection, desire and love for a woman are, today, some of the key aspects that constitute the bulk of his masculinity.

With their representation of Lysander in particular and, to a lesser extent, of Demetrius, Reinhardt and Dieterle, most likely unwittingly, succeeded in manifesting – albeit in fictional cinematic form – the worst fears of the early modern English people where gender and masculinity are concerned: a man beset by effeminacy because of his romantic interest in a woman. The main difference between Reinhardt and Dieterle's depiction and actual fifteenth-/sixteenth-century epistemology, as Orgel makes clear, is that the latter gave full credence to the incredible idea that a man's being effeminized would result in the literal evisceration of his penis, which would, because of the loss of the original strength and heat that pushed his genitals outward in the first place, morph back into the form of a vagina solely on account of his non-masculine behaviour, itself engendered by nothing more than his attraction to a woman. But it is crucially important to understand that what Reinhardt and Dieterle also succeeded in depicting in their *Midsummer*, especially through the character of Lysander, is the late nineteenth-/twentieth-/early twenty-first-century stereotype of the male homosexual. This stereotype, and all of its cognates, was built on the idea – explored by, among a number of others, the English sexologist Havelock Ellis – of sexual inversion: the view that male homosexuals were really women trapped in men's bodies that appropriated feminine behaviours in the areas of, for example, apparel, mannerisms, voice control and, most particularly of course, sexual desire for members of their own biological gender. So Reinhardt and Dieterle's Lysander, who takes delight in hopping, skipping and often speaking in falsetto, is coded effeminate in a specifically contemporary way because of those behaviours rather than because of his love for Hermia as would have been the case during the Renaissance in England. And that is a queer representation indeed.

V

Though not as extensive as the studies derived from Shakespeare's original playtext of *Midsummer*, a substantial body of criticism of Reinhardt and Dieterle's cinematic adaptation of the play does exist. A survey of this work reveals that critics have been particularly good at historicizing the film; considering how faithful it is to its source material; comparing it to other kinds of movies – screwball comedy and musicals most notably, as well as to other directors' film or television versions; assessing the performances of the actors and actresses, many of whom were well known for their successes in very different types of roles before their respective appearances in Reinhardt and Dieterle's *Midsummer*; and accounting for the fact that Warner Brothers turned to Shakespeare in order to make a prestige picture that the studio hoped would raise both its cultural and economic profiles. However, only a few of these essays, articles and book chapters direct attention of any kind to the issues at the heart of this study – and even they are rather perfunctory treatments.

For example, Babbington explains that

> Bottom's seduction by Titania, of which it may be said that whereas Titania's relationship with the Boy eroticises the mother–child relationship, Bottom's relationship with her de-eroticises the adult relationship or, rather, diffuses its eroticism within the primal pairing as Bottom becomes an infantile seeker of polymorphous pleasures and Titania loves him more like a mother than a lover.[78]

Of course, Babbington's interpretation remains well within the safe ground of Oedipal epistemology, safe because, in Freud's version of psychoanalysis, the Oedipal conflicts Babbington mentions will eventually sort themselves into the proper heterosexual categories. In a darker view of things, Robert F. Willson, Jr considers Titania's 'idyll with the ass-headed Bottom ... an example of grotesquerie in the play' and by extension in Reinhardt and Dieterle's film.[79] As these quotes make clear, though aware of the eroticism that attends Titania and Bottom's drug-induced dalliance, neither Babbington nor Willson choose to develop their pronouncements beyond statements of informed analysis. The result is that the erotic aspects of Reinhardt and Dieterle's *Midsummer* are glossed over in favour of other matters – quite possibly because of the queerness – the '*whatever* is at odds with the normal, the legitimate, the dominant', to cite Halperin yet again – inherent in the representations these critics single out for analysis.

Finally, Jorgens, in what Babbington characterizes as the first entirely sympathetic contemporary critical appraisal of Reinhardt and Dieterle's *Midsummer*, writes, '[a]longside the innocent playfulness, genial humor, and cotton-candy fantasy in Shakespeare's dream play are numerous undercurrents which are unfestive, grotesque, erotic'.[80] He adds that in contrast 'to the dominant comic movement are moments of murderous hatred, jealousy, threatened rape, sexual humiliation' threaded throughout the film, none of which are normally associated with feel-good comedy.[81] Interestingly, though Jorgens acknowledges the presence of the erotic in the movie, he does not find the erotic in the relations between Oberon, Titania and the changeling boy, or in the fantastical love affair that takes place between Titania and Bottom. For him the 'eroticism of the play has been transferred to still another couple who dance an allegorical conflict between Moonlight and Night to Mendelssohn's "Nocturne"'.[82] In a description that accompanies a still from the film that features Moonlight and Night in the midst of their intricate ballet, Jorgens refers to it as the 'erotic conquest of Moonlight by

Night',[83] a scenario that mirrors Theseus's erotic conquest of Hippolyta and Oberon's erotic conquest of Titania. There can be no denying that eroticism does infuse the stylized dance of these ethereal figures. Given the obvious genders of the dancers, as well as the black/masculine, white/feminine colour motif that pervades the movie, this eroticism is coded, specifically, heterosexual. This is all well and good, but it should be noted that the 'transference' of eroticism from *Midsummer*'s usual suspects to the dancers Moonlight and Night that Jorgens argues is key to Reinhardt and Dieterle's cinematic production of the play allows him to elide any mention whatsoever of the far more problematic eroticism evident between the fairy king and queen and their changeling boy, or the bestial eroticism evident between Titania and Bottom. Thus Jorgens renders these troubling forms of eroticism unintelligible in the critical discourse – a situation the reading of Reinhardt and Dieterle's *Midsummer* performed in this chapter seeks to complicate.

2

The queer director, gay spectatorship and three cinematic productions of Shakespeare's 'straightest' play – *Romeo and Juliet*

I

Since the early to mid-1590s, when it made its debut on the stages of Elizabethan London, *Romeo and Juliet* has been an enormously successful play. Not surprisingly, its success is reflected in the play's fortunes in the cinema. According to Kenneth S. Rothwell, *Romeo and Juliet* has been brought to the screen in various forms some twenty-five times since the beginning of the twentieth century.[1] The first of these productions was Vitagraph's fifteen-minute silent black-and-white version in 1908; one of the more recent films was penned by Julian Fellowes, directed by Carlo Carlei and appeared in 2013. Because they were made by, broadly speaking, queer directors, this chapter focuses critical attention on George

Cukor's *Romeo and Juliet* (1936), Franco Zeffirelli's *Romeo and Juliet* (1968) and Alan Brown's *Private Romeo* (2011).[2] In fact, given their directorial provenance, it is not unreasonable to infer that these movies approach the Shakespearean source material from some kind of a demonstrable queer perspective. Beyond that idea, the guiding principle here is that, even though received knowledge holds firmly to the notion that *Romeo and Juliet* is one of the most well-known and universally admired stories of thwarted *heterosexual* love in the world's archive of cultural, artistic, literary and theatrical inheritances, it still has a great deal to offer its queer viewers and their allies, particularly in its various cinematic forms. This has everything to do with the fact that *Romeo and Juliet*, out of all of Shakespeare's plays, repeatedly shows that heterosexual love is often imbricated in male homosexual love and vice versa.

II

From the moment of its premiere and well into the present era the response to George Cukor's lavish 1936 film of *Romeo and Juliet* has been rather mixed.[3] There can be little doubt that this is not the kind of history the studio, Metro-Goldwyn-Mayer (MGM), had in mind to make when it set out to bring *Romeo and Juliet* and Shakespeare to the screen in the wake of Warner Brothers' release of Reinhardt and Dieterle's *Midsummer* the year before. For instance, though he finds much to admire in it, in the end, Rothwell describes the film as 'a reverential but not warm and vibrant *Romeo and Juliet*, received respectfully but not lovingly by the critics, and ultimately too wrapped up in a high mimetic bardolatry for either Shakespeare's or Hollywood's own good'.[4] Meanwhile, Courtney Lehmann explains that '[f]rom its acclaimed director and Tchaikovskian score to its all-star cast, multi-million dollar financing, distinguished screenwriter (Talbot Jennings) and, above all, its visionary producer Irving Thalberg – the watchmaker who oversaw every aspect of the film', this particular *Romeo and Juliet* 'seemed predestined to make history as the Hollywood studio system's first "legitimate" Shakespearean masterpiece of the sound era'.[5] Alas, this decidedly lofty ambition was not, for the most part, attained. It seems that the main problem with the film was not with the myriad technical and artistic elements that went into its production, which were uniformly of the highest quality, but with the age of its actors who portrayed the key characters, all of whom are young teenagers in the original source text, with, focusing on the two most prominent examples, Romeo aged sixteen and Juliet not quite aged fourteen respectively. Even so, Lehmann writes, 'Norma Shearer played Juliet at thirty-seven while Leslie Howard played Romeo at forty-two' and, similarly, a 'fifty-five-year-old John Barrymore supplied the role of Mercutio while Basil Rathbone performed Tybalt at forty-four'.[6] Given the specificity of this information, Lehmann is left to conclude in what comes across, no doubt unintentionally, as a somewhat ageist assessment, that the 'film was a geriatric adaptation of Shakespeare's tale of teenage lovers; despite the garish sets, gorgeous costumes, and Tchaikovskian musical accompaniment, nothing could turn back time for these would-be youngsters'.[7] Stephen Orgel is perhaps even more blunt in his remarks about the film, which he considers to have been woefully 'miscast ... with a preposterously mature pair of lovers in Leslie Howard and Norma Shearer, and an elderly John Barrymore as a stagey Mercutio decades out of date'.[8]

But another point of view on this matter of age in Cukor's *Romeo and Juliet* is to be found in the work of Richard Burt, who speculates that the 'film's gayness [i.e. its queerness, insofar as Burt conflates the two] is also marked, one could argue, by the casting of actors much too old for their parts, most obviously a middle-aged Leslie Howard' as Romeo.[9] From a perspective that demands more or less complete fidelity to Shakespeare's text, the casting of Shearer, Howard,

Barrymore and several other mature actors in Cukor's *Romeo and Juliet* is anachronistic and remains so for contemporary viewers of the film. It seems however, that Burt's hypothesis can be pushed a bit further since he does not articulate exactly why the age of the actors in the principal parts of the movie signifies, in one respect at least, its 'gayness'. The only larger implication that makes sense is that love is just for the young and older people should not be engaging in the kind of romantic antics Romeo and Juliet engage in simply because they ought to know better after having experienced more of life – its arbitrary vicissitudes, its triumphs and defeats, its joys and its miseries – than mere teenagers have. Love between older people then becomes as forbidden as the love between the teenaged Romeo and Juliet and, much more significantly in the context of this book, as forbidden as the love between two people of the same gender. In this case age itself is the agent that brings forth the queerness, or the not quite (hetero) normativeness, of Cukor's *Romeo and Juliet*.

Moving just beyond the critical assessments and debates touched on above, Harry M. Benshoff and Sean Griffin note that 'films might be considered queer when they are written, directed, or produced by queer people or perhaps when they star lesbian, gay, or otherwise queer actors'.[10] Though none of its lead actors or actresses, its scriptwriter, or its producer fall into this category, by all accounts Cukor, the director of MGM's *Romeo and Juliet*, was gay. Patrick McGilligan, one of Cukor's major (if not always sympathetic) biographers, explains that in the early part of the twentieth century 'Hollywood was a haven for all sorts of artistic people, but for those among them who happened to be homosexual it was a vaguely hospitable oasis in a distinctly antagonistic world'.[11] It is all the more remarkable then that Cukor was able to carve out a career for himself in such a milieu. McGilligan goes on to point out, though, that what

> needs to be understood is that Cukor's standing in this context was unique. There were certain pockets of the

movie business where homosexuality thrived; among the creative crafts – sketch and design, decoration and sets, costume and makeup – it was almost ghettoized. However, at the top of everything in Hollywood, in creative authority, stood the director, among whose first rank there was only one homosexual ...[12]

That first-rank director who also happened to be homosexual was Cukor. As such, McGilligan speculates that 'Cukor must have felt that he had to protect his stature among the first echelon.'[13] He adds that the resulting 'secretiveness had to be partly shame. Even among the most enlightened Hollywood people, the liberal opinion of the era – an opinion that to some extent prevails today – held that homosexuality was a kind of psychological deficiency, an abnormal, perhaps "curable" condition.'[14] In other words, acceptance of homosexuality at this time and place in history was tainted by a thoroughly homophobic stigma that men like Cukor internalized as embarrassment and acted accordingly in order to survive. However, Emanuel Levy, another of Cukor's biographers, offers what seems like a more measured take on these circumstances: 'Working in a highly conservative setting,' he writes, 'Hollywood of the studio era, Cukor was extremely careful ("discreet" was the word he liked) about his gayness. But he didn't have a double life; everybody in Hollywood knew he was gay, and he was never ashamed of it.'[15] To support this assertion, Levy quotes Cukor himself as saying 'I never had any problems accepting myself.'[16] This suggests that Cukor was apparently savvy enough about the effect the mere idea of homosexuality had on at least some of those who were not so affectively, erotically or romantically inclined of his era to make the appropriate accommodations without sacrificing either his integrity or his basic sense of self.

Given these circumstances, Burt explains that the 'usual approach to a film like Cukor's [*Romeo and Juliet*] would be to read it either as closeted or as (perhaps obliquely) marked as gay'.[17] He later suggests provisionally that 'Cukor might be regarded as so closeted ... that his *Romeo and Juliet* might seem not to be marked by gayness at all.'[18] It seems then that Benshoff and Griffin's idealistic assertion that it is possible to queer films on the sole basis of a queer person's involvement in a production proves fruitless where Cukor's *Romeo and Juliet* is concerned in every sense but, perhaps, the anecdotal. Though certainly queer in that this kind of a strategy does not engender anything productive in terms of new knowledge, that is not really very satisfying in the larger critical/analytical context of this study. But Burt later suggests that gayness is evident in Cukor's production in three ways. One of these is the already discussed mature age of the actors cast in the lead and a number of the supporting roles. The other two involve the film's set design and portions of its musical score. Burt proceeds to note that the 'English and gay design consultant Oliver Messel was brought over to Hollywood at considerable expense to give the production a gauzy revue look' and the 'consummation [of Romeo and Juliet] scene is accompanied by the music of a gay composer, the famous opening theme from Tchaikovsky's "Pathetique" (Symphony No. 6 in B Minor, Op. 74)'.[19] Thus as a film directed by a queer man (Cukor), adapted from a play by a queer man (Shakespeare), with sets crafted by a queer man (Messel) and featuring music by a queer man (Tchaikovsky), Cukor's *Romeo and Juliet* can be considered quadruple queer(ed). The problem with the 'marks of gayness' that Burt identifies in Cukor's *Romeo and Juliet* is that such esoteric information is not necessarily readily available to average film viewers, queer and non-queer alike. Though accessible in the archives, interested audience members would need to know what to look for, where to look for it, and how to interpret it in relation to Cukor's movie. So for all but the specialist, then, the information Burt discusses here seems to have value only at, yet again, the anecdotal rather than the critical level given its unintelligibility in the film itself.

Where the cachet of a film subject like *Romeo and Juliet* itself is concerned, McGilligan and Levy appear to be in agreement as Cukor's biographers. McGilligan reveals that although 'he was regarded as the studio's most "cultural" director, in fact Cukor had no experience with, or special claim on, Shakespearean literature'.[20] He adds that if Cukor was 'going to direct Shakespeare, probably something such as the acid-etched *Taming of the Shrew*, a battle royal of the sexes, would have better piqued his sensibility'.[21] Levy concurs: 'A grand-scale production, *Romeo and Juliet* was Cukor's biggest assignment to date, and he took great care in planning the medieval sets and costumes. But the prestige of the literary source – the first and only Shakespeare Cukor ever directed – made him nervous.'[22] Shakespeare awed Cukor as a cinema director, in other words, and not, evidently, in a good way. Furthermore, if Cukor was drawn to *Romeo and Juliet* because it was a tale of forbidden love – something queer folk might well be apt to identify with considering, until very recently, the disapprobation with which they and their relationships have been subjected to in the modern era – no (auto)biographical record exists to confirm that fact. This does not mean, however, that the project of queering Cukor's *Romeo and Juliet* is a lost cause. One of the keys to pursuing this line of enquiry further lies in a set of observations put forth by McGilligan about the director and his work on Shakespeare: 'Whatever his own instincts might have been, Cukor seemed overwhelmed by the swollen prestige of it all. The sets tended to dwarf the actors, and in any case Cukor was not one to let his camera linger on scenery; he preferred the architecture of the human body.'[23] It can be argued that Cukor's preference for the architecture of the human body – particularly the male body – is apparent in a number of places throughout his *Romeo and Juliet*, though, in keeping with what seems to have been his almost obsessive-compulsive penchant for discretion where his homosexuality was concerned, the director is never anything less than subtle in his representation of the male body.

In his commentary on the costuming of Cukor's *Romeo and Juliet* Jackson notes that '[s]ome of the younger men wear small fringed sporrans – not quite cod-pieces – that decorate their lower abdomen without covering the genital area. Their outline is the smoothed-out and idealized one of the male ballet dancer.'[24] In addition, citing a 16 February 1936 piece that ran in the *Boston Globe*, Jackson reveals that Leslie Howard was selected to play Romeo on account of the shapeliness of his legs; it seems, in fact, that none of his competitors for the role filled out the tights the actor would be required to wear throughout the film as well as Howard.[25] What Jackson remains silent on is the male homoerotic appeal these masculine outfits have on those in *Romeo and Juliet*'s audience who recognize and appreciate such a quality. That male homoerotic appeal is evident in the image below (see Figure 3). In the near centre stands Romeo with his sword drawn; to the extreme right of him is Tybalt, who is jousting with Mercutio; and to the left of Romeo is

FIGURE 3 *From left to right, Mercutio (John Barrymore), Benvolio (Reginald Denny) with strategically placed sporran at his waist, Romeo (Leslie Howard) and Tybalt (Basil Rathbone) brawling in the streets of Verona.* Romeo and Juliet, *dir. George Cukor, 1936.*

Benvolio (Reginald Denny) and Mercutio, the latter being the initiator of the attack on Tybalt. Benvolio is the only character clad in the type of sporran Jackson mentions, but otherwise all four men in the forefront of the shot are wearing formfitting tights that emphasize the musculature of their thighs, calves and knees. For aficionados of the male body, of which Cukor was one, such a composition – punctuated as it is by the testosterone-charged drama of a bitter fight – is redolent with homoeroticism since only males are shown in the screen capture, and since it depicts a riotous physicality punctuated by the use of swords, which have long been interpreted as symbols of men's, in this case unseen, penises. In tandem these elements coalesce at this point into what can be described as an overdetermined homoerotic masculine tableau. Queer viewers of Cukor's *Romeo and Juliet* are thus encouraged by the means of artful and suggestive costuming and stage fight choreography, if they are so inclined, to engage in the transgressive act of imagining exposed male flesh being presented to them for their pleasure here and throughout the film.

Interestingly, Burt also claims that Cukor's Mercutio 'is pointedly made heterosexual: he regularly flirts with the local single women' featured in *Romeo and Juliet*.[26] From a queer perspective, there is reason to challenge this assertion. The way to begin doing so is by observing Mercutio's style of dress closely. Early in the film Mercutio wears a large, pearl teardrop earring in his left ear; later, he wears a prominent gold hoop earring in the same ear (see Figure 4). Though inconsequential in and of themselves, these accessories are significant given the gender of the wearer because of the earring's longstanding and problematic association with homosexuality. 'Earlobes, necks, wrists and fingers', Shirley Bury writes, 'are among the chief parts of the human anatomy which lend themselves to applied decoration.'[27] She goes on to explain that, like 'so many innovations in the field of jewellery, the practice of piercing the fleshy protuberances of the ears for the attachment of ornaments symbolic of race, tribe and status seems to have originated in Western Asia. A sculptured

FIGURE 4 *Mercutio (John Barrymore), centre, with a large gold hoop earring clearly visible in his left ear.* Romeo and Juliet, dir. George Cukor, 1936.

slab from the palace of Ashurnasirpal II (883–859 BC)' – a well-known male ruler of Ancient Assyria famous for having had constructed a library at his Nineveh palace – that sits 'in the British Museum depicts the king in profile wearing a long earring with an acorn-shaped terminal'.[28] Throughout the ages, Bury details, 'men, women and children have been subjected to the ordeal of ear-piercing, though the male fashion for earrings has been mysteriously intermittent and sometimes a national rather than a cultural phenomenon'.[29] One of the key points Bury makes in her brief summary of the history of earrings as a fashion item is that from their earliest appearance earrings were not solely for women – men wore them, too.

Ronald D. Steinbach adds to the history of the earring when he notes that they 'were very fashionable for men in Europe and to a lesser extent in the United States during certain periods of time extending from the 1500s to the early 1800s.'[30] Though not, in Steinbach's view, always reliable, much of the evidence regarding the male penchant for wearing earrings in the early modern period comes from surveys of the portraiture of the time. These images reveal that prominent English figures like King Charles I, Sir Walter Raleigh, the first Duke of Buckingham – and particular romantic favourite of King James I – George Villiers and, finally, Shakespeare himself all wore an earring in the left ear as a matter of course. At the time such a fashion item was not unusual for men; it did not as would be the case later in history cause anxiety as far as the demarcations between masculinity and femininity were concerned. In any case, Cukor's costume designers were likely aware of the fashion trends of the period they were asked to depict in *Romeo and Juliet*. This is enough to explain why Mercutio wears either the pearl teardrop or the gold hoop earrings in all of the scenes he appears. Nevertheless, the queerness of such a representation is not mitigated entirely by this concession because, as Steinbach details, earrings became, by the 1970s and onward, and not incidentally in the aftermath of the Stonewall Riots and the emergence of the modern gay rights movement, a signifier of homosexuality for those males who chose to wear them, regardless of individuals' actual sexual identity.[31] Earrings, like pantyhose, make-up and so forth, were for women only; individually and collectively, all three of these items were tangible identifiers that allowed for the necessary differentiation between males and females that society demanded of its members.

In many respects, of course, it does not really matter whether or not Barrymore wore earrings in Cukor's *Romeo and Juliet*. If viewers and critics thought about the subject of earrings appearing on a man – on an actor, for that matter – at all, they likely considered it no more than part of Hollywood's attempt to be accurate in its portrayal of sixteenth-century Veronese men. Today, however, the historically contingent baggage associated with what gender can and, perhaps more importantly, what gender cannot don earrings maps directly on to Barrymore as the gold hoop- and pearl teardrop-wearing Mercutio. Alas, Barrymore's subpar performance is prone to hyperbolic affectation and overacting, neither of which makes for a very compelling character. Beyond that, Barrymore's Mercutio does not come across, as Burt claims, as being particularly heterosexual. Yes, he does regularly flirt with the local women of Verona, and he even goes so far as to bestow a lengthy kiss on at least one of them during the movie. But this flirting and kissing is thoroughly unconvincing. Joseph A. Porter describes Barrymore's Mercutio as one whose 'gestures and wide-eyed manners are exaggeratedly effeminate' and later asserts that the actor's/character's 'persistent eye for the ladies is itself subverted by the conspicuous effeminacy of all his flirtatiousness'.[32] The Mercutio that emerges from these cumulative representations and interpretations is more like a gay man with a large coterie of devoted female followers – a bevy of 'fag hags' to put it more colloquially – rather than a randy, red-blooded, heterosexual playboy eager to conquer the opposite sex with his amorous prowess.

Beyond handsome men to gaze at (though that is not, of course, the absolute limit of queerness), it would seem that Cukor's *Romeo and Juliet* does not have much to offer its viewers who are queer or queer-allied. Burt points out, however, that 'what is more interesting about Cukor's film than whether it tries to mark itself as gay or disavow the marks of its (perhaps unconscious) gayness is the way the film passes as straight so that any knowledge of gay desire that it secretes comes as a surprise to its audiences'.[33] Burt's 'gay desire', in its broadest form, encompasses everything from the mature actors chosen for the roles of the young characters in Cukor's *Romeo and Juliet* to the fact that Cukor managed to provide at least one unbilled and silent cameo appearance in the film for a young man he had a brief romantic/sexual liaison with at some point, as well as all of the other things touched on thus far in this chapter. These are details that Rothwell, Lehmann, Orgel and Jackson do not comment on in their studies of the movie. By now, however, in the second decade of the twenty-first century, contra Burt, such knowledge should not come 'as a surprise to its [Cukor's *Romeo and Juliet*] audiences'. It should be out of the closet and in the open. Indeed, armed with such information, the experience of the picture might be inflected quite differently for all of its audience members. Yet, at the same time, therein lies the value of a queer reading of the film like that attempted here from the remove of almost eighty years. Queer and queer-allied audiences of Cukor's *Romeo and Juliet* in the second decade of the twenty-first century have the ability, indeed, the privilege if not the imperative, of claiming the film as a part of their history – a history that has all too often been elided in modern times by the myriad forces of suppression. Watching a film like Cukor's *Romeo and Juliet* from a queer position is in itself a powerful act of what Jonathan Dollimore has called sexual dissidence.[34] Furthermore, crafting the interpretive response that follows into a piece of discourse that extends that act of sexual dissidence into the public realm, where it can effect real change – particularly in ways of thinking, being, and understanding – by virtue of its very existence, is also a worthy endeavour.

III

Franco Zeffirelli's career as a film director proper was launched with the 1967 production of *The Taming of the Shrew*, starring then-acting giants and off-screen married couple with a decidedly stormy relationship, Richard Burton and Elizabeth Taylor. The movie was a success financially and was also generally well liked by both cinema and Shakespeare critics. A year later, Zeffirelli would turn his directorial attentions to *Romeo and Juliet*.[35] The resulting film, starring – significantly from cultural, aesthetic and critical perspectives – the age-appropriate Leonard Whiting and Olivia Hussey in the lead roles, proved to be, and remains, one of the most successful Shakespeare movies of all time. It also made Zeffirelli a household name and gave him the power as a director to pick and choose the projects he wanted to work on from that point forward. In later decades Zeffirelli would adapt and appropriate Shakespearean source material two more times and craft what Rothwell calls 'a dazzling Verdi's *Otello* (1986), and a thoughtful *Hamlet* (1990)', the latter featuring Mel Gibson in the title role and a host of other late-twentieth century movie stars of the highest calibre in most of the play's other parts, too.[36] Thus whereas Shakespeare intimidated Cukor, the dramas of the celebrated Elizabethan/Jacobean playwright were more than a worthy challenge for Zeffirelli, who rose to each occasion with both panache and a sensibility that appealed – and continues to appeal – to multitudes.

Colour is perhaps the first thing a contemporary viewer might notice when comparing Cukor's and Zeffirelli's *Romeo and Juliet*s. In accord with the respective technologies available to their directors, where black-and-white defines the first film, glorious colour animates the second. Indeed, it is not overstating the case to claim that colour infuses every aspect of Zeffirelli's production, from the rich textures of the buildings and the furniture it depicts to the blazing Renaissance-styled costumes the actors wear that look as if they were made of richly luxurious velvets, silks and other similarly sumptuous materials. Everywhere the eye looks as it drinks in the myriad delights of Zeffirelli's *Romeo and Juliet* it is greeted by a panoply of colour. In the context of this book, the obvious correlation regarding this aspect of the film is that colour sheds a multivalent kind of light on things that were once considered in only black and white binaric terms. Two of those things are desire and sexuality, which had been constructed within the strict-gay-versus straight dichotomy for at least as far back as the identification of the homosexual in the nineteenth century. In light of the circumstances with Cukor's sexuality and how it relates to his 1936 production, there is no small amount of irony in the fact that this wildly successful late 1960s adaptation of *Romeo and Juliet* was directed by a queer – a bisexual as opposed to a strictly homosexual – man, too.[37] In addition, given the thirty-two years between their respective films, it is not surprising that Zeffirelli was able to direct what can be considered, arguably, a queerer version of *Romeo and Juliet* than Cukor had been able to do in the earlier part of the twentieth century.

It is significant too that Zeffirelli's *Romeo and Juliet* appeared at the height of the Sexual Revolution. Peter S. Donaldson explains that the 'film participates in the general loosening of restrictions on the representation of sexuality on film of the period, and it seemed to endorse a number of the values of the international youth movement: pacifism, distrust of elders, and sexual liberation'.[38] Meanwhile, reviewing the movie for *The New York Times* in the fall of 1968, Renata Adler describes it as a 'lovely, sensitive, friendly popularization of the play' and the 'sweetest, the most contemporary romance on film this year'.[39] Though she expresses some concern with the inevitable loss of Shakespeare's language to visual effects, Adler nevertheless concludes that the film 'should become the thing for young people to see' and 'that it works touchingly'.[40] Coming from a movie critic of Adler's status, this is high praise indeed. Aside from superlatives and qualifications, however, Adler was among the first of the intelligentsia to comment on what she terms 'the softly homosexual cast over the film'.[41] This enigmatic and apropos remark was for its time an astonishing observation to make and to put into print in what was contemporaneously one of the most well-known and highly regarded newspapers in the world.[42] That being said, it is important to note that Adler does not develop this idea further. The task of doing that necessary work would fall to scholars like Donaldson, Porter and William Van Watson, each of whom fleshed out the notion of the 'softly homosexual cast', or ethos, of Zeffirelli's *Romeo and Juliet* in a trio of important articles and book chapters that complement the queer reading of the film attempted here.

Donaldson claims that when it appeared Zeffirelli's *Romeo and Juliet* was 'perhaps the most daring of all Shakespeare adaptations in its bringing to the surface homoerotic aspects of Shakespeare's art'.[43] However, he insists that the 'homoerotic side of the film seldom breaks the surface of the film or transgresses the limits of public taste, remaining as allusion, implication, subtext'.[44] This was because

> [h]omosexual desire could not be directly represented in popular film at the same period [the late 1960s] but hovers at the edges of the film, structuring Zeffirelli's presentation of patriarchal violence, charging the separation of the heterosexual lovers with the pain of sundered male bonds, and inspiring the film's treatment of intimacy, trust, and self-reconstruction.[45]

It is important to realize though that Donaldson's assertion rests on a not unreasonably limited view of 'homosexual desire' and its expression in visual form. Certainly, mainstream films of the late 1960s could not show explicit images of men being intimate or affectionate, much less having out-and-out sex, with one another. But there are multiple ways to represent desire aside from depicting sex acts themselves; as such, it can be argued that just the opposite from what Donaldson posits is evidenced in a highly visceral way throughout Zeffirelli's *Romeo and Juliet*. In other words, the homoerotic does indeed break the surface of the film; it does not merely hover at the edges. The homoerotic is, in fact, a blatant and palpable force throughout its 138 minutes' running time. This is apparent, for example, when the male gender and the attractiveness of the bulk of the cast; the specifics of the masculine costuming; the physical intimacy in which the male characters are often depicted engaging; the famous male nudity of Romeo in the morning-after-the-wedding-night, or the aubade, scene; and, finally, when the desires of viewers are all taken into account in a queer critique of the film.

As evidenced in part by the image below, there can be no question but that Zeffirelli's *Romeo and Juliet* is populated by a literal host of beautiful young men, from Leonard Whiting, the actor who plays Romeo, about whom Zeffirelli himself remarked 'his looks were perfect for the role; he was the most beautiful male adolescent I've ever met';[46] to Michael York, the actor who plays Tybalt; to Keith Skinner, the actor who plays Romeo's man, Balthazar; and many more besides. All are lean and in the bloom of health; are fresh-faced and clean-shaven; have bright, shining eyes and straight, white teeth that reflect the sun when they grin or smile fully; have thick, luxurious hair; have gleaming, bronzed, unblemished skin; and were blessed with shapely physiques that epitomize masculine strength, grace and appeal (see Figure 5). As Donaldson puts it, Zeffirelli's camera 'displays the men's bodies as objects of an engrossed, sensual appreciation. The young men are all trim and attractive ... they are presented, to use Laura Mulvey's useful phrase, "to-be-looked-at".'[47] Indeed, they are particularly swoon-worthy examples of the male form that many audience members, regardless of where they fall in terms of sexual and gender identity, may take great delight in observing in this film.

FIGURE 5 *Romeo (Leonard Whiting), in tights, attempting to reason with Tybalt (Michael York), in tights and with his back to the audience/camera. Both are surrounded by a cadre of Montagues and Capulets in* Romeo and Juliet, *dir. Franco Zeffirelli, 1968.*

Donaldson's somewhat casual invocation of Mulvey's notion of 'to-be-looked-at-ness' belies the specificities associated with this important concept. Drawing on psychoanalytic theory, Mulvey details that one of the ways the cinema creates a particular kind of enjoyment is through the phenomenon of scopophilia, or the pleasure in looking. Scopophilia involves the 'taking of other people as objects, [and] subjecting them to a controlling and curious gaze'[48] on the subconscious level. Thus scopophilia is an active function that provides the 'erotic basis for pleasure in looking at another person as object'.[49] More problematically, though, Mulvey claims that:

> [i]n a world ordered by sexual imbalance, pleasure in looking has been split between active/male and passive/female. The determining male gaze projects its fantasy onto the female figure, which is styled accordingly. In their traditional exhibitionist role women are simultaneously looked at and displayed, their appearance coded for strong visual and erotic impact so that they can be said to connote *to-be-looked-at-ness*.[50]

From this perspective, film can be seen in its 'proper' light as a simulacrum of the masculine, heterosexual human consciousness inflected by patriarchal, misogynistic and, by extension, homophobic values. The male spectator of film is thus enabled to identify with his fictional correspondent – the heroes or the anti-heroes – in the visual narrative being presented to him and to assume that their bond with one another is unassailable. On a symbolic level, then, the male spectator of film is able to identify so fully with the film's male characters, the figures that direct the action and, more to the point, make women do their bidding, that he inhabits the exact same psychic position. In other words, the male spectator of film and the male characters in film are for all intents one in the same and they wield the same kind of directorial power over women.

Taking all of this theorizing into account, Mulvey goes on to insist that the 'male figure cannot bear the burden of sexual objectification. Man is reluctant to gaze at his exhibitionist like.'[51] But it is crucially important to be aware of the fact that what Mulvey does not claim here is that man's exhibitionist like – the male equivalent to the female who always already occupies the representational space of *to-be-looked-at-ness* because that is where man has consigned her to be – does not exist in film or any other type of visual media for that matter. However, she does not comment on the reasons why men are reluctant to gaze at other men in the same way that they gaze at women – as objects of erotic desire subject to their control. Would that Mulvey had made it plain that it is only heterosexual man who is reluctant to gaze at his exhibitionist like and that this reluctance likely stems from the homoerotic implications such a gaze signifies. It is difficult to imagine, however, that a gay or queer person would experience such inhibitions when it comes to where he chooses to direct his attention in the pursuit of the kind of scopophilic pleasures film images can inspire. Hence Mulvey's assertions can be altered in two ways: 1) *heterosexual* man is reluctant to gaze at his exhibitionist like, and 2) *homosexual* man is *not* reluctant to gaze at his exhibitionist like. To the latter point it then warrants adding that the 'male figure *can indeed* bear the burden of sexual objectification'. Donaldson's appropriation of the concept of *to-be-looked-at-ness* into his homoerotic reading of Zeffirelli's *Romeo and Juliet* then succeeds at disrupting the dominant patriarchal order as surely as Mulvey's intervention into visual pleasure and narrative cinema did in its originary moment. And that in itself opens up more queer interpretive possibilities in relation to the film than Donaldson allows for in his important study.

The work of Brett Farmer, who has extended Mulvey's insights exponentially in a number of queer directions, helps to move the analysis attempted here forward in a productive way. Farmer explains that '[t]oo often the "anatomical fact" of gay and straight men's shared corporeality is used as the grounds for all manner of theoretical conflations. I argue that, far from being continuous, gay and straight forms of masculinity are, in many ways, discontinuous.'[52] He goes on to add that even though 'gay male subjectivities intersect dominant forms of masculinity in significant ways, they are frequently a site of a thrilling undoing or deconstruction of those forms'.[53] For Farmer, as far as film is concerned, it is 'gay subjectivities/spectatorships [that] perform a fantasmatic "ruination" of phallic masculinity, a simultaneous assumption and de(con)struction of its forms and significances'.[54] Putting all of this in another way, the lived psychological and ontological experience of masculinity is different for gay men compared to straight men. Therefore gay men are, by virtue of their particular ways of understanding it, positioned to critique masculinity – and thereby 'ruin' it – given the concept's inherent mutability, a mutability that is more often than not entirely elided in the discourses that surround and prop masculinity up as a universal and unvarying gender norm. Where gay film spectatorship is concerned, this 'ruinous de(con)struction' is accomplished through engagement with what Farmer calls the 'fantasmatic', or the:

> concept that refers to the variable networks of fantasy and desire that subtend and structure subjectivity. Different subjectivities are sites of different fantasmatic organizations. Thus one may speak of the gay male fantasmatic, meaning the various formations of psychocultural fantasy, desire, and identification specific to and constitutive of male homosexual subjectivities.[55]

Building on their idiosyncratic understanding of masculinity, gay men accomplish this feat of fantasmatic spectatorship of movies in two ways. The first involves viewing males in films as sex objects, a role, as Mulvey painstakingly explains, that is traditionally and normatively foisted on women; the second is by imagining themselves as either the active or the passive partners in erotic encounters with male characters and actors in films. The end results of gay fantasmatic spectatorship are queer to the nth degree insofar as they profoundly challenge what is, often far too uncritically, considered normative in regards to gender, desire and sexuality in all of their respective permutations. Theoretically grounded as such, gay and/or queer men are thus provided with the means to describe their experience of narrative cinema in general and Zeffirelli's *Romeo and Juliet* in particular.

Regarding the latter, this extends to how such viewers are invited to gaze at characters like Tybalt and Romeo at various points in the film. Zeffirelli's 'homosexual camera'[56] encourages a highly charged homoerotic response to the lingering images of these young and attractive males. Where Tybalt is concerned, in his first appearance early in the film, his feet come into view as they are striding purposefully across the dusty Verona square in which the Capulet and Montague men are about to engage in an out-and-out brawl. Those feet are attached to perfectly shaped knees, calves and thighs that are themselves encased in form-fitting green and black tights. As the camera pans slowly upward, audiences are treated to a view of Tybalt's midsection, which, not incidentally, features a very prominent codpiece that only serves to call particular attention to his penis and testicles – parts of the body in which most if not all gay and/or queer men have what can be thought of as a natural interest. At the same time one of his hands is grasping the handle of a sword, indicating that this is a man who is ready for action; a man who, in Mulvey's terms, is in fact ready to direct the action. Finally the camera moves even further upward to reveal Tybalt's chest, which is clad in flattering Renaissance-styled fine clothing that is open at the neck to expose a patch of smooth sun-kissed skin. His handsome, clean-shaven face bears a grin at, apparently, the mere possibility that a fight is imminent, while the brim of the hat on his head curls up on either side in a way that makes the edges look like little devilish horns. It is difficult not to surmise that gay and/or queer men, not to mention many other kinds of viewers, may take erotic delight in this blatantly sensuous extended display of the roguish Tybalt's hyper-masculine person.

With Farmer's insights in mind, as he is presented initially in Zeffirelli's *Romeo and Juliet*, Tybalt, in all of his phallic, masculine glory, should be one of the figures male audience members identify with in the film to the point that they wish to emulate him as he asserts himself in and on the world he inhabits. These males thus desire Tybalt, but only in the sense that they seek to learn how to do what he does so that they can mimic his manly acts and behaviours, such as always being ready to engage in a fight. Oedipal male same-sex desire in this case is channelled in platonic, heterosexually normative ways that encompass the idea that straight men need to be taught exactly how to be straight men by other straight men. However, as Farmer explains, 'the gay subject recognizes and takes on the paternal [i.e. the masculine] site' that Tybalt inhabits in the film, 'but then proceeds to subvert it through an aberrant reconfiguration. Like his theoretical heterosexual counterpart, the gay subject is positioned in a network of desire *vis-à-vis* the father [here represented by Tybalt], but unlike the heterosexual male subject he does not translate that desire into an idealizing incorporation'[57] that results in styling himself in a heteronormative way. Instead the gay subject plays the idealizing incorporation 'out in a transgressive scenario of paternal [masculine] seduction and subversion in which the father's [the man's/Tybalt's] position is undermined through its appropriative reconstitution as a "passive object" of and for the gay subject's erotic desires'.[58] Through the transformative alchemy of the fantasmatic gay and queer spectators of Zeffirelli's film are thus able to conceive of Tybalt as a welcoming object of their erotic, as opposed to platonic, same-sex desires which in turn robs him of his traditional heteronormative phallic power. Being able to control the figure of Tybalt in such a way can be seen as a very queer thing that encompasses the transgressive and the subversive in ways that are liberating for audience members of all kinds, but most especially perhaps for gay and/or queer male spectators of the movie.

Where the gay spectatorial fantasmatic is concerned that liberation has everything to do with the concept of anality. According to Farmer, anality, '[m]ore than any other "sign" of male homosexuality ... marks the gay subject's flagrant difference in a phallic economy, that which sets him apart from other men'.[59] In Freudian terms, Farmer continues to point out, the

> repression of anality is a vital prerequisite for the successful production of phallic masculinity. In part, this is because male phallic identification requires an unchallenged prioritization of the penis as the sole legitimate site of male erotic organization. It is also because the anus has strong psychosexual associations with a 'feminine' passivity that is anathema to patrocentric masculinity.[60]

This leads to circumstances in which the 'anal zone thus features psychically as a fundamental symbol of sexual passivity, penetrability, and castration, something that must be disavowed and repressed as part of a cast-off femininity of male phallic identification', and the resulting normative heterosexual identity it is supposed to produce 'is to succeed'.[61] Farmer puts all of this in more blunt terms when he writes:

> [a]ccording to the logic of (hetero)sexual difference, in which masculinity and femininity are bound to an active/passive division, to be fucked is to be placed in the despised position of femininity and, thus, to lose one's claim to manhood. This is why anal penetration features so prominently in the patriarchal imaginary as the ultimate humiliation of the phallic male subject.[62]

Hence the gay subject's power lies in the fact that he 'can take the received image of masculinity as active, impenetrable, and phallocentric and submit it to a violent subversion',[63] at least within the imaginative bounds of the spectatorial fantasmatic.

Tybalt's status as a sex object rather than a sex subject is also facilitated, at least in part, by the fact that, like nearly all of the young males featured in Zeffirelli's *Romeo and Juliet*, he wears a codpiece. Marjorie Garber describes the codpiece as a 'sign of gender undecidability, since it is the quintessential gender mark of "seeming"' and notes that it 'confounds the question of gender, since it can signify yes or no, full or empty, lack or lack of lack'.[64] Given its rather dubious specificity, this kind of garment cannot be ignored in the context of this study of queerness in the Shakespeare film. In addition, Will Fisher explains that in England the codpiece became a fashion item near the beginning of the fifteenth century and would remain as such for the next 200 years. Concomitant with the appearance of higher-waisted jackets, something was needed to complement the hose men wore as a matter of routine in the period that would protect and simultaneously conceal men's genital areas.[65] Thus, as Fisher puts it, in many ways the codpiece 'quite literally helped to fashion manhood' at this time in history.[66] The codpiece, then, is what made a man a man.

Codpieces were not, though, as Fisher details, without controversy. That they were prosthetic devices that could be worn and removed at will and, as plays of the era indicate, by either gender, was one reason why codpieces were problematic. They were not, in other words, garments that were, as originally intended, exclusive to men. For a society in which the male and female genders were strictly policed codpieces were dangerous because they could not in the end be relied on to signify the absolute truth about the physiology of those who wore them. On the other hand, some felt that wearing codpieces was basically the same thing as wearing nothing at all and, therefore, completely inappropriate as public attire.[67] Furthermore, drawing on the work of Jean Howard and Phyllis Rackin, Fisher makes the point that the codpiece appeared at a time when ideas about the nature of masculinity were undergoing a profound shift in early modern England. Prior to this point the marker of masculinity was the production of sons who would carry on the male patrilineal line. During the Renaissance the marker of masculinity became the number of women a man conquered sexually and without any pretence whatsoever of reproduction or marriage.[68] It is incredibly ironic then that though the codpiece would, for all intents, disappear by the start of the seventeenth century, the new conception of masculinity – of what made a man a man – lingers well into the present day.[69] This can be seen in the all-too-common notion that men who bed lots of women are celebrated as 'studs' while their female counterparts are derided as 'sluts', or worse, if they engage in the same kind of unbridled sexual behaviours. Regardless, with either the pre- or post-Renaissance conceptions of masculinity, men are the only beneficiaries of such constructed ways of thinking and being in terms of agency.

A close contemporary cousin of the codpiece is the jockstrap, a garment made of cloth, leather, rubber or other material(s) that has been, over time, completely fetishized by gay and/or queer men as erotic since they first appeared in the mid-1870s as a form of protective wear for athletes. Even the briefest of forays into the world of beefcake books and magazines, as well as gay pornography, is enough to confirm the widespread extent of the fetishization of the jockstrap-cum-codpiece. In any case, by their very nature, codpieces – in whatever form they take – call attention to themselves and to the crotch areas of those who choose to wear them, whether the wearer is a sixteenth-century figure like England's King Henry VIII or a twentieth-century actor in a Zeffirelli film of Shakespeare's *Romeo and Juliet* like Michael York. What the gay and/or queer spectator brings to the interpretive equation is the ability to disrupt conventional ideas of what the codpiece signifies. He, engaging in the strategies enabled by the fantasmatic, is encouraged to view Zeffirelli's Tybalt as sexually available to him rather than off limits because of his assumed status as a straight man. Hence, rather than the traditional director of the action who can make women do whatever he wants them to do, Tybalt, under the pressure of the determining gay male gaze, becomes a man who is fully capable of giving and taking erotic pleasure to/from another man – that man being the gay/queer spectator of this cinematic production of *Romeo and Juliet* who thus 'ruins' Tybalt's heteronormative phallic masculinity by replacing it with a queer imaginative anality in its active and/or passive forms.

Whereas Tybalt's initial appearance in Zeffirelli's *Romeo and Juliet* seethes with a barely repressed aggression that is simply waiting to spill out of him at the slightest provocation, Romeo's first appearance in the film is far more subdued, although no less erotically enticing. Van Watson describes his entrance in these terms: 'Romeo walks into a close-up, the camera then following him in profile until he sits. When he finally reclines beside his cousin [Benvolio], the camera again shoots his face in close-up from above, and he talks of love.'[70] He is in fact the very epitome of melancholic distress brought about by what he considers to be his romantic misfortune given that Rosaline does not return his love. In his state of repose he evinces an endearing vulnerability as well as a charming, innocence-infused, sexual availability that is only heightened by the fact that he too wears a codpiece. Given the specificities of his overall demeanour here, he occupies what Mulvey would consider the traditional position that women in film would usually take in their circumscribed role as the sexual objects of men who are culturally sanctioned to toy with them in any way they so desire.

Meanwhile, the skin of Romeo's hands looks like it would be soft to the touch; his pretty face betrays the barest beginnings of a beard; his brown hair is delightfully mussed. Furthermore the clothes he wears – grey, form-fitting tights complete with codpiece and a matching, elaborately crafted, grey velvet vest – do little to conceal and everything to accentuate the glories of his masculine form. With what Van Watson describes as 'some of the most gently romantic theme music in the movie'[71] punctuating the affecting homosocial moment between them with an almost sublime poignancy, Benvolio (Bruce Robinson) asks Romeo what it is that has made Romeo feel so sad.

Romeo replies with: 'Not having that which, having, makes them short' (1.1.162).[72] At this point in the film many gay and/ or queer members of Zeffirelli's audience may find themselves wishing to do everything in their power to comfort Romeo and to ease his sufferings by giving him the 'that' he bemoans lacking. Like Tybalt, then, when placed under the determining gay male gaze, Romeo becomes an object of desire that can be had by any one or all of those spectators in a homoerotic imaginative context. And once again, queer anality trumps phallic masculinity in the operation of the gay fantasmatic.

This queer triumph is rendered indelible in the extended aftermath of Romeo's vengeful slaying of Tybalt on account of Tybalt's killing of Mercutio. Having received an earful and then some wise guidance from Friar Laurence (Milo O'Shea), Romeo goes to his beloved Juliet. Zeffirelli provides his viewers with a close-up of the couple sleeping in bed, each of their bare shoulders visible, facing one another but with their eyes closed, and with Romeo's arm draped protectively over Juliet (see Figure 6). Given the specifics of this tableau there can be no doubt that Romeo and Juliet have consummated

FIGURE 6 *Romeo (Leonard Whiting) and Juliet (Olivia Hussey) in bed after consummating their marriage in* Romeo and Juliet, *dir. Franco Zeffirelli, 1968.*

their marriage as part of their mutual consolation for all that they have endured, all that they have lost, and all that they must soon sacrifice of their happiness. But where does such an 'instinctive' assessment – that Romeo and Juliet have indeed had sex and consummated their marriage – come from? For Christine Varnado, the sex that Romeo and Juliet are presumptively assumed to have had in both Shakespeare's play and Zeffirelli's cinematic adaptation of it takes place just off the page, off the stage, or off the screen. It must be acknowledged, however, that 'generations of readers and interpreters of the play have imagined that [sex] act taking place offstage, right before the aubade scene, *because they wanted to* – because that is what *they* would do, what they imagine a generalized "one" or "anyone" would do' in the same circumstances.[73] Varnado goes on to add:

> projection is the stubborn anachronism inherent in representations of sex acts, especially the 'invisible,' indirectly figured sex acts in early modern plays. The very notion of 'sex' can only be conjured in the audience's or reader's mind via erotic identification – or disidentification – with acts being suggested, and that fantasmatic act of identification is inevitably structured by the reader's or viewer's desire.[74]

It should come as no surprise that this desire on the part of *Romeo and Juliet* readers or viewers Varnado discusses is always constructed and interpreted in heteronormative ways: thus the sex act that emerges is always of the 'legally significant, penis-in-vagina variety'.[75] Even so, there are other queer kinds of sex that could have taken place between this Romeo and Juliet. In fact, Varnado points out that '*nothing* would have to be different in the text of the play [or in its various cinematic texts] to imagine the invisible sex act ... as something else: some nonpenetrative erotic act of a more diffuse and mutual *jouissance* or some suspended dilation of pleasure that gets cruelly interrupted by the lark'.[76] The same applies 'if the unseen act were an unclimactic fumble, a premature climax, an impossible penetration, or a dysfunctional episode. Nor would anything have to change if Romeo did the same thing (any of the things) with Juliet that he would do with a boy.'[77] There is in sum 'no textual reason that this offstage act of "sex" (whatever it is) follows the strict phallocentric plot telos that furnishes the patriarchal definition of sex'.[78] The sheer indeterminacy of the kind of sex Romeo and Juliet have had – indeed, if they have had 'sex' at all – transforms what was considered a heteronormative certainty into a queer uncertainty.

In any case, the depiction of assumed heterosexual erotic bliss of Romeo and Juliet is interrupted by what surely qualifies as some of the most obviously homoerotic – and therefore queer – moments in all of Zefferilli's film. As the camera slowly pulls back from the close-up of Romeo and Juliet's faces, Romeo's bare backside – including his buttocks and legs – comes into the full view of the audience. What is equally striking about the composition of this shot is the fact that Juliet remains almost entirely covered up by the bedsheets and her hair; thus, unlike Romeo, she is hidden from the gaze of the audience. In accord with the heterosexist imperatives of narrative cinema that Mulvey discusses in her work, the conventional expectation for a shot like this demands that Juliet's nakedness, rather than Romeo's, be on display for, always presumably, straight males to objectify. With the sound of the morning lark chirping outside the room's open windows, Romeo's eyes flutter open. He smiles contentedly at the still-sleeping Juliet before kissing her softly on the lips. Then he rolls over, exposing his smooth bare chest, and sits up while swinging his legs over the side of the bed. Upon standing, opening the curtains very nearby and rubbing his eyes, viewers – including gay/queer male viewers – are treated to yet another full shot of Romeo's bare backside. Granted, Zeffirelli does not present any full-frontal nude shots of Romeo; queer audience members must, perhaps with the memory of the film's repeated attention to the male characters' codpieces in mind, resort to imagining what Romeo might look like naked.

But the backside nude shots of Romeo the director does present instead are wonderfully homoerotic without being the least bit prurient and arousing without being salacious. Indeed, it is as if all manner of audience members are invited by Zeffirelli to gaze at Romeo in this sequence as if he were a drawing, painting or sculpture straight out of the Classical era, and the invitation proves to be irresistible.

Considering their prominence in Zeffirelli's production of *Romeo and Juliet* it is important to the larger project of queering the Shakespeare film to also consider the homosocial moments of masculine intimacy characters like Romeo, Mercutio (John McEnery) and Tybalt engage in at various points in the movie. These moments can be categorized in two broad ways: as affectionate and as aggressive, with both forms complementing each other. A pair of examples will serve to make the point, beginning with one that involves Romeo and Mercutio. When, fairly early in the film, Romeo confesses to Mercutio that he 'dreamt a dream' (1.4.50) that profoundly unsettled him, Mercutio proceeds to conjure for Romeo and the rest of the assembled Montague men the Queen Mab of fairy lore. In Mercutio's excessively fantastical view Queen Mab is the agent that 'gallops night by night / Through lovers' brains' (1.4.70–1) causing them to go mad with dreams of love – the kind of love that causes nothing but distress for the lovers which in turn leads to the disruption of civil society and all it holds dear; in other words, the kind of love Romeo is about to experience with Juliet. By the time he reaches the end of this powerful speech Mercutio is in a state of obvious distress over these ideas. According to Jorgens, '[t]here is deep friendship, even love, between [Zeffirelli's] Romeo and Mercutio. Mercutio's mercurial showmanship seems aimed at Romeo, and his anger, when Romeo is off sighing for love or making a milksop of himself before Tybalt, is tinged with jealousy. How could a friend abandon male comradery for "a smock?"'[79] Indeed, how could a true friend do such a thing? A true friend would not, perhaps, but a lover of someone else would. Mercutio's sense of impending loss – a loss that is homosocial and possibly homosexual as well – is a palpable force where his 'friend' Romeo is concerned.

Taking Mercutio's head in his hands, Romeo forces Mercutio to pay attention to him as Romeo tells him: 'Peace, peace, Mercutio, peace, / Thou talk'st of nothing' (1.4.95–6). After several seconds of consideration, Mercutio places his forehead on to Romeo's so that the two men are even closer to one another, almost embracing and almost about to kiss, and concedes to his friend: 'True, I talk of dreams, / Which are the children of an idle brain' (1.4.96–7). This moment is astonishingly intimate and affectionate and, because it involves two men who are evidently not afraid of being intimate and affectionate with each other, it also qualifies as being homoerotic and queer. For Porter, Mercutio's Queen Mab speech in tandem with Romeo's reaction to both its words and the person who speaks them emphasizes the 'conflicting claims of friendship and love'[80] that many scholars have identified as problematic for the kind of men Shakespeare characterized in his plays, men who inevitably found themselves torn between the other men they loved and the women society demanded they marry with and produce the next generation. Men's homoerotic bonds with other men, like those of Romeo and Mercutio, cannot survive the demands of heterosexist, patriarchal culture when put under this kind of pressure. This point is made horrifically clear by Zeffirelli when Mercutio, having been stabbed in the heart by Tybalt, dies cursing the houses of both the Montagues and the Capulets. As he is dying, and his vision moves in and out of focus (an effect Zeffirelli's camera cleverly presents from the audience's point of view), Mercutio only has eyes for Romeo; at one point while he is staggering around the square, Romeo catches Mercutio in his arms and in a deliberate repetition of the intimacy and affection the two experienced in each other's arms just before the Capulet ball, Mercutio rests his forehead against that of an unresisting Romeo, bringing them close physically one last time. Add this to the fact that Mercutio dies because he was trying to defend and protect his beloved Romeo, and his death can be seen as redolent with a wholly poignant, and wholly queer, homoeroticism.

Horrified by Mercutio's death on his behalf, Romeo is not to be prevented by his fellow Montagues from pursuing Tybalt. After smashing the handkerchief that is stained with the blood of Mercutio's heart into Tybalt's face, the two men enter an all-out brawl that will leave one of them dead by the time it concludes. In many respects their athletic grappling, wrestling, kicking, punching and fencing forms an example of the aggressive type of male homoeroticism Zeffirelli goes to great lengths to present – and to critique – repeatedly in his *Romeo and Juliet*. Not at all incidentally, it also parodies in the extreme the physicality of sex between men, qualifying it as demonstrably homoerotic, too. This homoeroticism reaches its macabre zenith when Tybalt impales himself on Romeo's sword, thereby allowing Romeo to succeed at symbolically penetrating Tybalt sexually – a penetration that, arguably, Tybalt had longed for and deliberately sought out since the very beginning of *Romeo and Juliet*. Heightening the homoeroticism even further is the fact that Tybalt falls into and dies in Romeo's arms, having reached the little death (orgasm) and the big death (end of life) at one and the same time.

What this critical survey of some of the queer elements evident in his *Romeo and Juliet* has attempted to show is that Zeffirelli was able to push the envelope as far as these kinds of depictions were concerned much further than Cukor was able to do thirty-two years earlier. In fact, Cukor is on record as saying, taking into account his viewing of Zeffirelli's later effort, '[i]t's one picture that if I had to do over again, I'd know how. I'd get the garlic and the Mediterranean into it.'[81] Apparently Cukor also felt that his Romeo and Juliet were too old, too stodgy and not sexy enough considering the actor and actress cast in those roles.[82] What Cukor does not comment on, however, is whether he would, like Zeffirelli, choose to incorporate any kind of visual male homoeroticism into such a movie. Perhaps, in this regard, Zeffirelli's triumph has everything to do with the moment in history in which his *Romeo and Juliet* was made versus the moment in history in which Cukor's *Romeo and Juliet* was made. For Zeffirelli, of course, the Sexual Revolution was by the late 1960s in full swing and the modern gay rights movement was only a few months from exploding into the consciousness of the general public via the 1969 Stonewall Riots in New York City. In other words, for Zeffirelli, the incipient moment for more honest and open representations of things homoerotic in film had arrived.

IV

Private Romeo is an American independent film by the openly gay writer and director Alan Brown that premiered on screen in 2011 and presents its audiences with an achingly earnest homoerotic version of Shakespeare's *Romeo and Juliet*.[83] This production is described at its corresponding website[84] and on its DVD packaging as follows: 'When eight young cadets are left behind at an isolated military high school, the greatest romantic drama ever written seeps out of the classroom and permeates their lives.' The copy continues with: 'Incorporating the original text of *Romeo and Juliet*, YouTube videos, and lip-synced indie rock music, *Private Romeo* takes viewers to a mysterious and tender place that only Shakespeare could have inspired.' That mysterious and tender place is one in which two young men – both military high school cadets no less – just happen to fall in love with one another, much like their star-crossed counterparts do in *Romeo and Juliet*. Given this fortuitous development, it is argued here that, with *Private Romeo*, Brown succeeds at fully queering – by which is meant that he poses a sustained and successful challenge to the always assumed heteronormativity that attends nearly every aspect of Western culture, including its most celebrated artistic creations, like the works of Shakespeare – *Romeo and Juliet* in the cinema for the first time in the history of the medium. Also considered are some of the larger implications of such an accomplishment, particularly as it relates to the queerness of the *Romeo and Juliet*s of Cukor and Zeffirelli discussed in the earlier sections of this chapter.

The way that Brown begins to queer *Romeo and Juliet* in *Private Romeo* is by drawing explicit attention to the all-male world the characters of his film inhabit. Early on in the movie it is explained through a combination of voiceovers and corresponding images that a group of eight high school cadets have been left behind at the McKinley Military Academy because they did not qualify to participate in a series of land navigation exercises that are taking place off-campus. This means that for a period of four days these cadets will be responsible for taking care of themselves; there will be no officers or faculty present to supervise them. They will, however, continue to follow a strict regimen of class work, homework and physical fitness, all under the direction of a pair of senior upper classmen. Thus Brown creates from the outset of *Private Romeo* a *mise en scène* that is over-determined by an excess of male homosociality. It was, of course, Eve Kosofsky Sedgwick who, borrowing it from the social sciences, defined the term homosociality in the way it is used here: 'it describes social bonds between persons of the same sex'.[85] As Sedgwick takes great care to make clear in her work, however, homosociality is not to be understood as being exactly synonymous with homosexuality; nevertheless, homosociality is almost always 'potentially erotic', potentially sexual, because, hypothetically speaking at least, homosociality and homosexuality exist on a 'continuum' that links these two ontologies in the realm of experiential possibility.[86] Hence, at a macro level, the eight male cadets remaining at the McKinley Military Academy are bound together socially by virtue of their attendance at such an institution and by their mandated participation in its rituals. At a micro level, furthermore, this homosocial association extends to include the cadets' individual and collective relationships with each other. Invoking Sedgwick's always potentially erotic hypothetical at this point allows for recognition of the fact that homoeroticism, whether in the form of unrequited or requited desire, or out-and-out homosexuality, is a constant factor that could be activated at any moment in these particular circumstances.

Another and perhaps even more significant way that Brown queers *Romeo and Juliet* in *Private Romeo* is by using his all-male cast to portray Shakespeare's male *and* female characters as part of their comprehensive study of the tragedy. Thus it is that Brown deliberately and unapologetically transgresses the traditional rigid gender binary that continues to haunt humanity as the second decade of the twenty-first century unfolds. In her famous deconstruction of gender Judith Butler argues that, while the biological sexes of male and female are natural anatomical formations individuals have no control over, at least in their original bodily manifestations, gender is not a natural occurrence; gender, in other words, does not follow automatically from biological sex. Gender is, rather, something that is learned over time and performed by real people – actual material bodies – again and again on the social and private stages of everyday life. On this key point Butler writes that '*gender is a kind of imitation for which there is no original*'.[87] She adds that 'heterosexuality must be understood as a compulsive and compulsory repetition that can only produce the *effect* of its own originality', which therefore must mean that 'compulsory heterosexual identities, those ontologically consolidated phantasms of "man" and "woman," are theatrically produced effects that posture as grounds, origins, the normative measure of the real'.[88] Hence among a nexus of intricately related items gender encompasses things like the kind of clothes a boy/girl or a man/woman wears, how a boy/girl or a man/woman acts towards and around others of the same or opposite sex, and how a boy/girl or a man/woman talks to his or her fellow human beings, among countless other interactions and behaviours. These are all things that most people, conditioned as they are from birth by the absolute strictures of heterosexism, believe occur naturally, as if they are predestined rather than learned behaviours.

Applying Butler's supple conception of gender being a mutable performance instead of an unchanging natural characteristic universal to all humans to Brown's *Private Romeo* allows for the understanding that the young men charged with reading the lines and acting the parts of Capulet's Wife, Juliet and the Nurse are, by the use of mere words and motions, enacting the female gender despite their obvious masculinity, a masculinity that is almost impossible to ignore given their short high-and-tight service haircuts, their khaki/camouflage military-style clothing, the lower register of their voices and the absence of protruding breasts on their bodies. They still look, in other words, very much like young men even as they are attempting to bring to life three women of varying ages and equally varying experience through the combined magic of language and gesture. Even so, borrowing Samuel Taylor Coleridge's proscription for the 'willing suspension of disbelief'[89] is hardly necessary to succumb to the seductive idea that, even if only for a number of moments within the length of a ninety-eight-minute film, the three young men under discussion here are indeed the female characters of Capulet's Wife, Juliet and the Nurse that Shakespeare created in *Romeo and Juliet*. Such is the power of even the most unlikely, impromptu and amateur performance of a dramatic fiction on the imagination of the viewer.

Despite the explication provided above it is not that gender does not matter in *Private Romeo*; it is that gender matters in a different way in the film than it would in the so-called 'real' world. It is, in other words, significant that the characters of Romeo and Juliet – played by an actor and an actress, respectively, in the majority of productions since the late-seventeenth century when the theatres were re-opened in England following the Puritans' closure of them in 1642 – are instead portrayed in *Private Romeo* by two young men. This is because two young men are not supposed to fall in love with one another like Romeo and Juliet do in the fiercely heterosexist world that has existed since, according to Foucault, the mid-nineteenth century,[90] when the male homosexual was first categorized as a species and thereafter demonized mercilessly well into the present day. Yet mirroring their characters in many ways, falling in love with each other is exactly what cadets Sam Singleton (Seth Numrich) and Glenn Mangan (Matt Doyle) – the student actors who play, respectively, Romeo and Juliet – do in *Private Romeo*. In fact, it is Shakespeare's *Romeo and Juliet* that provides the means by which Sam and Glenn discover their romantic interest in one another. To this end, Brown transforms the Capulet ball into a typical clandestine teenage party that includes a game of for-stakes poker, a fair amount of beer drinking and copious amounts of masculine braggadocio in the McKinley Military Academy dining commons. Feeling uncomfortable once his tormentor, Cadet Neff (Hale Appleman), arrives, Glenn wanders away from the crowd to be by himself on the far side of the room next to the floor-to-ceiling windows. Sam notices Glenn in his self-imposed isolation and, as Romeo, asks Benvolio/Gus, 'What lady's that which doth enrich the hand / Of yonder knight' (1.5.41–2)? While he makes this enquiry of his friend, the camera focuses on Juliet/Glenn, who is staring at nothing in particular with a pensive expression on her/his face. Once Benvolio/Gus insists that he does not know the person to whom Romeo/Sam is referring, Romeo/Sam proceeds to extol to himself and to the audience upon her/his (Juliet/Glenn's) virtues in verse:

> O, she doth teach the torches to burn bright.
> It seems she hangs upon the cheek of night
> As a rich jewel in an Ethiop's ear,
> Beauty too rich for use, for earth too dear.
> So shows a snowy dove trooping with crows
> As yonder lady o'er her fellows shows.
> The measure done, I'll watch her place of stand
> And, touching hers, make blessed my rude hand. (1.5.43–50)

Having uttered this short but powerful observation, Romeo/Sam walks toward Juliet/Glenn, leaving Benvolio/Gus behind.

While doing so he stares at Juliet/Glenn with a newfound intensity and says, 'Did my heart love till now? Forswear it, sight, / For I ne'er saw true beauty till this night' (1.5.51–2). This is where Brown's inspired blurring of gender and character names in *Private Romeo* starts to mean something unique and important, particularly in a queer context. It is, after all, the first time that Sam, via the medium of the characters of Romeo and his Juliet, has admitted out loud that he is in love with someone who is of the same gender as himself. Despite Romeo/Sam's use of the pronouns she and hers, as well as the noun lady in this brief speech, it is always clear that Juliet/Glenn is a young man, again because Brown does not force his actors to cross-dress in female garb when they are portraying female characters. Furthermore, in a patriarchal, heterosexist society, there really is no unique language for one man to remark upon the beauty of another young man. Shakespeare's words thus allow Romeo/Sam to say something about another young man that he could not otherwise say without opening himself to the wrath of institutional, societal and cultural disapprobation.

A short while later, using the deceptive physical/rhetorical manoeuver of 'What is that on your shirt?', Romeo/Sam taps Glenn/Juliet on the chin with his right hand after Glenn/Juliet looks down to see what the imaginary thing was that Romeo/Sam was pointing at. Although Glenn/Juliet seems to be annoyed with himself for being taken in by such a puerile ruse, it soon becomes clear that Romeo/Sam's real intent was to touch Glenn/Juliet in any way that would get the other young man's attention – and pave the way for something more intimate to occur between them. To apologize, Romeo/Sam turns to the text of *Romeo and Juliet* again and explains that:

> If I profane with my unworthiest hand
> This holy shrine, the gentle sin is this:
> My lips, two blushing pilgrims, ready stand
> To smooth that rough touch with a tender kiss. (1.5.92–5)

With the last line he speaks here, Romeo/Sam leans in and tries to kiss Juliet/Glenn on the neck; however, rather flummoxed by Romeo/Sam's actions, Juliet/Glenn pulls away from him. In the aftermath of these moments Romeo/Sam's gaze darts from one direction to another in an endearing mixture of shyness, embarrassment and hope. Romeo/Sam's palpable vulnerability is touching and it shows that the experience of discovering love crosses the lines associated with gender and sexual identity. Also, when one human being is attracted to another human being as Romeo/Sam is to Juliet/Glenn, one of the next logical steps is for that person to seek to extend that attraction in a physical manner by initiating a kiss – something our species has done to demonstrate interest and desire since it first appeared on the evolutionary scene. But just like one young man is not supposed to notice or remark upon the beauty of another young man in our heteronormative society, one young man is not supposed to want, much less actually to attempt, to kiss another young man as Romeo/Sam does here. Because it is non-normative, male–male kissing, even in the context of Shakespeare's *Romeo and Juliet*, definitely qualifies as queer behaviour that threatens the supremacy of heterosexuality by virtue of both its very existence and its representation in cinematic form.

Having reached an initial level of intimacy, Juliet/Glenn steps close to Romeo/Sam and – picking up on and continuing the saint and sinner conceit evident in Shakespeare's text – says,

> Good pilgrim, you do wrong your hand too much,
> Which mannerly devotion shows in this,
> For saints have hands that pilgrims' hands do touch,
> And palm to palm is holy palmers' kiss. (1.5.96–9)

By this point, having overcome his initial astonishment, Juliet/Glenn reaches out with his right hand and takes Romeo/Sam's left hand in his own so that their palms are in fact touching. The gentle intimacy of the moment is palpable. And suddenly there is not the slightest doubt that these are two people – two young men – who are mutually attracted to one another. Then, like their Shakespearean counterparts in *Romeo and Juliet*, Romeo/Sam and Juliet/Glenn continue to flirt playfully and verbally with one another:

> Romeo/Sam: Have not saints lips and holy palmers too?
> Juliet/Glenn: Ay, pilgrim, lips that they must use in prayer.
> Romeo/Sam: Why then, dear saint, let lips do what hands do – They pray; grant thou, lest faith turn to despair.
> Juliet/Glenn: Saints do not move, though grant for prayers' sake.
> Romeo/Sam: Then move not while my prayer's effect I take.
> (1.5.100–5)

Romeo/Sam then kisses Juliet/Glenn full on the lips (see Figure 7). When they separate, both young men are rather surprised by what they have just done. 'Thus from my lips by thine my sin is purged,' Romeo/Sam offers as another apology for being so forward as to kiss Juliet/Glenn without

FIGURE 7 *Left to right: Juliet/Glenn (Matt Doyle) and Romeo/Sam (Seth Numrich) sharing their first kiss*. Private Romeo, *dir. Alan Brown, 2011.*

specifically being invited to do so (1.5.106). But Juliet/Glenn smiles broadly at Romeo/Sam, steps closer to him and says evenly, 'Then have my lips the sin that they have took' (1.5.107). Emboldened by this response Romeo/Sam says, 'Sin from my lips? O trespass sweetly urged! / Give me my sin again' (1.5.108–9), then he reaches out and takes Juliet/Glenn's face between his hands and kisses him again – this time even more passionately. And Juliet/Glenn responds in kind by kissing Romeo/Sam back with just as much ardour. That two young men can and do kiss one another, and that there is nothing sick or disgusting or untoward about them doing so as those in some increasingly isolated quarters of Western society believe, that it is just as natural for them to do so as it is for a man and a woman to kiss one another, are parts of the larger message that is conveyed so powerfully by this sequence of images in *Private Romeo*. Indeed, in this context, it is not a stretch to assert that two young men kissing each other is no more of a sin than it is for Romeo and Juliet to kiss each other at this moment in Shakespeare's play. This is queerness at its most visceral and, at least potentially, its most transformative.

Brown's low-key treatment of the aubade scene opens with a shot of an institutional wardrobe seeming to stand sentinel in the corner of a McKinley Military Academy dorm room. The camera then slowly moves viewers' attention to the left. Two pairs of intertwined and lightly hairy male legs appear. A rumpled white sheet covers the thighs and midsections of the men. Next, a smooth bare back and two nicely muscled right biceps come into view. Finally, two heads with crewcut hairstyles, both turned away from the audience and toward the wall of the room, become visible. As the gentle music of a single piano plays on the soundtrack, Sam/Romeo protectively spoons Glenn/Juliet. The cumulative image is one of tenderness, affection and love; it is (homo)erotic without being pruriently sexual. It is, however, more likely than not that Sam/Romeo and Glenn/Juliet – just like Zeffirelli's Romeo and Juliet – have had sex somewhere off-camera prior to this moment in their story. Just as Varnado speculated in her work, '*nothing* [had] to be different in the text of the play' in order for the invisible sex act(s) that have probably occurred between Sam/Romeo and Glenn/Juliet to be homo rather than hetero in nature; the words are the same regardless. And the 'strict phallocentric plot telos that furnishes the patriarchal definition of [heterosexual] sex' is once again queered in yet another cinematic adaptation of *Romeo and Juliet*. The fact that this particular Romeo/Sam and Juliet/Glenn are in effect a married same-sex couple only adds to the larger, expansively queer-positive resonance of Brown's interpretation of Shakespeare's 'straightest' play. Indeed, it is a wholly palpable expression of a dream come true for many gay/queer men, especially those who have longed for decades to have equal marriage rights.

Having created an entirely believable fictional realm in which male same-sex desire and love are paramount in *Private Romeo*, Brown also manages to generate a significant amount of suspense for those audience members who have become invested in Sam and Glenn's (Romeo and Juliet's) characters and the outcome of their romance. This is because, of course, of the well-known fact that Romeo and Juliet are doomed to death from the opening lines of Shakespeare's play. Indeed, the tension over what will ultimately happen to Sam and Glenn – which has been steadily increasing since they each recognized their feelings for the other – continues until almost the very last moments of *Private Romeo*. Brown stages the portion of 5.3 of *Romeo and Juliet* that takes place in the Capulet monument in a large McKinley Military Academy lecture hall with amphitheatre seating. There, Romeo/Sam rushes in to find his beloved Juliet/Glenn seemingly dead and sprawled on the instructors' table. His anguish is immediate and heartbreaking to witness. Thus it is totally understandable when Romeo/Sam drinks the last of the drugged water that Juliet/Glenn left in her/his canteen, is quickly overcome and dies while spooning Juliet/Glenn in his arms in an all-encompassing embrace that epitomizes Romeo/Sam's love for and devotion to Juliet/Glenn. Moments later, Juliet/Glenn awakes to find Friar Laurence (Adam Barrie) hovering nearby and urging her/him to leave immediately before they are discovered in the tomb/classroom. Juliet/Glenn sends him away, insisting that she/he will not part from her/his beloved Romeo/Sam. When Friar Laurence is gone, Juliet/Glenn says, 'I will kiss thy lips. / Haply some poison yet doth hang on them / To make me die with a restorative' (5.3.163–6), and then she/he kisses him. What happens next calls to mind Nahum Tate's (in)famous re-interpretation of *King Lear* in the late seventeenth century that ends with the survival of the characters of King Lear and Cordelia and Cordelia's marriage to Edgar, someone she never even associates with in Shakespeare's original text. As Juliet/Glenn is kissing Romeo/Sam, Romeo/Sam starts to kiss Juliet/Glenn back seconds before his eyes flutter open (see Figure 8). The spell of a performance-within-a-performance is thus broken and *Private Romeo* leaves us with Sam and Glenn, two young men who are alive and well and who are in love with one another, seemingly ready to take on the world

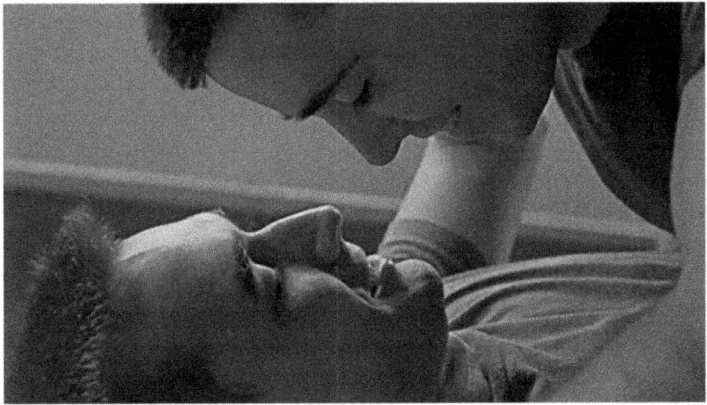

FIGURE 8 *Glenn (Matt Doyle) on the top, and Sam (Seth Numrich) on the bottom, alive, smiling and very much in love after their performance of Romeo and Juliet's death scene (5.3).* Private Romeo, dir. Alan Brown, 2011.

as a couple. This is perhaps the most significant moment of queering in the entirety of Brown's film because it features the triumph and the exaltation of homosexual or queer love instead of the reification of its traditionally triumphant heterosexual counterpart.

V

Where Shakespeare film is concerned Burt is the only critic who has explored in detail the ongoing queer fascination with the various cinematic productions of *Romeo and Juliet* that have appeared over the years since the invention of the medium in the late nineteenth century. After considering an impressive number of straightforward adaptations as well as more radical appropriations of the play that have been directed by or starred queer people, or reference *Romeo and Juliet* intertextually in some queer way, Burt wonders: 'How are we to account for this rather extensive gay and lesbian performance history of *Romeo and Juliet*?'[91] He goes on to point out that 'while we might expect *Romeo and Juliet* to have been of interest to gays and lesbians when same-sex desire was still closeted or when it was still, as in Oscar Wilde's case, a practice that could not yet speak the name "homosexual," we might wonder why the gay and lesbian romance' with *Romeo and Juliet* 'has persisted well after the need for a masked way of expressing gay and lesbian desire has significantly dissipated, at least when it comes to an increasingly queer-positive, mass-marketed cinema, theater, and fiction.'[92] Burt then proceeds to read the unabated queer investment in cinematic *Romeo and Juliet*s as a

> same-sex utopian impulse, a dream of what I call *homonormativity*. Far from mimicking heteronormative norms in order to resignify and possibly subvert them, these replays of *Romeo and Juliet* give expression to a gay utopian

fantasy whereby a no longer forbidden practice of gay male or lesbian sex is represented as 'normal,' heterosexualized, that is, according to the (queer) conventions of the genre of romance fiction.[93]

For Burt, the concept of homonormativity allows queer Shakespeare film to evade 'the categories by which gay and straight sexuality are [made] legible' in one of two ways: 'either by seeking to be unlegible as gay or by designifying gender difference'.[94] Both of these strategies that homonormativity makes possible 'can best be understood as a way of addressing the fact that gay and lesbian desire will always be read, insofar as it is signified and read at all, through the lens of heteronormativity'.[95]

Earlier in this chapter, Cukor's *Romeo and Juliet* was shown to be unlegible as gay, at least at a surface level. But if the, comparatively speaking, advanced ages of the actors/actresses – particularly Leslie Howard and Norma Shearer in the lead roles – can be read as gay as discussed here and in Burt's article, then a certain kind of queerness emerges and cannot be dismissed out of hand. That queerness is only extended further, is made even more apparent, when the fact that the film's director, one of its design consultants, one of its music composers and its originary writer were all gay/queer men is taken into account in the interpretive discourse that surrounds the production. In a very real sense where Cukor's movie is concerned, then, it is the queer that enables the heteronormative love between Romeo and Juliet to manifest fully. This specific example of heteronormativity cannot, in other words, exist without its queer counterpart(s). Meanwhile, the same-sex utopian impulse Burt mentions as part and parcel of the extensive queer reception history of *Romeo and Juliet* in the cinema can be understood as an altruistic impulse in regards to Cukor's adaptation. If gays like Cukor, Messel, Tchaikovsky and Shakespeare, not to mention gay audience members, support straight people – or representations of straight people like Romeo and Juliet – as they navigate the treacherous waters of forbidden love, then, perhaps, straight people will do the same in return and thereby put homosexual love on something of an equal footing with heterosexual love. Thus homosexual love would be queered in this instance because it would be potentially normalized or, to use Burt's term, heterosexualized, as totally acceptable rather than the opposite.

Though as a rule traditional Shakespeare film criticism does not concern itself with (auto)biographical matters, drawing on such materials as are available is as crucial to a queer reading of Zeffirelli's *Romeo and Juliet* as it was to Cukor's production. Indeed, there can be no question that Zeffirelli's appreciation of, attraction to, and love for other men infuses his *Romeo and Juliet* with a homoerotic ethos it would not otherwise have; the kind of homoerotic ethos that, in the mid-1930s, Cukor could only gesture at obliquely rather than openly like Zeffirelli was able to do. This queer homoeroticism is most apparent in the way Zeffirelli's camera lavishes extended attention on the male body throughout his *Romeo and Juliet*. This directorial strategy allows for a number of the male characters like Romeo, Tybalt, Mercutio and Benvolio – and the actors who portray them – to be perceived as sex objects, a role that women characters/actresses are, almost by default in patriarchal society, forced into in film. Thus, in one fell cinematic swoop, Zeffirelli manages to queer his *Romeo and Juliet* by subverting traditional heteronormative scopophilic conventions while telling the story of Romeo and Juliet's forbidden love – a forbidden love queer people can all-too easily understand. At the same time, Zeffirelli's directorial focus on the male body encourages, if not compels, a veritable constellation of queer homoerotic responses to the repeated images of young, masculine beauty that are presented to viewers in his film. Arguably, these responses are queer, too, because they challenge critical propriety given that they make plain, rather than shy away from, audience members' (including Shakespeare film critics) observations of and reactions to the attractiveness, the sexiness and/or the desirability of the male characters/actors that feature so prominently in Zeffirelli's *Romeo and Juliet*. Thus once again queerness is rendered normal in what Burt characterizes as the impulse toward the creation of a 'gay utopian fantasy' in which nothing, least of all male same-sex relationships, is forbidden.

Finally, presumably Burt's idea of the conventions of the genre of romance fiction has something to do with the following bare-bones plot outline: boy meets girl; boy and girl fall in love; boy and girl get married; boy and girl live happily ever after. Logically, then, the queer attachment to *Romeo and Juliet* in the cinema that Burt discusses in his article must involve the appropriation of this heteronormative master narrative and making it do its representational work in gay-positive contexts. Alan Brown's *Private Romeo* is particularly successful at this kind of appropriation, perhaps because it approaches queerness in *Romeo and Juliet* by designifying gender difference rather than, as is the case with the productions of Cukor and Zeffirelli, by making the gay more or less (un)legible. By using an all-male cast, Brown's film morphs the generic romance plotline evident in *Romeo and Juliet* to: boy meets boy; boy and boy fall in love; boy and boy get married; boy and boy live happily ever after. Re-visioning the master heteronormative romance/love narrative and refashioning it into a master homonormative romance/love narrative as Brown does in *Private Romeo* is a significant achievement. It shows that Shakespeare's 'straightest' play may not be so straight after all and, more importantly, it shows that love is not bound by the artificial constraints of gender or sexual identity. It just is. What could be more queer where the Shakespeare film is concerned?

3

The visual poetics of gender trouble in Trevor Nunn's *Twelfth Night*, Baz Luhrmann's *Romeo + Juliet* and Michael Hoffman's *William Shakespeare's A Midsummer Night's Dream*

I

As the numerous available critical studies testify, Shakespearean drama and poetry has taken a prominent place in the overall discourse of gender trouble – the revolutionary notion that gender is a changeable behaviour rather than an immutable characteristic that derives from biological sex. Indeed, gender trouble in relation to Shakespeare and his times has been thoroughly historicized according to the concerns of the late twentieth- and early twenty-first-century moment. However, the majority of this work focuses on Shakespeare's plays and poems as written texts. That being the case, the purpose of this chapter is to extend the discussion of gender trouble into the realm of the Shakespeare film. The cinematic texts that will be analysed in this overarching context are Trevor Nunn's *Twelfth Night* (1996), Baz Luhrmann's *Romeo + Juliet* (1996) and Michael Hoffman's *William Shakespeare's A Midsummer Night's Dream* (1999), each of which deals with gender trouble in ways that are complicated and enlightening from a queer perspective.

II

Whether because of its plot of twins separated by the vicissitudes of fate, its fanciful depiction of romantic courtship or its story of a servant who dares to imagine himself rising above his station in life through marriage to the countess who employs him, *Twelfth Night* has proven to be a triumph ever since its first recorded performance in 1601/2 in the great hall of the Middle Temple, one of the city of London's four prestigious law schools that comprised an educational institution known collectively then and still today as the Inns of Court. That success is reflected in the fact that – as Arden Series 3 editor of the play Keir Elam details – an astounding 120 stage, film and television productions of the play have been mounted in the 402 years between 1602 and 2004.[1] However, focusing on the latter two media, Rothwell identifies a total of only eight film or television adaptations of *Twelfth Night* that were produced in the last 102 years. Leading this short list is a ten-minute black-and-white silent production of the Vitagraph Company of America that appeared in 1910; the last is Trevor Nunn's sumptuous full-length feature film of the play that came to the screen in 1996.[2] After that, an appropriation of *Twelfth Night* entitled *She's the Man*, aimed at the notoriously fickle American teen movie audience, premiered in 2006. But otherwise filmmakers and television producers have – oddly, considering what is almost universally agreed to be the play's overall excellence and appeal – shied away from *Twelfth Night*.

Because of the paucity of screen examples, only Nunn's cinematic version of *Twelfth Night* will be discussed in this chapter. H. R. Coursen describes Nunn's production as 'one of the more straightforward translations of a Shakespeare script to film. It places itself squarely within the genre of Shakespeare film by telling the story pretty much as the First Folio tells it, as opposed to making it an allegory of our times'.[3] Yet at the same time Coursen notes that what he terms Nunn's metaphorical treatment of Viola's appropriation of male costume begs questions such as 'what is gender? what are the stereotypes of gender? what are the limits of stereotype? In this sense,' he claims, 'the film, for all of its fidelity to "Shakespeare," speaks directly to us. This is not an "imposition" on the script. Shakespeare was asking the same questions.'[4] In Coursen's view, because the playwright himself was concerned about issues with gender that continue to be vexing to audiences in the late twentieth and early twenty-first centuries, and because Nunn's *Twelfth Night* is equally attentive to those exact same issues, the supposed anachronistic folly of imposing present-day anxieties onto the past is totally avoided. Still, gender trouble persists in the film; it is, in fact, most evident in the way it inflects the relationship between the characters of Viola/Cesario and Orsino with a palpable form of queer, male, same-sex homoeroticism.

'What country, friends, is this?' Viola (Imogen Stubbs) asks in the first scene in which she appears in Shakespeare's playtext of *Twelfth Night*; she is informed by the Captain (Sid Livingstone) that she is in the land known as Illyria (1.2.1–2).[5] As their dialogue continues, it is made plain that Viola and the Captain are among the small number of survivors of a shipwreck that as far as they can discern has left Viola's beloved brother, along with many others, dead, swallowed by the angry sea (1.2.3–19). Nunn, making full use of the visual power of film to show rather than tell, transforms this bit of exposition into a series of moments that dramatize the chaos and the horror the passengers on the doomed vessel experience, the heartbreaking separation of the twin siblings Viola and Sebastian (Steven Mackintosh) and the eerie aftermath of the disaster in which those who came through it relatively unscathed must start to regain their bearings. Rothwell describes this extended interpolation as being akin to a '*Titanic* trope' that proves effective at conveying to the audience the extraordinary circumstances in which Viola suddenly finds herself.[6] To ensure her safety – she is, after all, in a place that she is not supposed to be without the protection of her beloved brother – after she is told it is unlikely that she would be able to enter into the service of the Countess Olivia (Helena Bonham Carter) while she remains in Illyria, Viola entreats the Captain to assist her in a rather unorthodox way: 'I prithee be my aid / For such disguise as haply shall become / The form of my intent. I'll serve this Duke' – Count Orsino (Toby Stephens), who rules over Illyria – and she intends to do so by presenting herself as a boy to him (Elam 1.2.49–53; Nunn 12).[7] When the Captain scoffs at this preposterous idea, Viola insists that 'It may be worth thy pains, for I can sing / And speak to him in many sorts of music / That will allow me very worth his service' (Elam 1.2.54–6; Nunn 12). Viola throws her arms around him and hugs him tightly when the Captain shrugs and smiles, indicating his acquiescence to her plan. Perhaps he realizes that, all things considered, she has no other options and, kind man that he is, decides to help her rather than hinder her.

In the montage that follows his agreement with her understandably necessary plan the Captain supervises Viola's transformation from female to cross-dressed male. In short order Viola allows her long hair to be cut so that what remains falls just above her shoulders; she removes her corset and exchanges it for a pair of naval cadet trousers; she pads her crotch with a folded cloth in order to create the appearance of male genitals; she binds her breasts tightly by wrapping her chest in a lengthy swathe of red fabric as if she were a living mummy; and she dons a formal military jacket that matches her pants and a pair of black men's boots. She then receives 'on-the-job' instruction from the captain in how to walk with the stride of a man and practises using her voice as a man would by bellowing at the Illyrian sea. Lastly, she places a faux moustache on her upper lip so that, in the end, she looks much like her (presumed) dead twin brother, Sebastian (see Figure 9). Thus Cesario, the young man that Duke Orsino (Toby Stephens) will fall in love with, is born (see Figure 10).

That female characters like Viola were played on the stage by boy actors during the early modern period in England is a matter of well-explored historical fact. As Phyllis Rackin writes, in a theatrical world governed by the convention:

FIGURE 9 *Imogen Stubbs as Viola before her transformation into the boy Cesario in* Twelfth Night, *dir. Trevor Nunn, 1996.*

FIGURE 10 *Imogen Stubbs as Viola after her transformation into the boy Cesario in* Twelfth Night, *dir. Trevor Nunn, 1996.*

where female characters were always played by male actors, feminine gender was inevitably a matter of costume; and in plays where the heroines dressed as boys, gender became doubly problematic, the unstable product of roleplaying and costume, not only in the theatrical representation but also within the fiction presented on the stage.[8]

To play a convincing Viola, then, a boy actor would have had to don clothing appropriate to a young woman and effect a feminine voice and mannerisms. To in turn become a convincing Cesario that same boy actor would have had to reassume masculine attire and the corresponding tone and behaviours evocative of a young man. The concept of gender, irrespective of biological sex, can, once again, be understood, borrowing Butler's paradigm, as a learned performance rather than a natural or innate characteristic that someone is born with and knows intuitively how to present to the world. Specifically, Butler writes that gender 'is the repeated stylization of the body, a set of repeated acts within a highly rigid regulatory frame that congeal over time to produce the appearance of substance, of a natural sort of being'.[9] Butler's insight leads to the supposition that it is in the theatre in general and in Shakespeare's and Nunn's *Twelfth Night*s in particular where the concept of gender is exposed as a wholly artificial construction. Viola proves that one is not born a woman, or a man, for that matter, and the implications of that fact are far reaching considering the representation of not only gender, but also of the inevitable resulting homosociality and male homoeroticism evident throughout Nunn's *Twelfth Night*.

Interestingly, little if any anxiety attends the intimate relationship that develops between Duke Orsino and his male servant Cesario. Indeed, it seems entirely acceptable that Orsino desires Cesario because Cesario is really no more than the fictional creation of the female Viola who is in turn the equally female Imogen Stubbs. On this point Maria F. Magro and Mark Douglas remark that viewers of Nunn's production, if they are so inclined, 'can safely indulge in some homoerotic titillation without guilt' where Orsino and Cesario are concerned because that titillation is really heteroerotic rather than homoerotic in nature given the actuality of Viola's, and the actress who plays her, female gender.[10] The attraction Orsino and Cesario feel is therefore at its heart based on essentially normative gender identities and, since audiences are in on the cross-dressing conceit from the outset, they can watch the Duke and his page's romance unfold with total assurance that the traditional man and woman will end up coupled in holy matrimony by the time the end credits roll. But it must also be acknowledged that it is just as possible to understand Nunn's depiction of the Orsino and Cesario relationship as one that is equally indicative of a substantive, as opposed to a merely titillating or laughable, form of male homoerotic desire given the gender trouble that lies at the heart of the representation. Initial authorization for taking this approach to the story of the Duke and his servant can be found in the available criticism of the film. For instance, two critics describe Orsino and Cesario's association in Nunn's production in what can be considered homoerotic terms. Coursen rather matter-of-factly declares that 'Orsino is very attracted to this boy',[11] while Rothwell makes a similar assertion when he comments on 'Orsino's falling in love with a boy'.[12] But the comments of Coursen and Rothwell can be taken further.

Turning back to the film itself, once he has been brought into being by Viola and the Captain, Cesario is next seen in Nunn's *Twelfth Night* after he has been in the service of Duke Orsino for almost three months. David Schalkwyk explains that service was a ubiquitous 'condition in early modern England' that 'tied people to each other'.[13] He continues by detailing the fact that service was primarily an economic institution whereby servants:

> worked for a master or mistress, in jobs ranging from domestic or personal service through crafts and cottage industries. These included weaving or brewing, sowing or harvesting, milking and tending animals, or trade and hospitality, in (ideally) mutually beneficial relationships through which the master or mistress received assistance in return for board, lodging, and wages (which were usually low).[14]

But as Schalkwyk also makes clear through the course of his argument, service often created an environment that fostered the development of various kinds of love, including eros, or the kind of romantic love that encompasses everything from infatuation to desire and sexual intercourse. So it is perhaps unsurprising that Shakespeare uses service as a plot device through which the characters of Orsino and Cesario are brought together in a set of dramatic circumstances that facilitates the evolution of their interpersonal relationship. This is an aspect of *Twelfth Night* that Nunn seems to exploit to the fullest in his cinematic text. Cesario is never seen in the film performing any of the comparatively menial tasks that Schalkwyk lists above and that real people in service in England would have been expected to carry out. Instead Cesario plays the piano for Orsino, functions as his sounding board, acts as an opponent in games of cards and billiards, and accompanies him on horseback on scouting missions in Illyria. Thus it is that Cesario's being in Orsino's service binds them to one another in a pragmatic sense but also, in due course, on an emotional level. Service sets the stage, so to speak, for each of these two men (men insofar as the concept of gender trouble is in play) to court one another in a roundabout way, something that likely could not or would not have occurred otherwise given the social/life stations they occupy in Illyrian society.

Though an affected melancholic because of what he obsessively describes as his unrequited love for the disdainful Countess Olivia, Orsino nevertheless cuts a dashing and masculine figure that many viewers of Nunn's film, in tandem with Cesario, might well find attractive. One morning the imperious Duke, his right arm in a sling for unexplained reasons, seeks Cesario out while Cesario is at fencing practice with the other men that make up Orsino's all-male company. As they leave the gymnasium Orsino unselfconsciously places his good arm around Cesario's shoulders in an action that indicates their intimacy, that embarrasses Cesario, and that, interestingly, does not go unnoticed by the rest of Orsino's people. This gesture also indicates that Cesario has, comparatively quickly, seemingly become Orsino's favourite subordinate. Thus, quite by chance it seems, Cesario occupies a highly privileged and influential position *vis-à-vis* Orsino that is analogous to the so-called 'royal favourite', a problematic figure during Shakespeare's time. For instance, King James I, as is well known, had a series of male favourites – and likely lovers – that those in his court who did not enjoy such intimate privilege always mistrusted. Curtis Perry explains that many in the period felt that the 'political intimacies of royal favoritism inhabit[ed] the dark corners of the state – the privy chamber or bedchamber and other sites of restricted access to the body of the monarch', hence they 'frequently imagined the influence of royal favorites in eroticized terms'.[15] Although *Twelfth Night* is not in any sense a political play or film, nor is Cesario out to bring down the Illyrian government, it is not difficult to suspect based on Perry's insights that Orsino's courtiers, retainers and counsellors might well think badly of Cesario precisely because of the intimate erotic connection they can plainly see exists between the Duke and this upstart who came out of nowhere and, through no fault of their own, managed to supersede them.

Orsino and his favourite Cesario proceed to have a private conversation that takes place on the bluffs overlooking the sea. There, as Orsino sits so close to Cesario that Cesario may as well be in his lap, Orsino reminds Cesario that he now 'knowest no less but all. I have unclasped / To thee the book even of my secret soul' (Elam 1.4.13–14; Nunn 16). With these lines audiences watching *Twelfth Night* can understand that the close relationship Orsino and Cesario have extends beyond physicality and into the realm of the personally revealing. It is doubtful that anyone, especially someone like Count Orsino, would confide his deepest thoughts and wishes to one in whom he does not have full faith, confidence and trust. That being the case, at this point in their story, Orsino wants to use his chosen one as a romantic go-between for himself with the Lady Olivia. When Cesario demurs taking on such an assignment because he thinks doing so might be an exercise in futility, Orsino once again wraps his left arm around Cesario's shoulders and holds him tightly. It is almost as if Orsino is trying to give Cesario some of his masculine strength through the power of human embrace so that Cesario will not fear approaching Olivia on Orsino's behalf. It is also yet another moment of obvious homoerotic physical closeness between these two men that would not be homoerotic if not for the gender trouble Viola's cross-dressing has created.

Orsino's actions toward Cesario become downright aggressive when Cesario still objects to attempting to woo Olivia in his master's stead. Orsino insists that Cesario is the only man for the job and then literally asserts his physical dominance over the frightened boy. While leaning ever closer to him and explaining that Olivia is apt to accept Cesario's entreaties on account of the fact that, being only a boy, he is not in the least threatening, the impassioned Duke suddenly looks at Cesario intently and says, 'Diana's lip / Is not more smooth and rubious' (Elam 1.4.31–2; Nunn 17). As he speaks these words Orsino rubs his thumb across Cesario's upper lip as if he is trying to confirm for himself that what he is saying is, in fact, true. Then, so emboldened, Orsino presses himself even more firmly against Cesario and comments: 'Thy small pipe / Is as the maiden's organ, shrill and sound, / And all is semblative a woman's part' (Elam 1.4.32–4; Nunn 17). It is only following the utterance of these words that Cesario, who has been struggling against Orsino the entire time Orsino has been so persistently forward with him, succeeds at throwing off Orsino. Orsino strikes his already hurt right arm against the rocks of the bluff because Cesario is able to push him away so forcefully. So much for Cesario being merely a non-threatening boy.

The physical homoeroticism evident in the relationship between Orsino and Cesario becomes even more pronounced in a pair of subsequent scenes in Nunn's *Twelfth Night*. In the first of these the director marshals bits of Orsino's and Cesario's dialogue from Acts 1 and 2 in Shakespeare's text; the innovation is the setting in which these lines are spoken and the stage directions that accompany them. After a hard early morning ride on horseback, Orsino beckons Cesario with 'Come hither, boy' (Elam 2.4.15; Nunn 54). At this order Cesario steps gingerly into a large dimly lit room with a fire burning in the fireplace against the far wall. In the centre of the space Orsino is soaking naked in a huge clawfoot tub.

The Duke's well-muscled shoulders and arms glisten in the shafts of light that are filtering in through the windows and falling upon him as if he were the subject of a great master's painting. Though Cesario is discomfited by this unexpected set of circumstances, Orsino exhibits no such concern. He seems in fact to have no problem being nude in the presence of his young male servant. As Cesario sits down in a nearby chair, Orsino waxes poetic about the Countess Olivia. 'How will she love, when the rich golden shaft / Hath killed the flock of all affections else / That live in her,' he muses (Elam 1.1.34–6; Nunn 54). Then he hands Cesario a puffy yellow sponge and leans forward in the bath. Cesario understands the wordless command and begins to wash Orsino's back. Within seconds Cesario becomes lost in his task. The repeated smiles that play upon his face serve to exemplify how one man can take delight in the body of another. That Cesario desires Orsino here is unmistakable in what qualifies as one of the most overtly homoerotic moments in all of Nunn's film.

The scene described above invites if not begs for a non-heteronormative interpretation, and performing such an interpretation involves what Alan Sinfield describes as 'reading against the grain, queering the text', here transformed into 'seeing against the grain, queering the cinematic text' of Nunn's *Twelfth Night*.[16] In other words, though audiences know that Cesario is being played by a female actress, they are nevertheless encouraged to see what is literally right before their eyes: the young male page Cesario – complete with moustache and military uniform – attending to the equally male Orsino's bathing needs. Those needs include being scrubbed with a sponge in a room where Orsino and Cesario are the sole occupants and which is crackling with the homoerotic energy of two characters that are in the process of falling in love with one another regardless of their actual and/or assumed genders. These images are punctuated by highly suggestive language. Orsino muses to Cesario about what kind of an effect his 'rich golden shaft' will have when it finally penetrates his beloved; there can be no mistaking such a metaphor as a verbal representation of sexual intercourse. A queer reading of the cinematic text lays bare the homoerotic possibilities such a staging and the corresponding dialogue present. With these elements operative queer viewers and their allies are free to indulge in the sensual depiction of one man seeing to the desires of another man in a way that is titillating without being crass. Such viewers may well find themselves giving in to the not unwelcome fantasy of being either Cesario or Orsino and, thus, vicariously experiencing an intimate moment with the object of their desire. They do not, in other words, have to read this bath scene in accord with the usual heteronormative paradigms that would erase the effects of any kind of a queer intervention from legibility.

Later in the film Orsino and Cesario race through the darkness to one of the barns on Orsino's property. There Orsino demands that Feste (Ben Kingsley) perform a solo for the Duke and his servant of a piece he is convinced will relieve his passion for the Countess Olivia (2.4.5). Though not referred to as such in Shakespeare's play, the song could be titled 'Come Away Death', and it is about the fate of an unrequited but defiant lover – a person not unlike Orsino himself. When Feste begins to sing, Orsino and Cesario are some ways apart from one another; Orsino is leaning on a towering stack of straw, while Cesario is across from him, standing with his back against the oversized wheel of a large horsecart. It is clear from the moment Feste launches into 'Come Away Death' that Orsino is deeply affected by the words and the music, but not in any way that accords with relief. Indeed, Orsino seems even more melancholy than ever. The expression on his handsome face morphs from one of joy to one of cynicism. His unhappiness is magnified when he glances over at Cesario and sees his servant in equally pensive thought. It may well be that in this moment Orsino understands that he and Cesario are sharing the same dark feelings about life, love and death, and that he feels a connection to the young man unlike any other he has felt for anyone else before.

Perhaps because he is simply unable to contain himself, or maybe because he is feeling guilty for making Cesario experience any kind of pain, Orsino leaves the haystack to go and stand right next to the young man. Then, as he has done twice before in Nunn's *Twelfth Night*, Orsino once again puts his arm around Cesario's shoulders and holds him firmly against his side. This is a decisive intimate move on Orsino's part and it is redolent with homoeroticism. Because Viola has presented herself as a boy, as Cesario, to Orsino, and the Count has accepted Cesario at face value, Orsino only knows Cesario as his male servant Cesario. At the level of character and narrative, then, what is happening here in the barn is happening between an older and a younger man. And as in the earlier bath scene this is another moment when Orsino seems to be perfectly comfortable being in such close proximity to someone of his own gender. Cesario, perhaps carried away by being held in the arms of the man he already desires so much, allows himself to relax and presses his back into Orsino's chest (see Figure 11). Slowly, he turns his head away from

FIGURE 11 *Duke Orsino (Toby Stephens) and his servant, the young man known by one and all as Cesario (Imogen Stubbs), about to kiss one another in* Twelfth Night, *dir. Trevor Nunn, 1996.*

the singing Feste and toward Orsino who, obviously content now, too, closes his eyes. By exquisite degrees Cesario moves his lips upward and ever closer to Orsino's. It could not be any more apparent that these two mustached men want to kiss each other in what appears to be an almost achingly homoerotic scene in Nunn's production. Nunn's cinematic text of *Twelfth Night* thus succeeds at conveying something vitally important in the context of the present chapter that Jean E. Howard insists the playtext does not. She claims that in Shakespeare's original, 'Orsino, in contrast to Olivia, shows no overt sexual interest in the crossdressed Viola', who is, after all, his male servant Cesario, and furthermore that 'the text makes his attraction to Cesario' unintelligible.[17] As the scene under consideration here attests, Orsino *does* show his attraction to, and sexual interest in, Cesario, and in a way that epitomizes the intelligibility of the homoerotic. On screen this desire *is* overt rather than oblique as in the written text of *Twelfth Night*. But when Feste's song comes to an end, in the sudden, deafening quiet, Orsino and Cesario realize what they were about to do and quickly pull apart from one another. What lingers, however, and most particularly, perhaps, for queer audience members of *Twelfth Night*, is the visceral memory of the male same-sex kiss that Orsino and Cesario almost shared.

Orsino and Cesario's homoerotic love for each other comes to the fore again in the denouement of Nunn's *Twelfth Night*, and in a way that dramatizes its physical and its romantic aspects. In order to take care of some necessary business associated with Antonio (Nicholas Farrell), who is being held under guard there by his soldiers, Orsino arrives on Olivia's estate. The moment the Countess herself appears Orsino rapturously tells Cesario 'now heaven walks on earth', and goes to greet her with a spring in his step (Elam 5.1.93; Nunn 115). Initially he is solicitous and respectful to Olivia, but when she cruelly rejects him yet again, and this time to his face rather than by Cesario as her proxy, Orsino loses his temper. The Duke's fury is centred on the fact that he knows that Olivia loves his servant Cesario rather than himself. As he stalks around the courtyard he hurls the following question at the uncivil lady: 'Why should I not – in savage jealousy / Like to th'Egyptian thief at point of death / Kill what I love?' (Elam 5.1.108, 113–15; Nunn 116). Not at all incidentally, Orsino is referring to Cesario in these lines. This is also the very first time Orsino speaks of his love for Cesario. The wonder is that he does so in such a public manner. The homoeroticism apparent here functions in a way that is quite similar to the way Bruce R. Smith describes homoeroticism at work in readings and performances of *Henry V*. Smith considers the Duke of Exeter's report of 'the battlefield deaths of the Duke of York and the Earl of Suffolk', which seem to Smith to be 'more appropriate to Romeo and Juliet than to two soldiers', referring, of course, to the two young lovers who die for each other rather than face the world alone or as the spouses of people they cannot countenance.[18] Significantly, Exeter's account does not even attempt to shy away from repeated mention of York and Suffolk kissing one another in their last moments. In fact Exeter's words both valorize and exalt this kind of same-sex intimacy.[19] For Smith, the 'fact that the expression of such love takes place between two men – and that it is narrated by a third man for the pleasure of several thousand others in the theatre – makes it an instance ... of *homo*eroticism'.[20] As in *Henry V*, Orsino's expression of love for Cesario occurs between two male figures – himself and his boy servant – and although it is not narrated by another man the fact that in this instance it happens in a film rather than on a theatre stage means that it is enacted for the pleasure of, potentially, millions of other men who have chosen to screen Nunn's *Twelfth Night*, many of whom might well be gay or queer and predisposed to be receptive to such passionate declarations of love between men.

Of course, Orsino does not stop posing questions to the Countess, who does not, indeed, cannot, love him. He vows with a sneer that he will remove Cesario from Olivia's presence once and for all: 'But this your minion, whom I know you love, / And whom, by heaven, I swear, I tender dearly, / Him will I tear out of that cruel eye' (Elam 5.1.121–3; Nunn 116). While uttering these words, Orsino stalks over to Cesario and takes Cesario's hand into his own, creating a visual exclamation point as it were of his intentions and his feelings. Meanwhile, the phrase 'tender dearly' could be glossed as another way of saying 'love', as in 'I love him'; it can, as textual editors often note, also be taken to mean that he simply cares deeply about Cesario. Regardless, he neither loves nor cares very much for Olivia, despite his many poetic declarations to the contrary. What Schalkwyk has to say about Orsino in this regard is apropos: the play, in tandem with Nunn's film, reveals the 'qualitative difference between Orsino's *desire* for Olivia and his *love* for Cesario, something which the character himself is deeply unaware' until these key moments in both the written and the cinematic texts.[21] Thus the punishment that Orsino intends to dole out to Olivia by irrevocably separating her and Cesario actually allows the Duke to secure what he most wants – and has most wanted all along – for himself: an exclusive relationship with Cesario, with someone of his own gender.

Throughout these dramatic moments in the denouement of the film Cesario is observing Orsino with nothing less than adoration animating his face. He is, it seems, beyond content to be claimed in such a physical, public and aggressive way by the man he loves. Echoing his master, he offers his own passionate avowal to Orsino: 'And I most jocund, apt, and willingly / To do you rest, a thousand deaths would die' (Elam 5.1.128–9; Nunn 117). Although Cesario has spoken of his love for Orsino before, his readiness to die again and again for that love, though certainly hyperbolic, nevertheless proves quite extraordinary to witness for queer and queer-allied viewers of Nunn's film. Arguably, this is a depiction of male homoerotic love of the highest order, and it would not have been possible to represent so vividly and so palpably were it not for the filmmakers of this *Twelfth Night*'s engagement with gender trouble.

II

In comparison to the *Romeo and Juliet*s of directors George Cukor (1936) and Franco Zeffirelli (1968) analysed in the previous chapter, Baz Luhrmann's *William Shakespeare's Romeo + Juliet* (1996)[22] is a wholly postmodern cinematic take on Shakespeare's original text that often verges on the psychedelic and the schizophrenic. Following its debut, a number of reviewers in the popular press complained about *Romeo + Juliet* being derivative, not Shakespearean enough despite the appearance of Shakespeare's name in the movie's title and, ultimately, more flamboyant style than substantive Shakespearean cinema. Academics were – and remain so today – just as divided in their opinions of the production. Rothwell, for example, offers the following equivocal response: 'This is watching Shakespeare's *Romeo and Juliet* under strobe lights. It has been filtered through John Woo's Hong Kong action movies, and the hiphop and gangsta rap of MTV, yet the characters speak in Elizabethan English. The verbal runs against the grain of the visual semiotics.'[23] And so it does.

Yet at the same time Rothwell finds a method to Luhrmann's madness in his *Romeo + Juliet*. He writes: 'The interplay between the crude actualities of television newscasts and MTV fantasies generates the film's *raison d'être*, which is the displacement into contemporary idiom the oxymorons of Shakespeare's oppositions of womb and tomb, love and death, youth and age, and so forth.'[24] *Romeo + Juliet* was, in other words, designed to appeal to the sensibilities of the young of the late twentieth century. On this subject Nicholas F. Radel points out, too, that Lurhmann's film 'does not interpret Shakespeare in a traditional way, representing his play's historical difference from modern concerns; instead, it focuses on seemingly anachronistic, modern social fantasies about race and sex, interpreting the famous "star-crossed" lovers within the social and sexual divisions of our own society'.[25] The irony of this reception history is that, within the larger project of critiquing Luhrmann's *Romeo + Juliet*, Zeffirelli's and even Cukor's *Romeo and Juliet*s were idealized as exemplars of cinematic fidelity to Shakespeare's original, although, in both of their respective historical moments, each was criticized just as harshly, albeit for different reasons.

While problematic and delightful on many different levels, if there is one thing that Luhrmann stumbles over in his *Romeo + Juliet* it is the simultaneous queering of the character of Mercutio (Harold Perrineau) and the homoeroticizing of Mercutio's relationship with Romeo (Leonardo DiCaprio); this failure can be attributed to the director's conventional treatment of gender in the film. A number of critics have touched on this aspect of the production, but have not otherwise explored it in detail. Rothwell asserts that the actor who plays 'a splendid Mercutio ... performs a virtuoso Queen Mab speech' and notes that his 'friendship [with Romeo] hints at a streak of homoeroticism'.[26] He then goes on to point out specifically the fact that '[f]or the Capulet ball, Mercutio cross-dresses in a mini-skirt.'[27] Similarly, James N. Loehlin explains that Mercutio 'vogues through a glitzy camp performance of "Young Hearts Run Free" that combines Busby Berkeley with *Paris is Burning*' before claiming that this 'memorable performance, atop a brightly lit staircase, in high heels, spangled bra and Jean Harlow wig, serves the structural function of the Mab speech, encapsulating the brilliancy, imaginative energy and homosocial bonding of Mercutio's world, just before Romeo meets the woman who will draw him away from it'.[28] Finally Lehmann states: 'Luhrmann's Mercutio is a black-skinned, white-sequined, drag queen who seems desperately disturbed by Romeo's heterosexual awakening.'[29] These critical assessments, individually and collectively, make the same empirical observations about the fact that Lurhmann's Mercutio is an impossible to ignore – Radel describes him as the 'most brilliant and attractive of Romeo's friends'[30] – black, gay drag queen, but they do not proceed to consider the larger implications of their summations. That being the case the purpose of this section of this chapter is to examine the significance of Mercutio's transvestitism and the homoerotic nature of his association with Romeo in *Romeo + Juliet* from a queer perspective – in this case a perspective that does not automatically accept representations at face value. The overarching argument is that gender trouble ultimately trumps the seemingly progressive nature of the interpretation of Mercutio that Luhrmann puts forth in the film.

The opening of Luhrmann's *Romeo + Juliet* is a slick montage of gritty and frantic images that tell the backstory of the Capulet and Montague feud. This sequence includes a visual representation of the film's dramatis personae. When Harold Perrineau appears as Mercutio his title card includes the following tag – 'Romeo's best friend' (see Figure 12). This is something of a cinematic elaboration on the lists of dramatis personae that appear in print versions of the play, most of which describe Mercutio as either Romeo's or Prince Escalus's kinsman and only as Romeo's friend rather than best friend. The concern here centres on the whys and wherefores of Luhrmann's decision to call specific attention to Mercutio's relational status to Romeo by using the superlative 'best' to

FIGURE 12 *Romeo's best friend Mercutio's (Harold Perrineau) title card*. William Shakespeare's Romeo + Juliet, *dir. Baz Luhrmann, 1996*.

modify 'friend'. Certainly doing so signifies that Romeo and Mercutio's friendship is more special and more important to them than their respective friendships with anyone else. At the same time, however, attaching such a modifier to 'friend' in this context seems like a not-so-subtle attempt to insist that Mercutio and Romeo are just best friends and nothing more. Put in another way, it seems like a not-so-subtle attempt to remove from the interpretive equation the mere idea that there is anything romantic, homoerotic or sexual between Mercutio and Romeo. Perhaps this is Luhrmann's way of circumventing the intertextual connotations that suggest otherwise (inclusive of, in particular, Zeffirelli's *Romeo and Juliet*, which establishes the fact of homoerotic intimacy as part and parcel of Romeo and Mercutio's relationship, as well as Porter's commentary on this aspect of Zeffirelli's film) with the visual rhetorical equivalent of a preemptive first strike. The effect of such a move seems to be to keep Romeo safely untouchable in the reified realm of the absolute heterosexual. Mercutio may not be straight, but Romeo is, and that is what matters most within the overall ideology of Luhrmann's production. As Radel writes, though, Luhrmann 'doesn't suggest that there is anything perverse about Mercutio's being gay. Rather he seems to be repeating what has become almost a cliché of modern interpretations of *Romeo and Juliet*' starting with Zeffirelli's 1968 production, which was the first to manifest a gay Mercutio.[31] Nevertheless, in 'both Zeffirelli's film and Luhrmann's, Mercutio definitely seems hung up on Romeo, even though – and this is crucial – his physical desire is apparently not returned'.[32] Still, these Romeos, it can be said in twenty-first-century colloquial terms, are just not that 'into' their respective Mercutios in Zeffirelli's and Luhrmann's adaptations.

Luhrmann's Mercutio is not just Romeo's best friend – he is also, significantly in the context of a visual poetics of gender trouble, a black, gay man who likes to dress up in women's clothing. Burt thoroughly describes one of Mercutio's appearances as follows:

In the spectacular, Las Vegas-style Capulet ball sequence in Baz Luhrmann's *William Shakespeare's Romeo and Juliet* (1996), a bearded Mercutio, played by black actor Harold Perinneau, is the 'very pink of courtesy,' performing in full drag on a staircase in front of a huge painting of the Virgin Mary and baby Jesus, surrounded by six male dancers (who flash their star-crossed buns to the camera) and flanked by two male go-go dancers. Shot as if he's in an MTV music video sequence in quickly paced zooms, zips, and pans, Mercutio wears a matching sequined cape, necklace, bodice, and miniskirt with exposed garters, stockings, and panties; white, long-sleeved, satin gloves; pumps; false eyelashes; heavy mascara and eyeshadow; bright red lipstick; and a large white fright wig. While dancing a showgirl number complete with above-the-head alternating leg kicks, Mercutio lip-synchs a pumping, Latin disco song entitled 'Young Hearts Run Free' (sung by Kym Mazell) and, extending his tongue at certain moments, makes a striptease-like address to the camera as well as to Romeo.[33]

In terms of imagery saturation, this is about as excessive and cinematically 'in-your-face' as it gets when it comes to non-normative gender representation. On one level, of course, the choice to present Mercutio as a drag queen seems both progressive and trendy. This aspect of *Romeo + Juliet* comes at a time in history when the cinematic and cultural zeitgeist brought such representations into vogue, as evidenced by films like *The Crying Game* (1992), *Mrs. Doubtfire* (1993), *The Adventures of Priscilla, Queen of the Desert* (1994), *To Wong Foo, Thanks For Everything, Julie Newmar* (1995) and *The Birdcage* (1996) – all very popular movies that took the figure of the (gay) male cross-dresser from the margins of Western society and placed him at its mainstream centre in what qualifies as, perhaps, the most accessible way possible in the period: via the medium of film.

But part of the problem with Luhrmann's transvestite Mercutio is that the director provides his viewers with no corresponding context that is intrinsic to *Romeo + Juliet* itself that allows for informed interpretation of this iteration of the character. They are in other words left to their own devices, and in that fact there is the potential for difficulty. This is because, as Butler revealed, 'gender is an identity constituted in time, instituted in an exterior space through a *stylized repetition of acts*. The effect of gender is produced through the stylization of the body and, hence, must be understood as the mundane way in which bodily gestures, movements, and styles of various kinds constitute the illusion of an abiding gendered self.'[34] The material representation of gender is therefore a set of performative acts having nothing at all to do with the biological sex of actual individuals. The concept of gender is strictly – even ruthlessly – policed along the masculine/feminine divide in the present historical epoch; as such, it only seems natural and unchanging. The very idea of cross-dressing, like the character of Mercutio does in Luhrmann's *Romeo + Juliet*, once again exposes gender as a fiction rather than a reality. And that, inevitably perhaps, creates trouble.

Of course, no one within the world of *Romeo + Juliet* reacts to Mercutio's penchant for cross-dressing in either a negative or a positive way; Mercutio is accepted by one and all with an admirable level of neutrality. Yet whether or not some, let alone all, of Luhrmann's viewers are capable of such equanimity is questionable – and this applies to viewers who span the sexual identity spectrum, from straight to gay or queer, transgender, intersexual, bisexual and beyond. Garber helps to contextualize these dynamics: '[i]n mainstream culture', she writes 'it thus appears just as unlikely that a gay man will be pictured in non-transvestite terms as it is that a transvestite man will be pictured in non-gay terms.'[35] Put in a slightly different way, Garber is arguing that, to many, gay men, simply because they are attracted to members of their own gender, are just like women, all of whom, from this perspective, are only ever attracted to men, too; hence it is no surprise that (some) gay men dress up like women. Furthermore, any man who enjoys donning women's clothes *must be* gay given his fetish for a certain kind of apparel even if his actual erotic and romantic interests involve people of the opposite sex. 'It is as though', Garber remarks, 'the hegemonic cultural imaginary is saying to itself: if there is a difference (between gay and straight), we want to be able to *see* it, and if we see a difference (a man in women's clothes), we want to be able to *interpret* it.'[36] In Foucauldian terms this is one way that the institution of heterosexuality seeks to contain anything that would attempt to subvert its various paradigms and proscriptions and, thereby, attempts to perpetuate itself ad infinitum. For individuals who are part of the material world – gay, straight or anywhere in between – this set of circumstances is equivalent to an ideological catch-22.

Significantly, what is also operative in this environment, as Garber explains, is the

> desire to *tell the difference*, to guard against a difference that might otherwise put the identity of one's own position in question. (If people who dress like me might be gay, then someone might think I'm gay, or I might get too close to someone I don't recognize as gay; if someone who is heterosexual like me dresses in women's clothes, what is heterosexuality? etc.) Both the energies of conflation and the energies of clarification and differentiation between transvestism and homosexuality thus mobilize and problematize, under the twin anxieties of *visibility* and *difference*, all of the culture's assumptions about normative sex and gender roles.[37]

Hence being neither as truly innovative nor as truly subversive as it pretends to be, Luhrmann's representation of Mercutio as a drag queen serves to reinforce the strictest of binaries between straight men and gay and/or queer men. Mercutio's transvestite appearance also only feeds into mainstream society's fears about its ability to differentiate itself from the Big Bad Wolf of the gay or homosexual Other. And because Mercutio is marked as a deviant cross-dresser on the very first instant he struts through the cinematic frame wearing what can be considered outlandish women's clothes, his difference from the norm(al) becomes an albatross around his neck from which he can never escape. While watching *Romeo + Juliet* some audience members may be encouraged by the subliminal effects of film to, as Garber puts it, *tell the difference* between what they can all too easily perceive to be a heterosexual Mercutio and a homosexual Mercutio, with the latter almost completely obliterating the former the second Mercutio appears onscreen for the first time in a glittering sequined dress. Such is the derogatory and ultimately destructive power of stereotypes where homosexuality and cross-dressing are concerned. Having said that, it must also be noted, however, that not even all gay, queer, or bisexual men in Lurhmann's audiences are off the hook. Those that are not would also include the legions of such people who have so internalized Western society's homophobia that they resolutely identify themselves as 'straight-acting' – with all of the attendant baggage such a phrase carries – and seek to distance themselves from their cross-dressing brethren.

All of what has been detailed here so far is why Luhrmann's *Romeo + Juliet* must be critiqued for its unmediated inclusion of a transvestite Mercutio. With no disrespect meant toward Perrineau – who really does give a virtuoso performance in the part – the Mercutio that emerges from the interpretive pressure applied in this analysis is not the, albeit qualified, celebratory figure that Rothwell, Loehlin and other critics identify in their commentaries on the film. Rather the Mercutio that emerges conforms totally to still pervasive stereotypes about the sad, unhappy and angry gay man who is the way he is because he is caught in the trap of forever pining over what he can never have: a true emotional, romantic, affectionate and sexual relationship with the straight man – in this case, of course, Romeo, who will always remain out of Mercutio's reach because he is unable to return Mercutio's feelings in kind. Luhrmann, it warrants adding, represents Mercutio as little more than the feminine gay foil for the straight, but problematically masculine, Romeo. Radel explains:

> A weak and vacillating character in the early part of Shakespeare's play and later a man made seemingly irrational by his love for Juliet, he [Romeo] hardly constitutes an ideal of early modern masculinity. That he grows to manhood in the play is arguable, but the fact that masculinity in our time is often (and homophobically) posited around heterosexuality provides a convenient type of cinematic shorthand for ... Luhrmann, who displace[s] homosexual desire onto Mercutio alone ... Mercutio's seeming homosexuality then, is used to mark by contrast the otherwise questionable sexuality of one of Shakespeare's most famous lovers.[38]

This overarching heteronormative ethos in turn colours what had the potential to be one of the most homoerotic parts of Lurhmann's production: Mercutio's death and Romeo's response to that irrevocable loss, which exemplifies Butler's insistence that 'gender is a performance with clearly punitive consequences. Discrete genders are part of what "humanizes" individuals within contemporary culture; indeed we regularly punish those who fail to do their gender right.'[39] Luhrmann's Mercutio, as a representative of all men who 'fail to do their gender right' in the realm of the cinema and the realm of the material, is punished by death for his unforgiveable transgression. The moral of Luhrmann's treatment of the tale could not be made more apparent.

The circumstances that lead to Mercutio's death begin when an already worried Benvolio states, after seeing them arrive at a park on the shore of Verona Beach, 'By my head, here comes the Capulets' (3.1.34).[40] Nonplussed, Mercutio places his feet on the table and proclaims 'By my heel, I care not' (3.1.35). This is a show of bravado on the part of Mercutio – foolhardy bravado perhaps, but bravado nonetheless. It is also the kind of action mixed with words that would be expected from a man who is spoiling for a fight. And that is just what he gets when the Capulets, led by the fiery Tybalt, walk up to the assembled Montagues. 'Gentlemen,' Tybalt says, 'a word with one of you' (3.1.37). Employing a mocking smile, Mercutio responds with, 'And but one word with one of us? Couple it / with something, make it a word and a blow' (3.1.38–9). As Weis points out in the footnote that accompanies these lines in his Arden 3 edition of *Romeo and Juliet*, the phrase 'a word and a blow' was proverbial in Shakespeare's day indicating how easy it was for words to morph into fisticuffs.[41] The problem is with the interpretive licence Luhrmann takes with the lines in *Romeo + Juliet*. The way Mercutio delivers them is deliberately provocative. The stage directions in Craig Pearce and Lurhmann's screenplay provide the following instructions: 'Leaning close to Tybalt' in the seconds before the last word, 'blow', is uttered, 'he [Mercutio] camps it up'.[42] Perrineau does not miss a beat as he delivers the word 'blow', after an ad-libbed dramatic pause, in a breathy falsetto voice that is dripping with bitchy sarcasm.

Word and gesture thus combine to make the bawdy meaning obvious – this Mercutio means 'blow' in its twentieth-/twenty-first-century sense of the performance of the sex act known as fellatio. But what remains unclear is if Mercutio is suggesting that Tybalt ought to 'blow' Mercutio along with the exchange of words Tybalt has requested or if, on the other hand, Mercutio is suggesting that Tybalt ought to allow Mercutio to 'blow' Tybalt in exchange for having words with him. The concern with Luhrmann's representation of the Mercutio/Tybalt dialogue here has everything to do with anachronism. Sources such as the *OED* reveal that 'blow' did not acquire the meaning of fellatio until the 1930s;[43] it would not have meant the same thing in Elizabethan or Jacobean parlance. Be that as it may, Mercutio's razor-sharp wit meets with success as evidenced by the laughter it generates from the Montagues and those of their surrounding allies. Tybalt, however, is enraged, presumably because Mercutio has triumphed at making fun of Tybalt in a public forum. At the same time, though, Tybalt could be upset because of the homosexual/

homoerotic implications inherent in the very idea of one man performing fellatio on another. It is also quite likely that both attitudes are influencing Tybalt. That being the case, Tybalt's explosive anger makes him seem like the stereotypical homophobic man who is so insecure with his own sexual identity that he must deal accordingly with any such threat to that identity in order to protect his reputation as a 'real' – not a gay, queer or bisexual – man.

Things go from bad to worse the moment Tybalt blurts out contemptuously: 'Mercutio, thou consortest with Romeo' (3.1.44). At that point all bets are off between the two men as Mercutio charges after Tybalt like an enraged bull, his anger matching if not exceeding Tybalt's in intensity. Mercutio demands to know if Tybalt dares to compare Mercutio and Romeo to minstrels. Once again drawing on Weis's footnotes in the Arden 3 edition of *Romeo and Juliet*, it becomes apparent that in the early modern period in England minstrels – not, ironically, unlike actors – were viewed by certain segments of the population as unsavoury figures with a penchant for both effeminacy and sodomy. Mercutio's rage over the accusation Tybalt may or may not be making about the nature of Mercutio and Romeo's relationship proves difficult to interpret within the overall context of Luhrmann's *Romeo + Juliet*. Certainly, on a homosocial level, Mercutio is looking out for Romeo and trying to defend his friend from being impugned in any way by Tybalt. But is Mercutio upset because Tybalt is denigrating both Mercutio and Romeo in general? Or is Mercutio upset because Tybalt is suggesting that Mercutio and Romeo have the kind of intimate relationship with one another that is undeserving of contempt? Or is Mercutio upset because Tybalt is implying that he knows Mercutio and Romeo do not have the kind of love relationship with each other that Mercutio longs for so desperately? The answers to these questions remain open-ended and thus a matter of interpretation, although all three lend themselves well to queer readings.

Luhrmann sets Mercutio's final battle with Tybalt on a dazzling open-air stage that is itself located on Verona Beach and bears the name Sycamore Grove Theatre. Though it may seem a heavy-handed sort of symbolism, it also has the effect of underscoring the fact that the story of *Romeo + Juliet*, like its source text, suddenly veers at this point from comedy to tragedy with Mercutio's death at Tybalt's hands, and that this is drama at its most theatrical *and* its most cinematic. Mercutio's evident desire to protect Romeo from Tybalt – inspired in no small part because of Romeo's pacifism where Tybalt's verbal and physical abuse of Romeo is concerned – signifies how deeply Mercutio feels about Romeo. It is not overstating the case to claim that Mercutio loves Romeo. But once again Mercutio's homoerotic longing for Romeo can only be viewed through the haze of the unrequited. Romeo may care just as much about Mercutio, and he may even love Mercutio, but in Luhrmann's vision Romeo's desire for Mercutio never crosses the line between the homosocial and the homoerotic. This is made plain the moment Mercutio dies as a result of Tybalt's having impaled him with a lethal shard of glass. Romeo grabs the lifeless body of Mercutio and wails and cries over the loss while he holds Mercutio in his arms (see Figure 13).

The moment is as affecting as it is disturbing; however, viewers of Luhrmann's *Romeo + Juliet* are aware, given the best friend title card flashed at the beginning of the film, that it takes place between two people who were best friends and not ever, even potentially where this Romeo is concerned, lovers. And although Romeo – not unlike Achilles taking vengeance on Hector for Hector's killing of Achilles's beloved Patroclus in Homer's *Iliad* – races after Tybalt and, before long, guns him down, he is only meting out justice because he is, homosocially speaking, one man looking out for another man, no more, no less. As in Shakespeare's play, Mercutio's death in Lurhmann's film, Radel writes, 'evokes a crisis of masculinity in which Romeo realizes that his love for Juliet has made him effeminate ... Revenging the death of his friend becomes a sign of Romeo's emerging masculinity, which is intimately connected in the play with violence, in advance of his consummating his marriage with Juliet', the latter being, of

FIGURE 13: *Romeo (Leonardo DiCaprio) cradling his dead best friend Mercutio (Harrold Perrineau) in his arms.* Romeo + Juliet, *dir. Baz Luhrmann, 1996.*

course, the most tangible sign of masculinity possible.[44] Thus it is made apparent yet again that Luhrmann uses the potentiality of the male homoerotic in *Romeo + Juliet* as a spectre that is always denied, that is always contained, in favour of the most adamant form of compulsory heterosexuality. Mercutio's gender trouble-inflected homoerotic desire for Romeo is brought to the fore again and again in Luhrmann's *Romeo + Juliet*, and every time this happens that homoerotic desire is suppressed and, finally, is snuffed out of existence entirely with Mercutio's death and his subsequent transformation into 'worms' meat'. All of which serves to reify heterosexuality as the be all and end all of human relationships – with Shakespeare appropriated as the authorizing cultural agent that secures such exaltation.

III

Audiences are made aware from the outset of Michael Hoffman's *William Shakespeare's A Midsummer Night's*

Dream (1999) that it is set in Monte Athena, a village somewhere in the photogenic Tuscan region of northern Italy rather than in Shakespeare's Athens, and in the Victorian era instead of either Antiquity or even the Renaissance.[64] They are also made aware early on that Bottom (Kevin Kline) has a shrew of a wife (Heather Elizabeth Parisi) who does not understand him and what she considers to be his foolish and irresponsible penchant for acting. Otherwise, the film is a reasonably straightforward cinematic retelling of Shakespeare's *Midsummer*. As is the case with nearly all Shakespeare films, reaction to Hoffman's *Dream* has been mixed. One critic appreciates the director's use of well-known Hollywood stars in the film, particularly Kline, Michelle Pfeiffer, Stanley Tucci and Calista Flockhart, along with his use of equally well-known operatic and symphonic pieces in the film's score, such as 'Brindisi' and Mendelssohn's 'Overture to *A Midsummer Night's Dream*', but faults Hoffman for overloading the visuality of the film. But another critic considers the film a visual masterpiece. Still others feel the film is weakened by its too-clever and too-creative use of emotional backstory where Bottom is concerned, but also feel that the performance of Flute/Thisbe is filled with a surprising and unexpected pathos. Yet another hails Hoffman's production as a Shakespearean heritage film in the high-class, cinematic art tradition of such Merchant/Ivory gems as *A Room with a View* (1985), *Maurice* (1987) and *Howard's End* (1992), but insists that it also shows the failure of theatre as a medium of mass entertainment in light of the success of film in the late twentieth/early twenty-first centuries. However, none of these critics takes up the subject of what can be considered the queerest aspect of Hoffman's *Midsummer*: the filmmaker's novel treatment of Shakespeare's Pyramus and Thisbe play-within-a-play plotline that has delighted audiences since the late sixteenth century. In so doing the director manages to transform the metatheatrical story involving the Rude Mechanicals' performance before the newly married Duke and Duchess from little more than a ridiculous, albeit funny, farce into a surprisingly poignant set piece that is informed by gender trouble and tinged with an unexpected touch of male homoeroticism.

Hoffman's innovative serious treatment of the Pyramus and Thisbe tale begins when, fairly early in the film, the amateur acting troupe gathers on the steps of a building undergoing refurbishment in the bustling village of Monte Athena. In accord with Shakespeare's playtext of *Midsummer* the company includes Nick Bottom the weaver, Peter Quince the carpenter (Roger Rees), Snug the joiner (Gregory Jbara), Francis Flute the bellows mender (Sam Rockwell), Tom Snout the tinker (Bill Irwin) and Robin Starveling the tailor (Max Wright). Having assembled, Bottom begs of Quince what play it is that they will endeavour to perform as part of the upcoming wedding celebration for Theseus (David Strathairn) and Hippolyta (Sophie Marceau). Quince informs the actors that their play is to be 'The most lamentable comedy and most cruel death of Pyramus and Thisbe', to which the irrepressible Bottom proclaims: 'A very good piece of work, I assure you, and a merry' (1.2.11–14),[40] although, in actuality, he has no idea what the Pyramus and Thisbe drama is even about. Nevertheless, Bottom is quickly cast by Quince in the part of Pyramus, the lover that 'kills himself most gallant for love' (1.2.20). The men respond to this description of Pyramus with a collective audible sigh of approval, indicating that playing the part of a man willing to kill himself for the love of a woman is a worthy assignment. Indeed, the impression made here is that any male actor not only would but ought to gladly take on such a *natural* role.

Having cast Bottom as Pyramus the director calls out for Flute. 'Here, Peter Quince' (1.2.39) Flute says in an unmistakably deep and masculine voice. Before responding to Flute Quince whispers something to Snout, who dashes away quickly after hearing whatever it is that Quince has to say. Clearly, viewers of Hoffman's *Midsummer* are meant to understand that Snout and Quince are in something of a conspiracy together against Flute, who is told by Quince 'You must take Thisbe on you' (1.2.40). With a touching smile (see Figure 14), Flute asks, 'What is Thisbe? A wandering knight?' and Quince, as he steps gingerly away from Flute, informs the man with a noticeable chuckle that Thisbe 'is the lady that Pyramus must love' (1.2.39–40). That Flute will be performing the role of Pyramus's lady love inspires a round of guffawing on the part of all of his fellow actors, with the exception of Bottom, who is too busy trying to figure out a way to convince Quince that he should be allowed to play multiple roles in the production to be at all concerned with Flute's immediate fate as a performer. To most of this group of amateur actors there is something inordinately amusing about the idea of a man playing the part of a woman on stage. A truly masculine, heterosexual male, the further implication

FIGURE 14 *Francis Flute (Sam Rockwell), with a genuinely innocent smile on his face, moments before being cast by Peter Quince (Roger Rees) as Thisbe.* William Shakespeare's A Midsummer Night's Dream, *dir. Michael Hoffman, 1999.*

is, would never degrade or humiliate himself by agreeing to portray a female character on the stage.

Hearing the role he is to play causes the ingenuous smile to vanish from Flute's face. Meanwhile, the ribbing of Flute by his fellows becomes even more pronounced when the camera turns viewers' attention to the character of Snout who, at Quince's instigation moments earlier, had hopped off the makeshift stage and retrieved the pink dress costume Flute will have to don when he portrays Thisbe. When Snout prances around below with the pink dress held up to his waist, mimicking how ridiculous he and the rest of the male actors think Flute will look wearing the dress as Thisbe, it engenders yet another round of spirited guffaws that become uproarious. Snout's juvenile actions also elicit Quince's non-verbal approval, as evidenced by the grin on his face in tandem with the 'good job' hand gesture he directs to Snout. Even the camera angle Hoffman uses in this shot makes explicit the idea that the dominant heteronormative portion of Western society literally looks down on men who dress up as women no matter the circumstances of such a gender performance. The shot is therefore neither neutral nor innocent. From a visual rhetorical perspective it seems like an attempt to persuade complicit audience members that cross-dressing on the part of a male is worthy of nothing more than scorn and derision.

An obviously disquieted Flute pleads with Quince: 'Nay, faith, let not me play a woman. I have a beard coming' (1.2.38). Bottom jumps into the conversation at this point and says, 'An I may hide my face, let me play Thisbe too. I'll speak in a monstrous little voice: "Thisne, Thisne!" "Ah, Pyramus, my lover dear! Thy Thisbe dear, and lady dear!"' (1.2.41–3). Bottom uses a falsetto voice that gets stronger and stronger as he improvises these lines to their end. Nearby stands Flute who, with each word Bottom speaks, becomes quite animated about the idea of Bottom playing Thisbe rather than taking on the role himself and being ridiculed for 'becoming' a woman in such a way. With a combination of comical eye and facial gestures Flute tries to convince Quince that Bottom would be the ideal actor for the part of Thisbe. But Quince disagrees: 'No, no,' he says to Bottom with evident asperity, 'you must play Pyramus, and Flute, you Thisbe' (1.2.44). Quince then calls out for Snout and together they lead Flute toward the back of the stage where Snout and Starveling begin fitting Flute into the pink dress with exaggerated coos of 'Thisbe' that make them sound a bit like mother hens fussing over a reluctant child in need of mollifying rather than the 'hard-handed men' (5.1.72) of Athens as the haughty Philostrate (John Sessions) later describes them.

With this particular representation of Flute's casting as Thisbe – and his colleagues' reaction to it – Hoffman is following cinematic tradition. In the *Midsummer* productions of Reinhardt and Dieterle (1935) and Peter Hall (1968), Flute's fellow mechanicals also laugh at him when he is made by Peter Quince to take on the role of Thisbe; they laugh at Flute for the exact same reasons in all three films – to them, there is something inherently funny about the idea of a man, especially, in this case, a comparatively young one like Flute, outfitted in female dress. However, as evidenced by two other screen productions of *Midsummer* by directors Elijah Moshinsky (1981) and Adrian Noble (1996), there is a different, equally viable, way to play the initial sequence involving Flute/Thisbe that is under discussion. Moshinsky's and Noble's Flutes, as well as their amateur-actor compatriots, take Flute's casting as Thisbe in their stride without bursting into mirth as happens in the films of Reinhardt and Dieterle, Hall and Hoffman. They seem in fact to understand that at times stage performance requires males to cross-dress as female characters and, as such, that cross-dressing is really no laughing matter in the world of the theatre that they are trying to enter, even if only temporarily. And thus an analytical crux reveals itself. Which is the correct interpretation? The one put forth by Reinhardt and Dieterle, Hall and Hoffman in which Flute is the butt of a joke? Or the one put forth by Moshinsky and Noble in which Flute's forthcoming drag performance before the Athenian court is not subject to ridicule? Considering the well-documented and thoroughly historicized fact that young male actors cross-dressing as female characters was a convention of early modern English theatre because of the laws in place that prevented women from working on stage, the extant research on the professionalism and range required of the boy actors of the period in order to portray totally convincing Katherinas, Lady Macbeths or Hermiones, among other female characters, and finally, Renaissance theatregoers' long-standing familiarity with these, to them, normative circumstances, it seems more likely than not that it is Moshinksy's and Noble's treatments of the early Flute/Thisbe material that are more authentic and more historically accurate than those of Reinhardt and Dieterle, Hall and Hoffman. Logically, then, the critical focus needs to shift somewhat into a consideration of what the latter set of *Midsummer* directors accomplishes as regards their individual and collective representations that encourage audiences to engage in heteronormative laughter at Flute/Thisbe.

Edward Berry explains that the act of laughing 'is deeply equivocal. At times, as when we laugh "with" someone, laughter may be a mechanism by which we identify with another human being, a means of psychological and social bonding. At other times, as when we laugh "at" someone, the same physical reaction may be a form of aggressive self-assertion.'[47] For Berry, laughing with someone is, in accord with the ideas of Mikhail Bakhtin, an exercise in the carnivalesque; on the other hand, laughing at someone is, in accord with the ideas of Thomas Hobbes, an exercise in the sharp Hobbesian distinction between the superior and the inferior. 'Both kinds of laughter, curiously, can strengthen certain kinds of social communion: the carnivalesque, by casting wide the net of community, implying that we are all, at some level one; the Hobbesian, by affirming the superiority of one community in opposition to an individual or group outside it.'[48] Berry proceeds to explain that Hobbesian laughter is often used 'as a form of social correction. By experiencing the humiliation of being laughed at, so the idea goes, the victim is led to recognize his or her social deviance and [possibly] rejoins the community reformed.'[49] Hence Hobbesian laughter 'works towards limited social communion through exclusion, forging group solidarity among privileged insiders through the mockery of outsiders, whoever they may be'.[50] In Shakespeare's comedies this mockery is directed at the 'Other', character-figures that were not 'aristocratic, male, white, English, heterosexual Christians'.[51] These 'Others' include Katherina from *The Taming of the Shrew*, Shylock from *The Merchant of Venice*, Jacques from *As You Like It*, Malvolio from *Twelfth Night*, Falstaff from *The Merry Wives of Windsor* and Caliban from *The Tempest*, all of which are mocked, abused, tormented and humiliated in one way or another in the plays they inhabit.[52] Interestingly, though Shakespeare's female characters like the shrew Katherina were considered 'Others', the boy actors who portrayed them on stage do not seem to have been considered 'Others'. Perhaps this is because, although unlikely to be or to ever become aristocratic, they were nevertheless still male, white, English, heterosexual and Christian.

All of the above information lends a great deal of credence to the notion that it is by no means certain that during the early modern period the mechanicals would have laughed at one of their own simply because he was going to have to perform his role cross-dressed as a woman in the Pyramus and Thisbe story arc as the characters do in Reinhardt and Dieterle's, Hall's and Hoffman's twentieth-century film versions of *Midsummer*. With this supposition in play, Reinhardt and Dieterle's, Hall's and Hoffman's respective depictions of the Pyramus and Thisbe material seem anachronistic in a specific way. Because the laughter directed at Flute is always shown from the point-of-view of his fellow mechanicals save Bottom, Hoffman's *Midsummer* is particularly good at making its audiences complicit in the kind of laughter Berry calls a Hobbesian form of social correction. Hoffman's viewers are thus in concert *with* most of mechanicals, encouraged to laugh *at* Flute because of the cross-dressing predicament in which, through no fault of his own, he finds himself. Since most men do not normally go around wearing women's clothing in today's world – and those who do are, in most cases, automatically assumed to be homosexual regardless of their actual sexual identity – the mechanicals' laughter (and that of the members of Hoffman's audiences who identify with them) at Flute is deployed in Hoffman's *Midsummer* to make sure everyone involved within and without the film knows that there is something not quite right, that there is something non-heteronormative, that there is something queer, about these circumstances.

As was the case with Nunn's *Twelfth Night* and Lurhmann's *Romeo + Juliet* discussed in the earlier sections of this chapter, gender trouble lies at the heart of Hoffman's representation of Flute/Thisbe. It is worth quoting Garber again on this point. When it comes to gender and sexuality in the late twentieth/early twenty-first centuries, as she explains, Western society is obsessed with the 'desire to *tell the difference*' between men and women and, more especially perhaps, between straight men and gay/queer men, in order 'to guard against a difference that might otherwise put the identity of one's own position in question. (If people who dress like me might be gay, then someone might think I'm gay, or I might get too close to someone I don't recognize as gay; if someone who is heterosexual like me dresses in women's clothes, what is heterosexuality? etc.)', hence 'the energies of conflation and the energies of clarification and differentiation between transvestism and homosexuality thus mobilize and problematize, under the twin anxieties of *visibility* and *difference*, all of the culture's assumptions about normative sex and gender roles'.[53] In Hoffman's *Midsummer*, laughing at Flute/Thisbe and making him feel the bitter sting of public humiliation seems to be one way of preserving the heteronormative status quo. But, as it turns out, Hoffman's agenda reaches beyond the simplistic containment of such 'disruptive' gender and sexual forces.

Just prior to the performance before the Duke and the Duchess and their guests, Flute appears for the first time in

Hoffman's *Midsummer* as Thisbe in full drag. The wig he wears provides him with a head of woman's hair that is brown and frizzy and features tangled braids that stretch almost to the ground. His white foundation makes him look almost deathly pale, yet at the same time makes both the pink lipstick and rouge he is wearing stand out prominently. He does not quite seem like a clown, but the overall effect of the make-up is close. In addition, Flute's costume consists of a gold dress, a red shawl, and a number of elaborate gold chains and other jewellery. Looking closely at Flute, however, two things threaten the illusion of femininity: the heavy workman's shoes that can be seen sticking out beneath the hem of his dress and the rather obvious fact that the wig he is wearing is not placed squarely on his head, revealing a bit of the close-cropped hairstyle a young man his age might be expected to wear.

As the actual production of 'The Most Lamentable Comedy and Most Cruel Death of Pyramus and Thisbe' unfolds, Flute as Thisbe arrives on stage only to discover his/her beloved Pyramus lying motionless on the ground. 'Asleep, my love? / What, dead my dove', he/she says using a pronounced falsetto, much to the merriment of the Duke and the Duchess and their courtiers (5.1.304–5). The condescending laughter which Flute/Thisbe bears with stoic equanimity continues as he/she gets stuck on saying the word 'O' (5.1.306). He/she says this one word several times, and each time he/she does so, he/she lowers his voice an octave. But by the time Flute as Thisbe begins to deliver his next lines, he speaks quite clearly and in his own natural voice; that of the young man he is underneath the exaggerated make-up and the multi-layered dress, rather than that of Thisbe, the woman he is attempting to portray. Interestingly, the lower Flute's voice gets as he performs Thisbe, the more emotional, heartfelt and real his words sound. As he continues with 'Speak, speak. Quite dumb? / Dead, dead? A tomb / Must cover thy sweet eyes', the laughter of the audience watching the play-within-the-film fades noticeably (5.1.306–9). First the camera focuses on the expressions of Lysander (Dominic West) and Hermia (Anna

Friel), then those of Helena (Calista Flockhart) and Demetrius (Christian Bale), and shows how they change from delight to seriousness within the space of just a few seconds.

As the scene continues, Flute says, 'O Sisters Three, / Come, come to me, / With hands as pale as milk'; then, in a surprising and extraordinary move, he pulls the woman's wig off of his head and flings it aside, exposing the short brown hair of the young man he really is (5.1.316–18). Thus in addition to dealing with the pathos of the moment, audiences of 'The Most Lamentable Comedy and Most Cruel Death of Pyramus and Thisbe', and of Hoffman's *Midsummer*, must somehow reconcile the fact that they are now watching a young man – albeit a young man still in a woman's dress, but a recognizable young man nonetheless – struggling with the fact that his beloved, Pyramus, another man, is dead (see Figure 15). Not long thereafter, Flute as Thisbe exposed as Flute grabs Pyramus's sword and stabs himself. 'And farewell, friends,' he says, 'Thus Thisbe ends. / Adieu, adieu, adieu' (5.1.325–7). Flute's fingers touch Pyramus's body lightly as he says his trio of goodbyes, and when he dies his head falls to its final rest on Pyramus's waist. At this point it is helpful to

FIGURE 15 *Flute as Thisbe (Sam Rockwell), sans wig, preparing to die so that he/she can be with his/her beloved Pyramus (Kevin Kline) in* William Shakespeare's A Midsummer Night's Dream, *dir. Michael Hoffman, 1999.*

recall that when the group of amateur actors first appeared in Hoffman's film, audiences were told that Pyramus is a lover who dies most gallantly for love. But as his death makes clear, it is actually Flute who is the lover, in this case of another man, who dies most gallantly for that love. What makes the interaction between Flute and Bottom/Pyramus homoerotic is that viewers actually see two men, as opposed to a man and a woman, enacting their passion, the spectacle of one man making good on his willingness to kill himself for another man with whom he happens to be in love, as a palpable reality on screen.

Hoffman's transformation of 'The Most Lamentable Comedy and Cruel Death of Pyramus and Thisbe' from farce to serious, indeed, almost tragic, drama was an inspired choice on his part. Given the cross-dressing aspect of this part of the film, which demands a young man to don female apparel in an illusion that fools no one in the audience about the real gender of Flute/Thisbe, the sequence has homoerotic potential. This potential morphs into vivid actuality the moment Flute removes his wig and begins speaking as one recognizable man to another of love, of mourning and of death. Nevertheless, the homoeroticism of this portrayal seems an accidental rather than a deliberate effect on the part of the filmmakers. Although they may appear in the final shooting script, the published version of Hoffman's screenplay for his *Midsummer* evidences no stage directions that indicate either Flute's removal of the wig or the lowering of his voice from a falsetto to a normal masculine tone, the two key factors that allow for the latent homoeroticism between Flute as Thisbe and Pyramus to manifest most noticeably on screen.[54] This suggests of course that these occurrences were spontaneous, in-the-moment, decisions on the part of either the director or Sam Rockwell, the actor responsible for bringing Flute/Thisbe to life. Whatever the case, it can be argued that these decisions work beautifully in the overall context of Hoffman's movie because they seem organic rather than contrived. They also serve to infuse this unique cinematic performance of the Pyramus and Thisbe play – a play-within-a-film that, as is the situation with earlier productions of *Midsummer* like Reinhardt and Dieterle's, Hall's and Noble's, is presented strictly as heterosexual farce – with a quality that is all the more affecting given this subtle, sophisticated and entirely unexpected emphasis on its homoeroticsim.

Two key transformations – one intrinsic, the other extrinsic, to Hoffman's *Midsummer* – occur during the latter part of the Pyramus and Thisbe performance. As they are touched by the genuine emotion the mechanicals manage to effect in playing their roles, it is made plain that Lysander, Hermia, Helena and Demetrius are all brought up short by their reactions to what they are witnessing on stage. The young nobles have in fact been made to see that their original derisive laughter at the mechanicals was uncalled for; they have been chastened, momentarily at least, by suddenly having to confront the fact that even though they are not professional actors, the hard-handed men of Athens are capable of extraordinary things in the theatre. Hoffman's cinematic audiences experience something similar as regards the cross-dressing Flute is required to do in order to transform himself into Thisbe. Meanwhile, in accord with the ideas of Berry on laughter, following the lead of Flute's fellow mechanicals, viewers of Hoffman's *Midsummer* are encouraged to laugh *at* Flute in concert *with* them given that the role he has been chosen to play demands that he disguise his masculinity in order to become a female character. Because of just how much of a threat the figure is in the heteronormative imaginary, the male transvestite must be mocked unmercifully so that he can be made to forego his transgressive behaviour in order to be accepted by society once again. But as surely as the young nobles are chastened by the real emotion Flute manages to engender in his performance as Thisbe, so are Hoffman's cinematic audiences. As human beings, cross-dressers do not deserve to be ridiculed, and love between two people of the same gender can be as affecting and meaningful as love between those of opposite genders – even in, or perhaps especially in, fictional form.

Hoffman's didacticism on these two points is light, but unmistakable in his overall treatment of the Pyramus and Thisbe play-within-a-film.

In their respective considerations of his production of *Midsummer*, scholars have had a great deal to say about Hoffman's obvious cinematic homages to Reinhardt and Dieterle's *Midsummer* and Kenneth Branagh's *Much Ado About Nothing* (1994), his shifting of the story's setting from Athens to the imaginary town of Monte Athena in Tuscany and his altering of the time period from antiquity to the Victorian era, and, above all, his decision to provide the character of Bottom with a backstory not found, or indeed even hinted at, in Shakespeare's original text. Focused as they seem to be on the details listed here, it is interesting to note that critics have had nothing to say about the homoerotic quality of the final moments of the performance of 'The Most Lamentable Comedy and Cruel Death of Pyramus and Thisbe' as detailed above. Samuel Crowl provides one example of this kind of analytical elision:

> On screen, less is always more with Shakespeare, which is nowhere made more evident than in Sam Rockwell's brilliant, moving Flute ... Rockwell gives us a heartbreaking Thisby, and he makes his delivery of 'his eyes were green as leeks' as tragically moving as Juliet's 'thy lips are warm.' ... Rockwell's Thisby genuinely grieves for her Pyramus ...[55]

Significantly, Crowl begins his remarks by bestowing praise on the *male* actor Sam Rockwell, whose understated performance as the *male* character of Flute he finds to be both exceptional and touching. It is furthermore the *male* actor Rockwell, as the *male* character Flute, who endows the female character of Thisby [sic] with an emotional pathos that finds its only equal in that of Shakespeare's Juliet, a female character who, as is well known, would have been played by a *boy* actor on the stages of early modern London. And it is the *male* actor Rockwell, again as the *male* character Flute, who transforms

Thisby into a figure whose mourning for the loss of her *male* lover Pyramus is gut-wrenching. Crowl's fastidiousness with the use of masculine proper names and pronouns for Rockwell and Flute in this passage is telling; *in toto*, these grammatical devices never let his readers forget that the only real gender at work in the scene he praises here is male. Given the subject matter at the heart of the scene, forbidden romantic love interrupted by sudden death, and given that it involves two sets of male actors – Rockwell and Kline and Flute and Bottom – the fact that Crowl does not mention male homoeroticism even in passing proves to be a curious oversight that the queer reading attempted here seeks to address in a way that yields an equally valuable interpretation informed by the deconstruction of the visual poetics of gender trouble.

IV

It is interesting that the three Shakespeare films analysed in this chapter – Nunn's *Twelfth Night*, Lurhmann's *Romeo + Juliet* and Hoffman's *Midsummer* – were made in the last years of the twentieth century. By this time in history the concept of gender was already in serious trouble; it was well on its way to being thoroughly queered by the forces of deconstruction, feminism, gay and lesbian studies, and queer theory. That being the case, it cannot be a coincidence that each of the movies studied features a character that expresses a gender identity that does not accord with traditional heteronormative expectations, from the winsomeness of Nunn's Viola/Cesario to the angry cross-dressing of Luhrmann's Mercutio and, finally, to the chameleon-like gender bending of Hoffman's Flute/Thisbe. Individually and collectively, these directors/characters attempt to make sense (and encourage their audiences to do the same) out of the idea that gender is neither a natural nor a predictable result of biological sex as was thought to be the case for the preceding millennia. If that understanding seems a bit muddled rather than unified in the films of Nunn, Luhrmann and Hoffman, that should come as no surprise; every paradigm shift in human consciousness happens in fits and starts rather than in one clean sweep. Even so, the *Twelfth Night*, *Romeo + Juliet* and *Midsummer* productions discussed above all seem to indicate that there is every reason to look forward to the day that might well be coming when gender is no longer trouble in the Shakespeare film.

4

Screening the male homoerotics of Shakespearean romantic comedy on film in Michael Radford's *The Merchant of Venice* and Trevor Nunn's *Twelfth Night*

I

Two groundbreaking articles from 1992 continue to draw attention to the subject of male homoeroticism in Shakespearean romantic comedy, specifically in plays like *The Merchant of Venice* and *Twelfth Night*.[1] In these pieces a fair amount of critical attention is directed to what Joseph Pequigney cleverly referred to as 'the two Antonios', the pair of characters that are linked to one another not only by name, but because both exhibit pronounced homoerotic desire for other male characters in the plays they appear; those being Bassanio in *Merchant* and Sebastian in *Twelfth Night*. Systematically comparing the relationships of these characters, Pequigney argues that the relationship between Antonio and Bassanio in *Merchant* is never anything but platonic and that, conversely, the relationship between Antonio and Sebastian in *Twelfth Night* is romantic and, more significantly, is also requited in some fashion in the space just off the margins of the playtext. Valerie Traub, though she only mentions *Merchant* briefly in her work (she more closely examines *As You Like It* and *Twelfth Night*) without touching on the characters of Antonio and Bassanio, seems to agree with Pequigney on the matter of the homoeroticism evident in the relationship between Antonio and Sebastian in *Twelfth Night*. However, she does not go as far as Pequigney and does not claim, at least explicitly, that there is any kind of romantic love, much less consummation of that love, apparent in the Antonio and Sebastian pairing. For Traub, the homoerotic part of Antonio and Sebastian's relationship exists only in the realm of the rhetorical rather than the material as exemplified by, most often, what Antonio says to and about his beloved Sebastian as Shakespeare tells their story. Ironically, Pequigney makes a similar claim about Antonio and Bassanio in *Merchant*; in his view their relationship is defined only by what the Antonio of that play says to and about Bassanio rather than by anything he actually does physically or otherwise with the younger man.

Pequigney and Traub also differ in their views on the matter of what exactly happens to the two Antonios by the close of their respective plays. Traub maintains that *Twelfth Night*'s Antonio is marginalized to the point of complete exclusion from the heteronormative utopia that results on account of the marriages between the male/female couples Sebastian and Olivia and Orsino and Viola. Pequigney, on the other hand, adamantly resists all such notions of marginalization for either of the two Antonios in *Merchant* and *Twelfth Night*. 'Why,' he questions rhetorically and with some asperity, 'the nearly universal assent to the mistaken critical view that both Antonios at the finish are excluded and unhappy? Since the Shakespearean text does not lend support to this view – quite the reverse – it must be imported and imposed by readers.'[2] According to Pequigney those readers err on the side of assuming that men who never marry women and never father children by their wives – men like the characters of the two Antonios in *Merchant* and *Twelfth Night* – are doomed to nothing but loneliness and despair because of their deviant (i.e. non-heteronormative) love object choices. Such an assumption, he adds, is not in the least justified by the textual evidence in the plays. However, as exhilarating as Pequigney's disavowal of conventional critical thinking about the fate of *Merchant*'s and *Twelfth Night*'s Antonios is, it is difficult not to wish that he had gone beyond verbal fiat and fleshed out more specifically how he thinks the two Antonios manage to avoid the exclusion and unhappiness that far too many readers, viewers and critics consign them to in the end.

Even after nearly twenty-five years since they were taken up by Pequigney and Traub, the problematics associated with male homoeroticism in Shakespeare's romantic comedies like *Merchant* and *Twelfth Night* have not yet been resolved, at least insofar as literary criticism ever allows for what can be considered definitive resolutions within its sphere of enquiry. These problematics have also not been addressed as fully as possible in extant work on the Shakespeare film. The purpose of this chapter then is to address that gap in the criticism by using Michael Radford's 2004 production of *Merchant* and, once again, Nunn's 1996 *Twelfth Night*, since it is as equally attentive to the homoeroticism of the Antonio/Sebastian relationship as it is to that of the Orsino/Cesario relationship discussed in the previous chapter. As such, this section is situated firmly on the traditional or the originary ground of queer theory with sex and sexuality as the prime markers of difference from the normative. That being the case it will be shown in what follows that, despite the lavish representation of male homoeroticism clearly evident in them, both

Radford's *Merchant* and Nunn's *Twelfth Night* end on strikingly similar notes that seem to serve not, as Pequigney points out, the ends of textual fidelity to Shakespeare's originals, but rather for the sole purpose of re-inscribing the supremacy of compulsory heterosexuality as their combined *raison d'être* in the late twentieth and early twenty-first centuries.[3]

II

Tempestuous relations between Christians and Jews. The convoluted minutiae of the practice of usury in a Christian-dominated and emergent proto-capitalist society. Female agency and the lack thereof in a patriarchal world. Love, money and family as influences on, as well as the determiners of, marriage choices. Contractual, moral and ethical obligations. True justice versus hypocritical self-righteousness. The state in opposition to the individual; the individual in opposition to the state. The conflicts that propel *Merchant* derive from a potent mixture of all of these dramatic motifs, elements and themes. Though highly troubling in the early twenty-first century because of its pronounced anti-Semitism, especially in the long aftermath of the Holocaust, the play has nevertheless enjoyed popular and critical acclaim since it was originally performed on the London stages in the late sixteenth century. This qualified success continues to be reflected in the various film and television adaptations of the play completed in the present historical epoch. Rothwell lists a total of twelve productions of *Merchant* having been made and shown in movie theatres or broadcast on television since the beginning of the last century, ranging from a ten-minute, silent, black-and-white film made in 1908 by the Vitagraph Studios Film Company to 2004's sumptuous full-length feature, *William Shakespeare's The Merchant of Venice*,[4] written and directed by Michael Radford and starring an impressive roster of veteran, accomplished and up-and-coming stars like Al Pacino,

Jeremy Irons, Joseph Fiennes and Lynn Collins.[5] Having been created, distributed, screened, consumed and critiqued in the twenty-first century, Radford's *Merchant* seems to be sympathetic to the male homoerotic potentialities inherent in its source text where the characters of Antonio (Jeremy Irons) and Bassanio (Joseph Fiennes) are concerned. In this regard the movie also seems to be demonstrably aware of the insights of gay and lesbian and queer scholarship that their practitioners have contributed to the study of Shakespearean drama since their advent nearly fifty years ago. Ultimately, however, this *Merchant* seems to abruptly abandon its engagement with male homoeroticism in a way that proves completely jarring to viewers from a queer perspective.

One extended sequence early in the movie is particularly evocative of the overall male homoeroticism Radford depicts in his *Merchant* and, thus, warrants specific attention in the present context. It begins with Antonio's second appearance in the production, which finds the merchant pacing around his Venetian palazzo with a brooding look on his face while Salerio (John Sessions) and Solanio (Gregor Fisher) eat a meal at the dining table set at the centre of the room – a meal that Antonio is unable to touch given his distracted state of mind. 'In sooth I know not why I am so sad', Antonio confides to his companions (1.1.1).[6] 'It wearies me,' he continues as Salerio and Solanio exchange glances, 'you say it wearies you; / ... and such a want-wit sadness makes of me / That I have much ado to know myself' (1.1.2 and 5–6). Arthur L. Little describes this brief speech as part of what he terms Shakespeare's 'broader challenge to heteronormativity', a challenge that he finds particularly evident in *Merchant*.[7] He goes on to make the point that Antonio is not merely sad; he is in mourning. The way Irons plays Antonio in Radford's *Merchant* finds accord with Little's insights; he does indeed seem like a man given over entirely to grieving the inevitable separation from someone he holds particularly dear. Antonio, according to Little, 'mourns the impending loss of Bassanio' and he mourns how his own culturally unsanctioned desires [for Bassanio], those of same-sex intimate friendship, push him outside the presumptions of what increasingly in the early modern culture becomes *the* civil institution, *the* institution of valuation and belonging; he mourns because he sees the institution of heterosexual marriage working not only to displace but to replace same-sex communing.[8]

The broader challenge to heteronormativity Little discerns in Shakespeare, which, given how, in many cases, closely the cinematic text adheres to the playtext, can be extended to Radford's *Merchant*, lies in the very fact of Antonio's 'culturally unsanctioned desires' for Bassanio.

The psychoanalytic work of both Janet Adelman and Coppélia Kahn supports the assertions Little makes about *Merchant*'s Antonio. Adelman, for instance, claims, 'Shakespeare explores male identity and friendship felt as necessarily prior to marriage', hence real-world individuals, represented by characters like Bassanio in *Merchant*, 'do not move directly from family bonds to marriage without an intervening period in which friendships with same-sex friends help ... to establish our [their] independent identities'.[9] Same-sex friendship then proves a, if not the, crucial factor in the early psychological and emotional development of human beings, a development that does not – indeed, cannot in Adelman's view – reach its ultimate manifestation absent a heterosexual marital union. Along similar lines, Kahn writes that in 'Shakespeare's psychology, men first seek to mirror themselves in a homoerotic attachment ... and then to confirm themselves through difference, in a bond with the opposite sex – the marital bond'.[10] The larger point of the insights Little, Adelman and Kahn offer is that, while homoerotic relationships like that which Antonio and Bassanio share with one another are acceptable, eventually they must be set aside in favour of taking a wife and having children in order for either man to reach his full potential. That means, as Little explains, that Antonio's entire world, complete and fulfilling with same-sex intimate friendship – and love – at its centre, is falling apart around him because of what seems to be Bassanio's complete and unquestioning acceptance of the increasing demands placed on him by the rapid institutionalization of heteronormativity. Yet it warrants pointing out that in both Shakespeare's and Radford's *Merchant*s Antonio does not give Bassanio up without the proverbial fight. Indeed, it is arguable whether or not Antonio really lets Bassanio go entirely by the time the last line of Shakespeare's play is uttered and the end credits of Radford's film roll.

Antonio's two business acquaintances speculate that the merchant's sadness is caused by the uncertain status of his various commercial ventures, all of which are dependent on trading ships still at sea and, thus, are subject to the whims of nature and fate. While Salerio and Solanio are discussing this possibility they are oblivious to the fact that Antonio ignores them and stops pacing long enough to look through the large multi-paned windows of the house. Doing so, he spies a gondola with three young men plus the pilot in it making its way through the canal outside. Glancing back at Salerio and Solanio, Antonio shakes his head and says, 'Believe me, no', and thus denies that his cares have anything to do with his ventures in trade (1.1.40). Undeterred, Solanio suggests with undisguised mirth that Antonio is in love and then both he and Salerio erupt into raucous laughter over such a prospect. A now obviously irritated Antonio's response to his friends' intimation is a vehement, 'Fie, fie, fie' (1.1.46). However, this retort comes perhaps a little too quickly from Antonio, indicating that Salerio and Solanio may be closer to the truth with their supposition than Antonio wants to admit, at least not to them. The question becomes then, with whom is Antonio in love? Radford soon makes it clear that it is Bassanio whom Antonio loves. In fact, immediately after denying being in love with anyone, Antonio turns to look out through the glass again only to fix his gaze on the young and dashing Bassanio who, at that moment, happens to be standing in the lead position with his friends Graziano (Kris

Marshall) and Lorenzo (Charlie Cox) in the gondola that is approaching Antonio's residence. Given the cross-cutting shots of the two characters in this part of the film, it is quite obvious that Antonio only has eyes for Bassanio.

Though certainly a logical cinematic move given both the text and the subtext of Shakespeare's *Merchant*, Laury Magnus considers this part of the scene to be the result of what she terms a questionable 'visual oversimplification' on the part of director Radford.[11] For her, the manner in which the film presents Antonio's 'glimpse from the casement window of his beloved Bassanio' reveals one of the play's key mysteries – the nature of the relationship between Antonio and Bassanio – too early in the film because it explicitly links Antonio's 'sadness and its most likely cause; we see it emanating from what his eyes have lit upon and cannot have', which is Bassanio.[12] It seems that Magnus would prefer audiences to be convinced that Antonio's sadness emanates from nothing more than the everyday travails of the 'Renaissance venture capitalist' she characterizes Antonio as being for a longer period of time than Radford allows in what she considers to be the director's overall 'dumbing down' of the original Shakespearean narrative logic.[13] Partly because she provides no criteria for her assessment, of equal concern here is Magnus's insistence that Antonio 'cannot have' Bassanio in, it can be presumed, a romantic/sexual sense. This assertion seems to be infused with an all-too casual heteronormative certainty that overlooks historical evidence presented in the work of scholars like Sedgwick, Bray and others who have shown that same-sex male friendships like that represented by Antonio and Bassanio in *Merchant* could very easily involve general affection, intimacy and sexuality on the physical – as opposed to the merely platonic – levels. In addition, as will be explored below, Magnus's assertion elides consideration of the other, even more explicitly homoerotic, aspects in Radford's production that are key to a more complete interpretation of the director's overall representation of Antonio and Bassanio's relationship.

Surrounded as they are by attendants in the house after his arrival, Antonio leads Bassanio from the dining area and into his large bedroom filled with ornate furnishings where they can presumably have the privacy to speak candidly with one another. Each moves to opposite sides of the room of their own accord; an elaborately carved and dressed four-poster bed separates them. Situated as such, Antonio coaxes Bassanio to talk with the words, 'tell me now ... / That you today promised to tell me of' (1.1.119 and 121). At first Bassanio seems reluctant to reveal to Antonio whatever it is he has already agreed to divulge to the merchant prior to this meeting. Bassanio opens his mouth to speak, but no sound escapes from him. Restlessly he takes his gloves off and tosses them onto the bed, still without saying a word. Then Bassanio gives Antonio a brief, rather impish smile. Before long though, he spreads his arms out with his palms up in a gesture of surrender and begins to confess: "Tis not unknown to you, Antonio, / How much I have disabled mine estate' (1.1.122–3). He goes on to say that his only concern at the moment is 'to come fairly off from the great debts / Wherein my time, something too prodigal, / Hath left me gaged' (1.1.128–30). Bassanio has, as he makes plain to Antonio, spent the bulk of his money and is trying to figure out how he can pay back his obligations to his creditors.

Significantly, while beginning to unburden himself to Antonio, Bassanio removes his cape, tosses it aside, then lies down and stretches his legs out along the length of Antonio's bed as if the bed belongs to him too, and that he has every right to make himself comfortable in it. Antonio, meanwhile, raises no objections whatsoever to Bassanio being in his bed. It is almost as if Bassanio's presence there is a common enough occurrence that it warrants no special comment from either of them. Setting aside the fact that Shakespeare's playtexts are notorious for their lack of stage directions, it must not be overlooked that Radford places this important scene in, specifically, Antonio's bedroom. This is a location that is not indicated in Shakespeare's words that form the conversation that Antonio and Bassanio have in these moments in the film, so it can only be a deliberate choice on the part of the director. Regardless, the bedroom setting suggests the physically and emotionally intimate nature of the homoerotic relationship between Antonio and Bassanio. Bedrooms have, after all, long been understood as places where couples retire to in order to have the privacy in which to, among other things of course, engage in sexual congress with one another.[14] Just because they are two men does not mean that Antonio and Bassanio would never do the same as their heterosexual counterparts. Indeed, erotic encounters in Antonio's bedroom are very nearly a surety for them given the love, intimacy and desire that they have for each other and that is evidenced by them in their words and actions in this lengthy scene alone.

Antonio smiles at Bassanio with knowing affection when Bassanio continues to castigate himself for the spendthrift ways that have put him in serious financial difficulty. He then tells Antonio, using words that only call specific attention to the depth of the intimacy they share:

... To you, Antonio,
I owe the most in money and love,
And from your love I have a warranty
To unburden all my plots and purposes
How to get clear of all the debts I owe. (1.1.130–4)

Following such a preamble Antonio calmly says, 'I pray you, good Bassanio, let me know it' (1.1.135), meaning he wants to know how Bassanio intends to achieve solvency. Having said this Antonio walks to the head of his bed, fiddles for a moment or two with the door of a tall cabinet situated next to it, turns to Bassanio and adds, '... if it stand as you yourself still do,' then he pauses, reaches out and tenderly cups Bassanio's chin in the palm of his hand before continuing, 'Within the eye of honour, be assured / My purse, my person, my extremest means / Lie all unlocked to your occasions' (1.1.136–9). From Antonio's perspective it seems that Bassanio has not shamed himself in the least because of his carelessness with money. In fact, Antonio may well enjoy Bassanio's dependence on him. The larger point in any case is that Antonio remains supportive of Bassanio regardless. But it warrants noting too that Antonio's response to Bassanio and the predicament Bassanio has managed to get himself into goes beyond casual acceptance of this reality. Antonio is willing to offer Bassanio all the wealth he has access to via his own assets or his credit, his non-material assistance if it is required, and, above all, his very *self* so that Bassanio can put himself into a better position in life. Borrowing an apropos phrase from elsewhere within both Shakespeare's and Radford's *Merchant*s, Antonio is prepared to 'give and hazard all he hath' for Bassanio (2.7.9). Even so, this is a significant commitment for Antonio to make to Bassanio, particularly if their relationship is only a platonic one. If, however, their relationship is a romantic and an intimate one, if they are, indeed, lovers, then what Antonio is willing to sacrifice for Bassanio makes rather more sense.

Encouraged by Antonio's response so far, Bassanio rises to his knees in the(ir) bed and begins to tell Antonio about the rich heiress, Portia. Antonio peers up at and intently watches Bassanio as he speaks. After mentioning the array of suitors who have already travelled to Belmont in order to court Portia, and those who are sure to do so in the future, all of whom he could never hope to compete with given his squandered fortune, Bassanio declares: 'O my Antonio, had I but means / To hold a rival place with one of them, / ... / That I should questionless be fortunate' (1.1.173–4 and 176). The first three words of this pronouncement, 'O my Antonio,' deserve comment since by using them Bassanio lets it be known that, in some vital, tangible way, Antonio belongs to him and him alone. The strong note of possession in this phrase is unmistakable. Furthermore, Antonio registers no problem with being so claimed by Bassanio; he seems, in fact, totally content to be Bassanio's Antonio.

Furthermore, Antonio does not seem to be in the least perturbed or jealous about Bassanio's sudden newfound interest in Portia. Antonio takes this development in stride and without any undo angst. Seymour Kleinberg offers pertinent insight here with his explanation that during the early modern period all 'upper-class men married. Their duties to property, propriety and posterity demanded an heir. After that, their romantic predilections were less important socially as long as they were reasonably discreet'.[15] There can be no question that Antonio understands the pragmatics of these circumstances and, since Bassanio's marriage to a woman does not necessarily mean that Bassanio will renounce Antonio and their relationship once he has met, or while he is in the process of meeting, his marital, familial and societal obligations, Antonio has no reason to feel threatened. He and Bassanio remain, after all, part of a staunchly homosocial world in which bonds between men are paramount. Thus Little's assertion that Antonio is mourning the impending loss of Bassanio comes into question. Another equally valid possibility is that Antonio's sadness and melancholy stem not from the fact that he is going to lose Bassanio, but rather from the fact that he has been unable to figure out a way to help Bassanio secure a stable future for himself economically and otherwise. Being a Venetian merchant of some repute and success, it is conceivable that Antonio's failure to accomplish such a task on behalf of the man he loves is actually what proves deeply troubling to him on both emotional (apparent in his sadness/melancholy) and physical (apparent in his weariness) levels. It may well be, then, a marked concern over his inability to be innovative rather than his fear of loss that fuels Antonio's profound concern for Bassanio.

With this possibility in play it is only a small wonder that Antonio jumps at the chance to provide Bassanio with the funding he needs in order to go to Belmont to woo Portia despite the considerable personal risk he incurs by putting himself in Shylock's debt. If Antonio was as afraid of losing Bassanio as so many critics believe him to be, it seems that he would do everything in his power to prevent Bassanio from leaving Venice and going to Portia; instead, he does the exact opposite. Indeed, Antonio starts to consider in earnest what options are available to him as far as how he may best help Bassanio and, in so doing, to keep Bassanio as close to him as possible, at least emotionally if not physically. He swallows deeply before saying with more than a hint of regret in his voice, 'Thou knowst that all my fortunes are at sea'; then he swings his legs over the edge of the bed, stands and slowly begins to walk to the other side of the room (1.1.177). While he is doing so he adds more detail to his initial statement: 'Neither have I money, nor commodity / To raise a present sum' (1.1.178–9). Hearing this, Bassanio, still in Antonio's (and, arguably, his) bed, looks both guilty and dejected at the same time – guilty for having brought up the subject of his interest in pursuing Portia while being unable to sustain such an enterprise by his own means, thus placing Antonio into a difficult position, and dejected because Antonio, Bassanio's last resort, cannot help him on account of Antonio's own trading ventures. But then Antonio, while writing a brief communication of some kind on a piece of parchment, unexpectedly gives Bassanio new hope when he tells him to go out and 'Try what my credit can in Venice do; / That shall be racked even to the uttermost / To furnish thee to Belmont to fair Portia' (1.1.180–2). Given Antonio's current financial situation, the fact that he is willing to go into a significant amount of debt in order to assist Bassanio in Bassanio's hour of need is extraordinary, but only if Antonio and Bassanio's relationship is purely platonic. Few would be comfortable risking so much, particularly when money is involved, for a mere friend. A lover, however, might well do for his beloved what Antonio decides to do for Bassanio in this scene.

Bassanio is completely taken aback by Antonio's decision to help him. He walks open-mouthed from Antonio's bed to stand before Antonio. Without saying a word Bassanio grabs Antonio's right hand, lifts it to his mouth and kisses it with his lips. Bassanio then places his own right hand on Antonio's bearded face so that Antonio's chin lies between Bassanio's thumb and forefinger, while his other fingers rest on the better part of Antonio's left cheek. Bassanio looks into Antonio's eyes and then proceeds to lean toward the other man; Bassanio is soon kissing Antonio full on the lips. As the kiss occurs, the eyes of both men close while each enjoys the pleasure of their mouths coming together (see Figure 16). Magnus complains that Bassanio bestows the kiss 'somewhat too knowingly upon Antonio.'[16] Perhaps, but, since it was Bassanio who spontaneously initiated the contact, it is clear that he wanted to kiss Antonio and wanted Antonio to kiss him in return. Antonio, furthermore, does not pull away from Bassanio; he appears to welcome Bassanio's kiss. What makes this moment so intriguing in the present context is that, in the early twenty-first century West, at least, men do not normally go around kissing members of their own gender on the lips in the way that Bassanio kisses Antonio here unless such men are capable of and interested in engaging in relationships with other men that transcend mere friendship to encompass the romantic, the erotic and the sexual. In Radford's *Merchant* both Antonio and Bassanio fall into this latter category as evidenced by the palpable display of intimacy and affection this kiss represents. Given the homophobia – the irrational fear and hatred of homosexuals and the behaviours in which

FIGURE 16 *Bassanio (Joseph Fiennes) kissing Antonio (Jeremy Irons) in Antonio's bedroom in* William Shakespeare's The Merchant of Venice, *dir. Michael Radford, 2004, DVD screen capture.*

their sexuality enables them to engage – that is such a pervasive aspect of society today, men who kiss other men like Bassanio kisses Antonio risk being branded as deviants, with all the negativity that term implies, from the expected heterosexual norm. However, as the work of Bray in particular shows, such physicality between two male friends like Antonio and Bassanio was not only socially acceptable, but also strongly encouraged by Elizabethan and Jacobean culture at large. Indeed, on this point, Bray writes, '[w]hen two men kissed or embraced, the gesture had the same meaning' as that indicated by their sleeping together; being 'someone's "bedfellow" suggested that one had influence' over another.[17] There can be no question but that Antonio has such emotional and romantic influence over Bassanio and vice versa.

Moving briefly to Act 2, Scene 8 of Shakespeare's *Merchant*, Salerio reports to Solanio on Bassanio's departure from Venice for Belmont and fair Portia. Radford, however, shows audiences this leave-taking rather than providing the information secondhand. The scene begins with Bassanio reaching out to embrace Antonio while a heavy rain falls and lightning flashes. After Bassanio jumps aboard his ship Antonio tells him: 'Be merry, and employ your chiefest thoughts / To courtship and such fair displays [ostents] of love / As shall conveniently become you there' (2.8.43–5). Upon receiving such counsel Bassanio blows Antonio a kiss from the boat as it starts to pull away from the dock. Antonio, in turn, 'catches' Bassanio's kiss between his clasped hands and then presses them against his lips (see Figure 17). He closes his eyes tight as if savouring the kiss, opens them again and then raises one hand in farewell to Bassanio as the multi-manned oared craft carrying him pulls away and into the ever-flowing canals of mighty Venice. Once again, no stage directions in Shakespeare's dramatic text call for the exchange of air-kisses on the part of Antonio and Bassanio. Yet, without question, this scene, in all of its particulars, fits perfectly within the context of Radford's cinematic text. It serves, in fact, as nothing less than a pointed reminder of the queer homoerotic nature of Antonio and

FIGURE 17 *Antonio (Jeremy Irons) 'catching' Bassanio's (Joseph Fiennes) kiss and holding it to his lips in* William Shakespeare's The Merchant of Venice, *dir. Michael Radford, 2004, DVD screen capture.*

Bassanio's relationship, even as Bassanio heads off to claim a rich and beautiful heiress for himself in Belmont.

Considering the specific male homoerotic content in the scenes discussed above, Irons' comments on how he as an actor approached the role of Antonio in Radford's *Merchant* are surprising. In 'The Merchant of Venice: Shakespeare through the Lens,' one of the special features on the DVD version of the cinematic text, Irons states, '[h]e [Antonio] finds himself very happy in the company of young men ... ah, particularly one young man [Bassanio], who is sort of everything he'd like to be'. Not long thereafter Irons insists: 'I didn't play Antonio gay'. Rather, he portrayed Antonio as only a very great friend of Bassanio's – nothing more, nothing less.[18] Irons has something of a reputation for making controversial statements like this. Even so, whether or not Antonio envies Bassanio in the way Irons claims he does is debatable. It is a point of view that seems too dangerously close to the extant stereotypes about homosexual males being forever unhappy simply because they are not straight and because they are always attracted to often younger men who are unable to respond in kind. Arguably, Antonio wants to be together with Bassanio as a romantic couple is together; he also does not emulate Bassanio out of any kind of jealousy. More importantly, Irons' words belie the images – images that include Antonio kissing and fondling Bassanio, as well as images of Antonio clearly feeling pain and happiness depending on whether or not he is in Bassanio's presence – of the Antonio/Bassanio relationship that made their way into Radford's *Merchant*. These images make it seem that Irons did, in fact, 'play Antonio gay' and they do so in part because of the proscriptions of heteronormativity that attempt, without ever fully succeeding, to circumscribe (un)acceptable homosexual and homosocial behaviours – behaviours that have changed in terms of meaning, of signification, between the sixteenth and the twenty-first centuries. As, once again, Bray and others have made clear, during the early modern period it was perfectly acceptable for men to kiss one other, to hold hands and even to sleep together regardless of their sexual object choices and desires; but in the present, such behaviours are considered bisexual if not homosexual. A queer reading of Radford's *Merchant* must therefore register this interpretive tension.

But what of Bassanio's feelings towards Antonio? Even critics who are willing to grant that Antonio's interest in Bassanio crosses the line that is supposed to separate friendship from romantic affection and sexual desire make haste to assert that, because he marries Portia and therefore must love her, and her only, Bassanio is using Antonio merely for his own purposes and does not really reciprocate Antonio's romantic feelings. In other words, Bassanio does not love Antonio in the same way that Antonio loves Bassanio. However, taking into consideration the feelings Bassanio experiences on account of his love for Antonio – and how those feelings are represented in visual form in Radford's *Merchant* – calls such a hypothesis into serious question. As the film begins Bassanio is frankly desirous that Antonio will consent to help him pursue Portia; this desire morphs into grave concern fuelled by guilt for Antonio when Antonio agrees to Shylock's pound-of-flesh proviso in order to guarantee his loan. 'You shall not seal to such a bond for me;' Bassanio exclaims, 'I'll rather dwell in my necessity' (1.3.150–1); but Antonio tells the younger man that there is nothing to be worried about since his ships, with all their valuable merchandise, will return to Venice long before the debt to Shylock comes due (1.3.153–5, 177). As such, Bassanio's concern turns into out-and-out horror when, in Belmont, Bassanio learns that all of Antonio's ships have miscarried and Antonio faces death because he cannot afford to make good on the loan from Shylock. With a deeply pained expression on his face Bassanio explains to Portia:

> I have engaged myself to a dear friend,
> Engaged my friend to his mere enemy,
> To feed my means. Here is a letter, lady,
> The paper as the body of my friend,
> And every word in it a gaping wound
> Issuing life-blood. (3.2.260–5)

Bassanio's use of the term engaged in this passage proves intriguing. The word can, of course, refer to a bond – legal or otherwise – agreed to by two or more parties. It can also signify a betrothal in the marital sense. Invoking this meaning suggests that Bassanio is as betrothed to Antonio as he now is to Portia; in fact, he was betrothed to Antonio first. In addition, the letter from Antonio may as well be Antonio himself in spectral form. Nevertheless, in its paper form it is not unlike a marriage certificate that symbolizes as well as validates the relationship that exists between Antonio and Bassanio. It is not surprising then that all Bassanio wants to do is to staunch the flow of Antonio's blood.

Portia asks to hear what Antonio has written in his letter to Bassanio. Antonio's words are as poignant as they are affecting, and Bassanio reads them out loud to Portia and to Graziano, Lorenzo, Jessica and Salerio with no hint of either reluctance or embarrassment. 'Sweet Bassanio', he begins:

> *my ships have all miscarried, my creditors grow cruel, my estate is very low, my bond to the Jew forfeit, and, since in paying it, it is impossible I should live, all debts are cleared between you and I if I might but see you at my death. Nothwithstanding, use your pleasure; if your love do not persuade you to come, let not my letter.* (3.2.314–20; italics in the original)

Though not erotic in an overtly sexual sense, Antonio's words are nevertheless intended to seduce Bassanio into leaving Belmont and Portia in order to return to Venice to be with Antonio during what may well be the latter's final hours on earth. Indeed, Antonio's emotional manipulation of Bassanio with his choice of words in this letter echoes the speaker's emotional manipulation of the young man in Sonnet 72, 'O, lest the world should task you to recite'. The third line of this poem presents the following entreaty: 'After my death (dear love) forget me quite'.[19] Of course the last thing the speaker wants is to be forgotten by the young man, and by saying the exact opposite, remembrance on the young man's part is what the speaker hopes to effect. Antonio uses the same rhetorical tactic; if Bassanio's love for Antonio alone does not persuade him to come to Antonio's aid in Venice, may his written communication go unheeded. But, again, it is very apparent that the last thing Antonio wants is for Bassanio to leave Antonio to suffer his fate without him. From a visual as opposed to a textual perspective, it is just as crucial to understand here too that all throughout Bassanio's sombre, heartfelt recitation of Antonio's letter, it is never less than clear from the expression on his face that Bassanio feels responsible for the terrible predicament in which Antonio now finds himself. The strength of their relationship remains unbroken despite the physical distance between them and the fact that Bassanio is now betrothed to Portia.

With a spirit of generosity that parallels Antonio's generosity to Bassanio earlier in Radford's cinematic narrative of *Merchant*, Portia outright tells Bassanio to, 'Dispatch all business and be gone' (3.2.321). Portia wants, as this instruction makes very clear, Bassanio to leave her and return to Venice with all due haste so that he can attempt to rescue his beloved Antonio from the unyielding Shylock. But then, interestingly enough, Portia makes Bassanio's departure from Belmont and herself dependent on his going to church with her at that very moment and becoming her husband, after which, she insists, he shall 'away to Venice to your friend, / For never shall you lie by Portia's side / With an unquiet soul' (3.2.302–5). In these lines Portia seems to understand that her own happiness rests in large part on Bassanio's peace of mind. And unless Bassanio does everything within his power to save Antonio from the fate to which Shylock intends to hold him, Bassanio will never be able to be truly close to Portia given his 'unquiet soul.' Furthermore, while Portia speaks Radford and his team supply her words with a corresponding set of complementary images. These include: Portia and Nerissa in full bridal dress walking down the aisle of a church side by side; a priest enfolding the joined hands of Portia and Bassanio within his own; Portia and Bassanio standing next to one another as they are joined in holy matrimony; and finally, Bassanio and Graziano waving goodbye to Portia and Nerissa while their boat moves off as it begins the journey to Venice. Of particular interest in this sequence of cross-cut scenes is the pained expression on Bassanio's face as he and Portia are being married to one another by the priest. Distracted, Bassanio does not seem to be in the moment of his marriage. Bassanio's thoughts are undoubtedly with Antonio rather than with Portia, suggesting that – and despite the fact that Portia has just become his wife – Antonio is, and perhaps will always be, more important to Bassanio. On the latter point Sinfield, drawing on the work of Bray, explains that even though 'marriage was involved in alliances of property and influence, male friendship informed, through complex obligations, networks of extended family, companions, clients, suitors and those influential in high places'.[20] The effects of male friendship like that the characters of Antonio and Bassanio share, were, in other words, pervasive and more powerful than the marital bond between a man and a woman.

Antonio and Bassanio are obligated to one another through, among other things, Shylock's bond; arguably, they also form an extended familial unit; they are companions, clients and suitors to each other; in the respective social, cultural and economic arenas they inhabit they are highly influential. No wonder then that Bassanio is not focused on his marriage to Portia at this moment in Radford's *Merchant*. Indeed, Radford's cinematic treatment of the late sixteenth and early seventeenth century English exaltation of male friendships like that between Antonio and Bassanio highlights the supremacy of such relationships in the intensely homosocial world of Elizabethan and Jacobean England. Through Antonio and Bassanio, both Shakespeare and Radford offer audiences a highly visceral dramatic representation of one way that the historical practice of homosocially inflected male friendship may have manifested itself in the early modern world. Antonio and Bassanio appear as concerned about each other as two very good friends – or lovers – would be; their relationship operates in a way that is completely understandable as opposed to a way that seems alien or abstract because, even 400 years later, men still act in a similar manner when it comes to other men. What makes their relationship (homo)erotic as opposed to merely homosocial is its intimacy, physicality and affective intensity – all of which, as evidenced in this chapter, Radford does not shy away from representing in his cinematic text.

In Venice itself, not long after his appearance in the crowded judicial chambers, Bassanio comes to Antonio's defence after Shylock tells the court that the reason for his prosecution of the bond involves no more than the 'lodged hate' and 'certain loathing' he has for Antonio (4.1.59). In response to this declaration Bassanio tells Shylock, 'This is no answer, thou unfeeling man, / To excuse the current of thy cruelty!' (4.1.62–3). Bassanio then goes on to debate the moneylender on the concepts of love and hate and what each would or would not compel a rational man to do. Antonio, though obviously grateful for Bassanio's intervention, remains the epitome of fatalism; he tells Bassanio and the court as a whole not to bother arguing with Shylock. Antonio wants to bring this unpleasant matter to an end since the conclusion is foregone. To him there is no point in prolonging the inevitable. But Bassanio, determined to not give up on the fight for the man he loves, has a pair of men carry a large heavy chest into the centre of the chambers and place it on the floor directly in front of Shylock. 'For thy three thousand ducats', Bassanio spits at Shylock, 'here is six!' (4.1.83). The lid of the trunk is then thrown open, revealing an enormous pile of coins that causes one and all present for the trial to gasp audibly.

With the 6,000 ducats he is offering to give to Shylock on Antonio's behalf, Bassanio is also making it clear that, to him, Antonio is worth at least twice what Antonio originally secured for Bassanio on credit in the spirit of willingly sacrificing his purse, person and his most extreme means for Bassanio. Hence, in a very real sense, Bassanio's putting up the 6,000 ducats for Antonio proves that he, too, is just as willing to risk as much as Antonio was for him prior to Bassanio going off to Belmont. That being the case, the look of astonished anger on Bassanio's face when Shylock refuses to accept the money Bassanio has pledged to give him in order to settle Antonio's bond would whither any other character but Shylock to the bone. Yet Bassanio's protective instincts reach beyond the verbal when Shylock pulls out a long and lethal carving knife from its sheath after insisting that the Duke pronounce his judgement on the case at hand; Bassanio pushes, jostles, pleads and otherwise does everything he can to get past the court guards so that he can defend Antonio, but they do not let him pass.

Following the justly famous quality of mercy speech made by a Portia dressed in the severe black robes of the young lawyer called Balthazar, Portia/Balthazar questions whether or not Antonio is able to discharge Shylock's bond. Bassanio once more jumps into the fray and shouts:

> Yes, here I tender it for him in court,
> Yea, twice the sum. If that will not suffice,
> I will be bound to pay it ten times o'er,
> On forfeit of my hands, my head, my heart. (4.1.205–8)

Having made this pronouncement Bassanio finally breaks free of the court guards, races past Antonio, kneels before the Duke and implores him to 'do a great right' even if it means doing a 'little wrong,' by which he means that the Duke should deny Shylock the bloody judgement he is demanding in accord with the terms of the bond and thereby spare Antonio's life (4.1.212). Throughout Bassanio's impassioned entreaty Antonio is both astonished and grateful for the other man's efforts. Bassanio's plea furthermore serves to confirm yet again all that he will put at stake for Antonio; this includes not just 3,000, but the sum of 30,000 ducats and, complementing Antonio's earlier sacrifices for Bassanio, his hands, his head and his heart. It seems that the love Bassanio bears for Antonio knows no bounds as evidenced by these avowals. In fact, this entire episode can be understood as being an extended, thoroughly public declaration of Bassanio's love for Antonio.

When Balthazar/Portia asks if Antonio has anything to communicate before the court's judgement against him is carried out, a totally resigned Antonio answers with, 'But little. I am armed and well prepared' (4.1.260). Though he claims to have little to say, that little proves to be of great import in a queer context. First, Antonio requests that Bassanio give him his hand. Bassanio surges forward and holds out his hand to Antonio; Antonio grabs Bassanio's hand and kisses it as he shudders in fear. This is nothing less than an intense physical expression of love for Bassanio on Antonio's part. Antonio slowly, almost reluctantly, pulls away from Bassanio's hand then looks up at Bassanio and tells him, 'fare you well', before burying his face in the crook of Bassanio's welcoming shoulder (4.1.261). After having composed himself Antonio continues with, 'Grieve not that I am fall'n to this for you', then adds:

> Commend me to your honourable wife;
> Tell her the process of Antonio's end,
> Say how I loved you, speak me fair in death,
> And, when the tale is told, bid her be judge
> Whether Bassanio had not once a love.
> Repent but you that you shall lose your friend
> And he repents not that he pays your debt.
> For if the Jew do cut but deep enough
> I'll pay it instantly with all my heart. (4.1.262–77)

Though undoubtedly frightened, Antonio's words are heartfelt and filled with emotion. He wants to make sure Bassanio knows how deeply Antonio loves him. Beyond that, Antonio wants Bassanio to speak of Antonio and their love to others in general and Portia in particular. There is no need for their relationship to be hidden away in euphemism or silence. Thus it can be understood that Antonio meant what he said when he told Bassanio that he would unlock his purse, person and most extreme means to and for Bassanio. Dying for or because of Bassanio certainly qualifies as the most extreme means Antonio could use to prove his love.

Tears running down his cheeks and otherwise being only just able to control himself, Bassanio responds to Antonio with:

> Antonio, I am married to a wife
> Which is as dear to me as life itself;
> But life itself, my wife and all the world
> Are not with me esteemed above thy life.

> I would lose all, ay, sacrifice them all
> Here to this devil [Shylock], to deliver you. (4.1.278–83)

Again, just as Antonio was willing to give all for Bassanio, Bassanio is willing to give all for Antonio. Indeed, he would forego his wife and marriage, all of his monetary and material possessions *and* his very existence, if necessary, to spare Antonio from Shylock's vengeance. This seems like far too much for a mere friend to sacrifice for another; a lover, on the other hand, would likely sacrifice all this and more. And as Shylock is about to slice into Antonio's breast with his lethal carving knife, Bassanio holds Antonio's head in his hands in order to steady his beloved merchant. With this gesture it seems that Bassanio will see to it that Antonio is able to die within the space between Bassanio's arms – a place that he has likely inhabited many times before in other, happier circumstances – since Bassanio could not by the laws of Venice die in Antonio's stead.

Even Balthazar/Portia can see how much Bassanio and Antonio love each other as the two men exchange words and attempt to comfort one another given what is about to happen. Though Radford, making a more powerful impression with visuals than with words, cuts Balthazar/Portia's lines in which he/she insists in an aside that 'Your wife would give you little thanks for that / If she were by to hear you make the offer', referring to Bassanio's swearing to give up all for Antonio, the director has Balthazar/Portia drop her eyes to the ground upon hearing Bassanio's vow to Antonio (4.1.284–5). She cannot be unaware that Bassanio's love for Antonio is stronger than his love for her. Such knowledge may well provide her with the motivation she needs to allow, rather sadistically it seems, Antonio's life to hang in the balance until quite literally the very last possible second when she finally screams for Shylock to '[t]arry a little,' thus stopping the moneylender from slicing into Antonio's bosom and very likely killing him in the process (4.1.301). For characters and audiences alike the drama of these moments is beyond intense.

It is also threaded throughout with male homoeroticism. On screen, with Jeremy Irons and Joseph Fiennes bringing the roles of Antonio and Bassanio to vivid, emotionally-charged life, that male homoeroticism is visible – and knowable – in a way that is far more palpable than even Shakespeare's words alone could convey on the page.

III

Though a decidedly melancholy work, *Twelfth Night* is a bit lighter of a play in comparison to *The Merchant of Venice*. This may well be because of its focus on gender and class rather than usury and religion. In any case, Nunn points out in the 'Introduction'[21] to his screenplay for *Twelfth Night* that both he and Shakespeare were concerned with the related problematics of (homo)eroticism and desire. On this subject the director elaborates with his own set of queries that informed the philosophy of his production: 'how are men in love different from women in love; what is attractive to men about the male in women; what is attractive to women about the female in men; is love between two people of the same gender of the same kind as between people of opposite gender?'[22] Throughout most of the film, *Twelfth Night* answers the latter question posed here in the affirmative; same-sex love *is* equivalent to opposite-sex love. But as is the case with Radford's *Merchant*, it is not until the movie draws to a close that same-sex love is suddenly devalued in a way that ultimately proves disappointing, particularly for queer viewers and their many allies. Rather than Orsino and Cesario, here the analytical focus will be on Nunn's treatment of *Twelfth Night*'s other male couple, Antonio (Nicholas Farrell) and Sebastian (Stephen Mackintosh).

Considering Antonio and Sebastian in Nunn's *Twelfth Night* first requires a look at the prologue that serves as the opening scenes of the film.[23] In these the director dramatizes the harrowing events that brought the two men together in the first place, circumstances that Shakespeare mentions only in snippets of dialogue early in the playtext. As such, on the ship bound home to Messaline, in the vessel's grand salon, two young twins with long black hair, who are dressed exactly alike in exotic, androgynous outfits complete with veils covering their faces, entertain the assembled company with a lively ditty. The vocal high jinks on the part of the performers that ensue reveal that one of them is in fact a male, the other a female. This bit of good-natured gender-bending comedy seems to delight everyone but the man standing removed and aloof at the back of the crowd. The man is dressed in formal maritime uniform and he has brown shoulder-length hair and a neatly trimmed beard. He is neither smiling nor frowning; but in fact his bright blue eyes are focused with laser-like intensity on the twins and their antics on the makeshift stage across the room. This man with the severe countenance and bearing is Antonio. And although it seems as if at this early point that he has not yet made Sebastian's acquaintance, he is nevertheless mesmerized by the young man. Why? It is just possible, given Sebastian's uninhibited cross-dressing in feminine garb, that Antonio's fascination with him derives from the fact that said cross-dressing signifies Sebastian's possible sexual availability; that Sebastian may be willing to play the woman in bed for Antonio since he is comfortable with being thought of as a woman by others in order to amuse them in an impromptu stage show.

The fun and games come to an abrupt end when, in the voiced-over words of the film's narrator (Ben Kingsley as Feste), the steamer, having strayed off its course because of a storm, runs into serious trouble when it hits 'upon submergèd rocks'. Everyone is thrown into a state of panic; people are being wrenched about as if they were toys, tables and chairs are tipping over, terrified shrieks are heard as the vessel lists violently to and fro. After changing clothes and gathering what they can of their belongings the twins venture to the ship's main deck where, within moments, things go from bad to worse. Viola is ripped out of her brother's grasp due to the violence of the wind and the rain swirling around them. Having lost hold of her, Sebastian screams in horror as his sister is tossed into the churning sea. He is momentarily stopped from throwing himself off the deck in order to go after Viola by none other than Antonio. But Antonio is only able to keep the younger man secure in his arms for a second or two before Sebastian hurls himself off the side of the ship so that he can try to save what turns out to be his only living family member. Antonio is next seen after having climbed onto the ship's rigging so that he has a better view to look at the roiling sea below. It is obvious that he is hoping against hope to catch a glimpse of the twins and, no doubt, of Sebastian in particular. This also makes it plain that Antonio already – even this early on in Nunn's *Twelfth Night* – has a significant emotional investment in Sebastian, one that would drive him to save the young man's life if he could even at great risk to his own. Furthermore, as the narrative of the homoerotic love these two men share continues to unfold, this motif of self-sacrifice on Antonio's part will be repeated in two other equally dramatic sets of circumstances.

Some forty minutes later in Nunn's *Twelfth Night* the audience learns that both Sebastian and Antonio survived the wreck of the steamer, the former because of the latter's determined efforts. The scene in which this information is revealed opens in an idyllic but unnamed location where, presumably, the two men have spent the better part of the previous three months while Sebastian recovered from the trauma he suffered in the disaster that as far as he knows claimed the life of the sister he tried to rescue. Sebastian is walking toward a quay at the mouth of a river where a group of men are busy building a ship. Hurrying after him Antonio asks, with distress evident in his voice, 'Will you stay no longer?', then he reaches out and grabs Sebastian by the arm, forcing the younger man to stop and face him (Nunn 37; Elam 2.1.1).[24] When he is certain that Sebastian is paying attention to him, Antonio pleads: 'Let me yet know of you whither you are bound' (Nunn 37; Elam

2.1.8-9). Pequigney seizes on these lines from Shakespeare's playtext, that Nunn uses without change, in order to argue that Antonio's 'openly amorous language habitual to him whenever he speaks to or about Sebastian – and rarely does his attention turn to anything else – is the foremost clue to the erotic nature of their friendship'.[25] As such it supplements the visual evidence of Antonio's desire for Sebastian – signified by Antonio's insistent attendance to Sebastian – that Nunn provides in both the prologue and this particular scene of his *Twelfth Night*. In addition, the way Nicholas Farrell plays him, Antonio's face is almost always a study in longing for Sebastian. Nevertheless, in response to Antonio's entreaty, Sebastian takes his black overcoat from him and says, 'No, sooth, sir,' then he turns his back on Antonio and starts to walk away from him (Nunn 37; Elam 2.1.10). But he only goes so far before practically collapsing in evident frustration or despair on a nearby bench.

Within a moment or two Sebastian turns to Antonio once again; Antonio looks at him with the deepest compassion. It is clear that all Antonio wants to do is to somehow make any and all of the pain Sebastian is feeling go away. For Sebastian, the time has come for him to confess the truth: 'You must know of me then, Antonio, my name is Sebastian. My father was that Sebastian of Messaline whom I know you have heard of' (Nunn 37; Elam 2.1.15-17). Antonio allows himself the briefest of smiles, indicating that he is indeed familiar with Sebastian's father, if only by report than by any other means. Sebastian continues, explaining that his parent 'left behind him myself and a sister, Viola, both born in an hour – would we had so ended! But you, sir, altered that; before you took me from the breach of the sea was my sister drowned' (Nunn 37-8; Elam 2.1.17-21). As he is speaking here, it is obvious that Sebastian is only just able to keep from bursting into tears because he loved his sister so deeply; he likely wishes that he, too, were dead so that he could be with her in the afterlife. The only thing an honestly affected Antonio can say at this point after hearing Sebastian's revelations is, 'Alas, the day,' but then he sits down right next to the grieving young man (see Figure 18). In a trembling voice, Sebastian continues by describing his sister as a 'lady, sir, though it was said she much resembled me, was yet of many accounted beautiful' (Nunn 38; Elam 2.1.23–4). Then, apparently worn out from mourning, Sebastian lets his tears burst forth while simultaneously burying his face in Antonio's chest. Antonio welcomes the chance to comfort Sebastian by wrapping his arms around the young man and holding him tightly.

Sebastian remains in Antonio's arms only until the sound of an approaching carriage being pulled by a team of horses is heard. After drying his eyes with his hands and steadying himself with a deep breath he leaves Antonio who, once again, hurries after him. As Sebastian strides toward the coach with grim determination he attempts to apologize to Antonio by tossing over his shoulder the following words: 'O good

FIGURE 18 *A compassionate and adoring Antonio (Nicholas Farrell) attempting to comfort an extremely distraught Sebastian (Stephen Mackintosh) in* Twelfth Night, *dir. Trevor Nunn, 1996, DVD screen capture.*

Antonio, forgive me your trouble' (Nunn 38; Elam 2.1.31). Antonio will not accept being dismissed in such a way, and yet again grabs Sebastian by the arm and forces the younger man to turn around and face him. 'If you will not murder me for my love', he says, 'let me be your servant' (Nunn 38; Elam 2.1.32–3). Here, Antonio longs to be Sebastian's servant in much the same way that Cesario sought out a similar position in the household of Duke Orsino. As Schalkwyk has pointed out, service in the context Antonio uses it here was a fact of life for many during the early modern period in England and it was something Shakespeare often used in his plays as a way of bringing his characters together and into dramatic situations involving courtship and romance. On these lines in *Twelfth Night* in particular he writes that Antonio's:

> demand stems from the necessary mutuality that is entailed by the concepts of friendship and service. Sebastian's acknowledgement of Antonio as either friend or servant would necessarily create a mutual bond between them. If he cannot continue to be his friend, service will allow Antonio to prolong intimate contact with Sebastian, and perhaps even gain some affective hold on him.[26]

There can be no disputing the fact that the dynamics Schalkwyk outlines in this passage in regards to Shakespeare's and Nunn's representation of the Antonio/Sebastian relationship are operative. Antonio does not wish to be parted from Sebastian regardless of the circumstances, even if that means placing himself in a subordinate position to the younger man. And it is more than likely that by so doing he does indeed hope to secure Sebastian's romantic affections. But his plea is, or so it seems, in vain, as Sebastian firmly, though not unkindly, tells Antonio: 'Desire it not. Fare ye well at once' (Nunn 38; Elam 2.1.35–6). But after he has boarded the carriage and seated himself he looks down at Antonio, sighs and reveals, 'I am bound to the Count Orsino's court. Farewell' (Nunn 38; Elam 2.1.38–9). At this point the only thing Antonio can do is watch the coach as it takes Sebastian away from him. 'The gentleness of all the gods go with thee,' he says softly to himself, then adds, 'I have many enemies in Orsino's court, / Else would I very shortly see thee there –' (Nunn 38; Elam 2.1.40–2). Thus it appears that a hapless Antonio has been abandoned by his beloved Sebastian. Or does it?

Arguably, this is one instance where Nunn's screenplay of *Twelfth Night* does something of a disservice to those viewers who are familiar with Shakespeare's original. In the source text Antonio utters two additional lines that prove key to any queer study of the male homoerotic aspects of the relationship he has with Sebastian. Following the mention of his Illyrian enemies Antonio goes on to say: 'But come what may I adore thee so / That danger shall seem sport, and I will go' (Elam 2.1.43–4). There can be no mistaking that the words 'I adore thee so' attest to the fact that Antonio, in accord with the insights of Pequigney, desires if not outright loves Sebastian in a romantic and sexual sense by this point in their story proper (i.e. exclusive of Nunn's appended prologue). For audiences, the antidote to this elision lies in remembering that the Antonio who seems to give up here in Nunn's film is the same Antonio who dove into the roiling sea in order to save Sebastian's life despite the risks to his own person. This may alert them to the possibility that, regardless of what he says in this scene about having many enemies in Orsino's court, he will indeed pursue Sebastian. And it is, of course, to the director's credit that he trusts them to recall that information and to speculate on just such a scenario coming to pass. But the excision of the 'I adore thee so' phrase is troubling. Without it viewers of Nunn's production are given too little of an indication of the tenaciousness of the homoerotic nature of Antonio's interest in Sebastian. The filmmaker thus makes it far too easy for them to rest on the assumption that it is simply in most humans' nature to come to the aid of others when they are in danger regardless of where they may fall on the affective spectrum in terms of their love object desires. Put in slightly different terms, the absence of Antonio's 'I adore thee so' threatens to render any hint of non-normative desire and sexuality where he and Sebastian are concerned almost unintelligible.

Further into Nunn's *Twelfth Night*, Sebastian, with a *Baedeker Guidebook to Illyria* in hand, a detail Rothwell approvingly describes as a nice 'touch of whimsy' on the filmmakers' part,[27] is seen making his way through the bustling streets of the market town that sits in the shadow of Duke Orsino's palatial residence. Within seconds it is made clear that Sebastian believes he is being followed and that he is trying to escape from his unknown pursuer. However, Sebastian fails to elude the man, who catches up with him rather quickly. The man happens to be dressed somewhat oddly in the comely garb of a Christian cleric, but as soon as he removes his hat and glasses, he reveals himself to Sebastian to be none other than his savior, Antonio. Indeed, Cynthia Lewis describes Antonio as the ultimate Christian priest: 'If any figure in *Twelfth Night* calls Christ to mind,' she writes, 'it is Antonio', whose role is to be a 'Christ-like giver of love' in the play.[28] It is interesting to consider that insofar as Antonio's having usurped the attire of a man of the cloth, Nunn's thinking was on the same wavelength as Lewis's. But it also demands arguing that Antonio's love for Sebastian is far more secular than religious. Indeed, he looks at Sebastian with a sheepish expression and confesses, 'I could not stay behind you', by which he means that he was unable to remain separated from Sebastian (Nunn 71; Elam 3.3.4). Though taken aback by the presence of someone he did not expect to see again so soon, Sebastian is nevertheless thrilled to see Antonio. In point of fact he exclaims, 'My kind Antonio,' then he flings himself into Antonio's arms (Nunn 71; Elam 3.3.13). Caught up in the moment Antonio squeezes his eyes shut and holds Sebastian tightly, indicating how profoundly satisfying being so intimate with Sebastian is for him. This is the reunion of friends ... and of lovers (see Figure 19).

When their hug reaches its end Antonio continues his explanation about why he came in pursuit of Sebastian: 'But

FIGURE 19 *A thrilled Sebastian (Stephen Mackintosh) and an equally happy Antonio (Nicholas Farrell) reunited in Illyria in* Twelfth Night, *dir. Trevor Nunn, 1996, DVD screen capture.*

not all love to see you – you sir are / A stranger in these parts,' he says, by which he means that he came to Illyria not only because of his love for Sebastian, but also so that Sebastian would have the comfort of a familiar face while he pursues his quest, whatever that quest may entail (Nunn 71; Elam 3.3.6–11). Sebastian, as his response suggests, is grateful for Antonio's having sought him out: 'I can no other answer make but thanks, / And thanks. And ever oft good turns / Are shuffled off with such uncurrent pay' (Nunn 71: Elam 3.3.14–16). He wishes in fact that he could thank Antonio for the kindness Antonio has shown him with something other than words. That being the case, after glancing at his guidebook, he presents Antonio with the following rather curious suggestion:

> I am not weary, and 'tis long to night.
> I pray you, let us satisfy our eyes
> With the memorials and the things of fame
> That do renown this city. (Nunn 71, 73; Elam 3.3.21–4)

On a literal level Sebastian is merely proposing that he and Antonio spend the rest of what is left of the afternoon sightseeing in Illyria. But it does not require a huge leap of the imagination to also understand that, on another level, what Sebastian is really asking Antonio qualifies as the late twentieth- and early twenty-first-century equivalent of his asking Antonio out on a date. This understated romantic moment between these two men is crucially important as it, in tandem with Sebastian's spontaneously throwing himself into Antonio's arms moments before, testifies to the fact that Antonio's homoerotic feelings for Sebastian are not entirely one-sided as many critics of *Twelfth Night* have been all too quick to insist.

Alas, Antonio must refuse Sebastian's offer because he has risked enough by appearing in Illyria in the first place. That being the case, Antonio leads Sebastian to a spot very nearby that affords a bit more privacy in order to explain why he is declining to go sightseeing in the city with him. Once out of the earshot of passersby he proceeds to confide to Sebastian:

> I do not without danger walk these streets,
> Once in a seafight 'gainst Orsino's galleys
> I did some service – of such note indeed
> That were I ta'en here, it would scarce be answered. (Nunn 73; Elam 3.3.25–8)

Awestruck by this revelation Sebastian responds with, 'Belike you slew a great number of his people?' (Nunn 73; Elam 3.3.29). Indeed, this line registers the fact that Sebastian is wholly impressed by the notion that Antonio was valorous enough to take on a cadre of Orsino's troops; it seems like this is something he finds attractive about Antonio. Diverging somewhat from Shakespeare's text, Nunn allows Antonio to confirm Sebastian's supposition when he comments, 'For which, if I be lapsed in this place, / I shall pay dear', which causes Sebastian to become immediately concerned for Antonio's welfare: 'Do not then walk too open', he says as yet another verbal indication that his feelings for Antonio are on a par with the older man's for him and encompass the homoerotic as well the homosocial (Nunn 73; Elam 3.3.36–7). At the very least, if Sebastian did not admire and care for Antonio on some level, he would not be so quick to express his wonder at the nature of Antonio's exploits or his worry about Antonio's well-being.

In any case, being in something of a rush to conceal himself from the Illyrian authorities, Antonio goes on to tell Sebastian breathlessly that he shall find him 'at the Elephant,' then he hands the younger man a small black bag that is obviously filled with money (Nunn 73; Elam 3.3.39). Understandably, Sebastian is confused about why Antonio has just given him his purse, so Antonio explains: 'Haply your eye shall light upon some toy / You have desired to purchase; and your store, I think, is not for idle markets, sir' (Nunn 73; Elam 3.3.43–6).[29] Antonio starts to rush off, but stops himself long enough to reiterate excitedly to Sebastian, 'At th'Elephant;' in response Sebastian chuckles and says, 'I do remember' (Nunn 73; Elam 3.3.48). Then the two men part and go their separate ways. But viewers of Nunn's *Twelfth Night*, who, after all, lack the benefit of textual glosses, would do well to pause here and consider in more detail the implications of what they have just witnessed in this exchange between Sebastian and Antonio.

At first it might seem surprising that Antonio would simply hand over his purse containing any of what can be thought of in late twentieth and early twenty-first century colloquial terms as his 'hard-earned money.' But this is the same Antonio who risked his own life to save Sebastian in the shipwreck that brought them together and who has overseen the younger man's three month recovery from nearly drowning in the sea. This is also the same Antonio whose obvious desire for Sebastian extends beyond shared traumatic experience or homosocial camaraderie and into the realm of the affective, the romantic and the homoerotic. Pequigney makes the claim that Antonio does what he does here with his money 'with the ulterior motive of pleasing if not purchasing the desired youth'.[30] Unfortunately, this assessment serves to perpetuate the tiresome notion that the only way an older (gay) man like Antonio can secure the affections of a younger (straight) man like Sebastian is to buy those affections, which does not paint either Antonio or Sebastian in the most flattering of lights. In fact, this rather cynical idea makes their relationship seem both predatory and mercenary when neither adjective seems to describe the truth. In keeping with his generous character, Antonio gives his purse to Sebastian for no other reason than so that the latter will have sufficient funds to purchase a luxury item if he happens to come across one that he fancies during his wanderings in Illyria. And Sebastian seems to accept it in kind.

A great deal more suggestiveness attends on the Elephant, the location Antonio instructs Sebastian to rendezvous with him at after he has completed his sightseeing tour of the Illyrian capital. Uninformed viewers of Nunn's *Twelfth Night* will undoubtedly be content with thinking of the Elephant as roughly equivalent to their contemporary ideas of what a hotel or a motel is: a place to rest for the night. However, citing an essay by Gustave Ungerer in a footnote to Shakespeare's reference to the Elephant and the London suburbs, Arden 3 editor Elam reveals that 'there was indeed an Elephant Inn on Bankside' during the early modern period 'which was in practice "an inn-cum brothel".'[31] In any study of the male homoerotics of *Twelfth Night*, textual or cinematic, this bit of information cannot be ignored. Yu Jin Ko considers the subject of the Elephant further than does Elam: 'It is not at all clear what kind of brothel the Oliphant [the Elephant] was, though it does seem clear, as Alan Bray has demonstrated, that Elizabethan London had its share of homosexual brothels'.[32] The implications of this insight are unmistakable: the Elephant at which Antonio and Sebastian are going to meet could well be a place where sex between males was not only encouraged but actively sought out. Whether or not such liaisons were little more than financial transactions is, in this specific case at least, beside the point. Antonio and Sebastian can certainly take a room at the Elephant if they wish without participating in its larger sexual economy. Doing so would, not incidentally, afford them the privacy in which to (re)consummate their relationship on a physical level without fear of interruption or censure. From this perspective, the fact that Sebastian does not outright refuse to meet Antonio at a place like the Elephant proves significant as yet one more indication that his desire for Antonio matches Antonio's desire for him.

In accord with Shakespeare's play, following their night at the Elephant, Antonio makes a dramatic reappearance in Nunn's *Twelfth Night* when he intervenes in the duel that the rascals Sir Toby Belch (Mel Smith) and Fabian (Peter Gunn) have engineered for their amusement between the foppish Sir Andrew Aguecheek (Richard E. Grant) and a clueless Cesario. Given that Cesario looks exactly like him, Antonio thinks he is entering into this manufactured fray in order to protect his beloved Sebastian. Seeing what is taking place between Sir Andrew and Cesario in one of the orchards on the estate of the Countess Olivia, a look of horror spreads across his face and from his perch on the top of an outer wall ringing the grounds he shouts to the utter surprise of one and all, 'Put up your sword' (Nunn 98; Elam 3.4.307). Then, grim-faced, Antonio leaps off the wall and down into the orchard, strides over to the person he is certain is Sebastian, takes Sebastian's sword, and forcefully moves the young man behind him so that he is the one facing Sir Andrew. In a flat, determined voice he says, 'If this young gentleman / Have done offence, I take the fault on me' (Nunn 98; Elam 3.4.307–8). When asked by Sir Toby to explain exactly who he is, Antonio, while making a pointed show of assuring himself that Sebastian's sword will work the way it is intended, tells the crafty man that he is someone 'that for his [Sebastian's] love dares yet do more / Than you have heard him brag to you he will' (Nunn 98; Elam 3.4.311–12). These are the words and actions of high romantic chivalry. Antonio may as well be the fantastical knight in shining armour and Sebastian his 'damsel' in distress. Hyperbole aside, though, the Antonio defending Sebastian here is the very same Antonio who rescued Sebastian from the sea and followed him to Illyria at equally great peril to himself, both the actions of a man who loves another man so much that he would, quite literally, do anything for him, including die for him if necessary. Again, from a queer perspective, this qualifies as male homoeroticism at its most palpable.

No wonder then that Antonio's sense of betrayal is so intense when 'Sebastian' refuses to help him by returning his purse after he has been apprehended by Duke Orsino's militia and stands in desperate need of his money. 'Will you deny me now?', Antonio roars at the perplexed young man; then, in one swift movement, he pushes him away, causing the coins Cesario was attempting to give to Antonio to go flying every which way (Nunn 100; Elam 3.4.344). Sure that they have a situation on their hands, Orsino's men choose that moment to punch Antonio in the stomach and he doubles over in pain. After he recovers, he looks at 'Sebastian' with barely concealed contempt in his eyes. After saving his life, after coming to be with him and him only in a foreign land, after spending at least one night in which their passion for each other was likely given free reign, and after having placed himself into the middle of a duel not his own on behalf of 'Sebastian,' he is certainly justified in feeling as if he deserves better treatment from him.

Cesario, not surprisingly considering the circumstances, remains mystified by Antonio's behaviour while the soldiers and Sir Toby, Sir Andrew and Fabian could not care less about why Antonio is so upset with 'Sebastian.' When confronted later by Orsino, the count demands to know how Antonio came to be in the predicament in which he now finds himself: as a long sought after prisoner. Once again Antonio looks darkly at 'Sebastian' and claims in a voice tight with emotion, 'A witchcraft drew me hither. / That most ingrateful boy there by your side', then he erupts in total anger when he adds, 'For his sake / Faced the danger of this adverse town' (Nunn 114 and 115; Elam 5.1.78

and 80). For those familiar with Shakespeare's later play *Othello*, the word witchcraft might well resonate when they recall that, according to her incensed father, Brabantio, the only thing that could have made Desdemona fall in love with what she feared to look upon is Othello's spells and enchantments.[33] Othello insists however that stories about himself and his experiences were the only form of witchcraft he used on Desdemona.[34] On this point Antonio's feelings are akin to those of Brabantio; the only way he could have been fooled into believing, trusting and, ultimately, caring so deeply for someone as 'ugly' as Sebastian has turned out to be – despite his considerable physical beauty – is through some sort of witchcraft. From his point of view there can be no other explanation. And in the painful moments discussed here, the depth of Antonio's emotion at being so callously cast aside serve, if it is needed, as a final exclamation point in Nunn's *Twelfth Night* to the homoerotic nature of his desire and love for Sebastian.

IV

It is not an overstatement to assert that with *Twelfth Night* in particular, among all his plays, Shakespeare succeeds at blending the melancholic, the vicious, the mirthful and the joyful in a way that uncannily mirrors the human experience of life. So, it can be said, does Nunn in his cinematic adaptation of the play. As Rothwell notes at the conclusion of commentary on the film in relation to the original play, 'Shakespeare created a verbal structure that probes the sadness and sweetness in the mystery of life, and Nunn has gracefully and wittily put that daunting challenge into moving images.'[35] True enough; yet where Nunn errs, and Shakespeare does not, at least not in the same way or to the same extent, is at the end of his otherwise outstanding production. Coursen agrees with this assessment:

Where does this film not work? – at the end. But then it often does not work on stage either, where the ending can be crowded. It calls for exquisite blocking. Here, it could have been condensed, with film solving some of the traffic problems and giving us shorthand for some of the language.[36]

For Coursen though, the reason Nunn's *Twelfth Night* does not succeed at the end is because it is unwieldy, featuring as it does too many characters, too much stage business and too much dialogue all crammed into a few minutes' time. But it is crucial to understand that what Coursen is commenting on here is the movie's denouement – which does follow Shakespeare's text quite closely – not what can be considered its actual finish. For reasons that are not explained in the published screenplay, Nunn includes a coda that serves as the true conclusion to his film, and it is this coda that is quite problematic, at least for queer audiences and their allies, considering all that precedes it.

In the *Twelfth Night* cinematic coda Nunn presents a collage of scenes immediately prior to the scrolling of the credits. Most prominent among these images are those that depict the double wedding celebration of the couples Sebastian and Olivia (Helena Bonham Carter) and Orsino (Toby Stephens) and Viola (Imogen Stubbs). At the same time, audiences are made privy to the silent departures of Feste (Ben Kingsley), Malvolio (Nigel Hawthorne), Sir Toby and Maria (Imelda Staunton) and, finally, Antonio, from the Countess Olivia's residence. When he comes into view Antonio appears utterly alone on the path leading from the estate. Given the evident fog and dampness it cannot but be a raw and inhospitable time of day. He pauses long enough to bundle himself further into his coat as a defence against the cold temperature. Thus fortified, Antonio trudges on his way without looking back at the house where, presumably, his beloved Sebastian remains with Oliva in wedded bliss. In its specificity, such a depiction of Antonio's fate comes across as the cinematic equivalent of a slap-in-the-face directed toward Nunn's queer viewers. In the playtext of *Twelfth Night* there are no stage directions or verbal mentions of Antonio's departure from Olivia's domain. Magro and Douglas articulate the issues at stake in the close of Nunn's film as follows, 'it rehearses homosexual desire and then disavows it in order to postulate the naturalness and transparency of heterosexual relations'.[37] It also exposes the fact that 'it is heterosexuality that is the dependent concept, relying on homosexuality to provide it with its seeming authenticity'.[38] The rehearsal of the homosexual desire Magro and Douglas mention in this cogent statement of the problem at hand has, it is to be hoped, been explored as fully as possible in this chapter. As was detailed above, Antonio's interest in, and later devotion to, Sebastian, is a function of his requited love for the young man. So when Nunn shows Antonio stalking away – alone – from Olivia's estate into the cold gray twilight, queer viewers of the movie and their allies have every right to feel betrayed and with a distinct longing for what could have – indeed, should have, been.

Following Pequigney's only partially tongue-in-cheek query about a *ménage à trois* between Antonio, Sebastian and Olivia resulting from the latter's marital union near the end of *Twelfth Night*, Alan Sinfield comments that:

> Sebastian's marriage to a stranger heiress need not significantly affect Antonio's relationship with him ... They might all live together in Olivia's house ... So Antonio need not appear at the end of *Twelfth Night* as the defeated and melancholy outsider that critics [and Nunn] have supposed; a director, reading only partly against the grain, might show him delighted with his boyfriend's lucky break.[39]

While it is a far-fetched idea that the Antonio, Sebastian and Olivia triad would set up permanent housekeeping in the manner Pequigney and Sinfield put forth, Sebastian, though married, was, as Kleinberg revealed, free to do as he pleased given his position as, now, a gentleman of the nobility. He could in other words elect to prolong his relationship with Antonio indefinitely and without necessarily risking his vows as long as he made at least some effort to keep up normative appearances. But Sinfield is right to point out that there is no reason whatsoever why Antonio would not be happy that Sebastian had managed to secure a living for himself that could when all is said and done benefit both of them in ways neither imagined before. With his penchant for interpolation, as evidenced by the thoroughly imagined prologue, it seems that Nunn could have easily included a scene or a montage at the end of his *Twelfth Night* that shows Antonio and Sebastian embracing as the former prepares to depart, but agreeing to meet in Messaline, perhaps, where they can once again enjoy all of the emotional, affective and erotic pleasures that two men can share with each other if they are so inclined. Still, his queer audiences and their allies will always have the comfort of screening *Twelfth Night* in the way that Sinfield advocates for, 'against the grain, queering the text', and thus in a way that makes perfect sense to them from their unique perspective.

Similarly, with the amount of sustained and sympathetic attention Radford devotes to the male homoerotic subtext that is more than evident in Shakespeare's *Merchant*, it proves more than a little disappointing that the director chooses to finish Antonio and Bassanio's story in a pointedly heteronormative manner. Indeed, Radford's *Merchant* concludes in total, seemingly unquestioned, accord with Bruce Smith's observation that 'all of Shakespeare's comedies and tragicomedies end with male friendship yielding place to heterosexual love'.[40] This can be seen in that, not long before the closing credits of the film begin to scroll, Portia turns back toward Bassanio before walking out of the room at her estate in Belmont and says in a voice that can only be described as determinedly, even triumphantly, seductive:

> It is almost morning,
> And yet I am sure you are not satisfied

> Of these events in full. Let us go in;
> [...]
> And I [we] will answer all things faithfully. (5.1.293–7)

From the way Portia speaks these lines it seems as if she and Bassanio are going to 'go in' not only to talk, but also to make love. Bassanio slowly follows her into another part of the mansion as if he is in a daze. In so doing he quite clearly forgets, or just plain ignores, Antonio, who stands watching them from only a few feet away as Bassanio walks past him and after Portia.

Moments later, the last time Antonio is seen in the film, he is obviously alone and unsure of what to do with himself now that Bassanio and Portia and Graziano and Nerissa, the male and female couples, have gone off to consummate their marriages. He paces to and fro like he did when he was so consumed by sadness in his palazzo back in Venice prior to Bassanio's arrival. This demonstrates in cinematic form how, as Little describes it, 'Shakespeare's romantic comedies end not only with the reifying and presumed stability of heterosexuality but with Shakespeare's audience being coerced into witnessing the end of queer desire and queer marriage'.[41] In all fairness, however, it must be remembered that Shakespeare's *Merchant*, as has been pointed out many times before elsewhere, does not provide any definitive insight about what exactly happens to Antonio by the time the curtain closes or, in this case, as the screen fades to black. Even so, Radford's choice to depict Antonio in the manner he does serves to perpetuate only negative stereotypes about gay men who are, in this conception, always assumed to be doomed to a life of loneliness and despair because the men they choose to love cannot or will not return that love in either kind or quality.

Given that Radford shares Nunn's talent for creating scenes that do not technically exist in Shakespeare's *Merchant*, as well as his facility with depicting stage directions and textual cues in visual form that make logical sense in tandem with the context – and more particularly, the male homoerotic context – of the original dramatic text, such a pessimistic end to Antonio and Bassanio's relationship seems rather odd. Further scrutiny of Shakespeare's playtext makes it clear that Antonio, and therefore the male homoerotic itself, remain very much a part of its concluding fabric. There is no word from Bassanio, or Portia for that matter, of exiling Antonio from their home in Belmont. It is also mentioned, by Bassanio himself no less, that he foresees absenting himself from Portia at various times in the future. There is more than sufficient reason to suspect that Bassanio will be in Venice, in the arms and the bed of his beloved Antonio. Would that Radford had created a scene or even a montage for the closing of his version of *Merchant* that capitalized on these potentialities and was as attentive to the male homoerotics in these moments as he was in the balance of his otherwise excellent cinematic production of the play. And once again, a queer experience of the film depends on viewers' ability to screen this *Merchant* by watching it 'against the grain' and thereby 'queering the text' to their satisfaction rather than passively accepting the heteronormative status quo it presents.

5

'I am your own forever': Iago, queer self-fashioning and the cinematic *Othellos* of Orson Welles and Oliver Parker

I

Arguably, *Othello* stands as one of the most celebrated – and one of the most disturbing – tragedies in the Shakespeare canon.[1] Almost certainly written immediately after *Hamlet*, the first documented performance of the play was on 1 November 1604. It might, as Lois Potter explains, 'have been finished in time to be acted before the death of Elizabeth I and the plagues that closed the theatres for much of 1603–4, or the recorded performance may have been one of the first in James I's reign'.[2] Regardless, *Othello* 'belongs to a period when the London theatres were competing to produce plays of an apparently new genre, domestic drama'.[3] Although the action unfolds in both Venice and Cyprus, and there are hints of nationalistic themes in the war that never materializes between the Venetians and the invading Turks, *Othello* qualifies as a domestic tragedy simply because of the fact that it charts the terrible disintegration of a marriage – perhaps the most insular and intimate, and vulnerable, of human social institutions. And, given his gifts for originality and innovation, it makes perfect sense that Shakespeare was involved in his own idiosyncratic way with both the genesis and the evolution of what then constituted a form of theatrical representation unlike that which had come before and that Elizabethan and Jacobean audiences embraced with their characteristic enthusiasm for all things theatre.

As it travelled through time from the early seventeenth to the early twenty-first century, *Othello* would remain a popular but increasingly troubling work of drama. Concerns with the coarseness – particularly where sexual matters are involved – of the play's language were noted in the 1700s and 1800s. The offending lines were dealt with accordingly, usually by the means of elision in performance and publication.[4] Furthermore, because of the unavoidable legacy of slavery as well as the institutionalized misogyny that pervades Western culture at large, *Othello* became even more of a problem play by the twentieth and early twenty-first centuries. But, despite the evident difficulties related to the concepts of race, postcolonialism, gender, feminism and sexuality that the play traffics in, directors and actors have not shied away from bringing *Othello* to the big and the small screens alike. Including appropriations and more or less literal adaptations of the tragedy, Rothwell lists a total of twenty-five film and television productions of *Othello* as having appeared between 1908, when Vitagraph's ten-minute black-and-white silent version made its debut, and 2001, when Tim Blake Nelson's teen-oriented, Columbine-affected *O* once again brought the play to the attention of cinema audiences.[5] This chapter will consider two of these movies: Orson Welles's *Othello* (1952) and Oliver Parker's *Othello* (1995). Both of these productions, it will be argued, deals with the queerness that is so clearly a part of Shakespeare's original playtext in specific ways that are indicative of the historical periods from which they emerged and that represent, most particularly where the character of Iago is concerned, a specific form of what can be considered, appropriating the idea from Stephen Greenblatt, queer self-fashioning that has been overlooked in the extant criticism of these films.

II

Beyond the issues raised and explored on account of racial, postcolonial, gender, sexual and feminist concerns, *Othello* has also been the subject of a great deal of what can be in the broadest sense characterized as queer critical inquiry. Indeed, before delving into the specifics of the queerness and queer self-fashioning evident in the films that will serve as the exemplars for this chapter's discussion, it proves instructive to consider a few of the interventions that have been made into *Othello* as a written theatrical text from a queer perspective. This is useful because many of the insights and questions raised by this kind of analysis find their way into *Othello* in the two cinematic productions discussed below. As such, to start with, it can be noted that the queer line of interpretation of *Othello* is traceable back to the work of Stanley Edgar Hyman who, forty-five years ago, wrote that the character of Iago is 'motivated by strong latent homosexuality (or acts as does a person so motivated). This is not only abundantly clear in the play, but it is clearly of Shakespeare's deliberate contrivance' rather than a facet the playwright derived from his source materials.[6] Directly comparing Iago to the character that, in Cinthio's *Hecatomithi*, served as Iago's prototype, Hyman goes on to insist that Shakespeare's Iago 'neither loves Desdemona nor believes for a moment that she loves Cassio ... It is he [Iago] who unconsciously loves both Othello and Cassio; that love is repressed and, by the defense mechanism called "reaction formation," turned into hate' – creating a set of circumstances not to be found in Cinthio's story.[7] This is a classic Freudian/psychoanalytic reading of Iago and, while there is no doubt that it was an insightful interpretation forty-five years ago, in the early twenty-first century it comes across as problematic.

It also seems that Hyman's analysis could only have been produced from a presumptively normative heterosexual reading position that results in a view of homosexuality as always already the opposite – rather than any kind of an equal in and of itself – of heterosexuality. This may be why Hyman's interpretation perceives Iago's homosexuality in the quasi-negative: as latent, unconscious and repressed. Within the superstructure that is hegemonic heterosexuality, homosexuality can only ever be hidden, unknown and regulated, as opposed to open, above board and uninhibited like its oppositional counterpart. Indeed, this is how, as Foucault has explained, especially in the first volume of *The History of Sexuality*, heterosexuality perpetuates itself as the gold standard of human interpersonal relations. By peremptorily defining and policing homosexuality, heterosexuality can control what it considers to be an alien Other on its own terms. Thus in Hyman's reading, because he is classified as a homosexual rather than a heterosexual, there is something inherently and fundamentally unnatural and wrong about Iago from the outset. He is, in Hyman's words, filled with 'contempt for women' and 'disgust with heterosexual love and marriage', three of the cornerstones at the heart of the patriarchal system that defines Western culture.[8] Homosexuals, from this normative perspective, can only have dislike for women and an extreme discomfort with the very idea of opposite gender sexual activities and the institution of holy matrimony. Hyman seems to give no thought at all to the possibility that homosexuals can and do like women without wanting or needing to have sex with them, or to the possibility that there are other ways for human beings to love and to have stable, long-term relationships (the equivalent of heterosexual marriages) with people of the same gender.

Hyman proceeds to claim that Iago's supposition that Othello is having an ongoing sexual affair with Iago's wife, Emilia, is nothing less than Iago's 'unconscious wish that Othello go to bed with him' instead, and that Iago is thus jealous of Desdemona because she is the one Othello goes to bed with rather than Iago himself.[9] But the unwritten assumption here is that Othello and Iago have never slept together as lovers prior to, or even at some point during, for that matter, the action of *Othello* proper. Given that both are part of an all-male milieu – military service – known throughout recorded history for the prevalence of homoerotic couplings within its ranks – such a conjecture warrants some qualification. Be that as it may, Cassio's dream about making love to Desdemona that Iago 'reluctantly' relates to Othello then becomes the fantastical means by which Iago transforms himself into the imagined object of sexual desire that is, in turn, pursued by both Cassio and Othello – two exceptionally virile men that Iago longs to be ravished by, perhaps simultaneously – while in a state of decadent homosexual excess. Taking all of these forces into account leads Hyman to the perhaps inevitable conclusion that Iago's suggestion to Othello that, rather than poison her, Othello should strangle Desdemona in the very bed where they sleep and have sex, is 'in this context a strikingly homosexual wish, the transformation of the heterosexual act into murder', a murder that would for all intents and purposes remove Desdemona as an impediment to Iago's sublimated desire to be with Othello as his one and only friend and, more importantly, lover.[10] A 'strikingly homosexual wish'? This disturbing pronouncement serves in effect to stereotype all homosexuals – as opposed to only just Iago, a *character* in a Shakespearean tragedy – as psychopaths whose sole option is to kill women in order to have the opportunity to be with the men they desire and cannot secure for themselves in any other way than by eliminating the competition. Later quoting Desdemona's last words, Hyman manages yet again to equate the 'homosexual motivations' that brought about her death at Othello's – and, by extension,

Iago's – hands with the unnatural and the foul.[11] There can be no question that Iago is the villain of *Othello*; however, he is not, as Hyman seems to believe, villainous solely because he is a homosexual in the (out)dated psychoanalytic sense of that word. He is evil simply because he is evil and regardless of his sexual desires.

Ben Saunders' more recent discussion of Iago's use of the term 'clyster-pipes' (2.1.176) in reference to Cassio's kissing of his fingers while he talks to Desdemona after their arrival on Cyprus seems to pick up the psychoanalytic thread where Hyman left off despite Saunders's disavowal that he does 'not see Iago's clyster-pipes as a means to reintroduce ... a traditional Freudian interpretation of the character as a "repressed homosexual".'[12] This is because, Saunders explains, while such a reading comes across to him as being 'perceptive in its acknowledgement of the dynamic role played by male-male desire', it is also a critical practice best avoided given the fact that the resulting 'dogmatically Freudian accounts of sexuality are frequently homophobic and dependent on categories of sexual identity that cannot be applied to Renaissance texts without anachronism'.[13] Nevertheless, Saunders proceeds to construct an elaborate gloss of Iago's clyster-pipes as symbolic of enema tubes that would be used in the purgation of bodily waste. Hence by conflating clyster-pipes and enema tubes together in this manner, Cassio's fingers become instruments that have been in, significantly at the outset of Saunders's argument, an unidentified character's anus.[14] What follows is Saunders' attempt to convince his readers that Iago represents 'a portrait of the villain as anal-retentive artist'[15] who, quite queerly, absolutely revels in the myriad pleasures of clyster-pipe/enema tube-induced eliminations.

The detritus Iago enjoys expelling in this manner is Desdemona, with her 'excessive [heterosexual] desire'[16] for Othello, as well as Othello himself, whom Iago cannot countenance because of his status as a Moor whose dark skin brands him the equivalent of a waste product unworthy of participating in civilized, white, patriarchal, Christian culture.[17]

Thus, as Saunders concludes, Iago's "monstrous birth" [Iago's plan to destroy Othello by convincing him that Desdemona is cuckolding him with Cassio] is no welcome and innocent baby, then, 'but rather a tremendous evacuation—the inevitable and horrific consequence of a "diet of revenge". And the complete success of Iago's enema is attested to when this masterful' manipulator refuses to speak after all of his misdeeds have been revealed and he stands in the custody of the Venetian authorities[18] at the very end of the play. There is, in other words, nothing left for him to expel at this point from his mind or body. The thorough purge of wastes that Iago sought and took such pleasure in effecting has been achieved; he is left to wallow in the satisfied silence and relief of a post-enema-induced bliss – or stupor.

But it can be argued that Saunders' psychoanalytic reading of Iago's clyster-pipes is not so far removed from Hyman's as he would have his readers believe. The ultimate purgation of Desdemona and Othello that Iago has given such monstrous 'birth' to could also be seen, in Hyman's words, as a 'strikingly homosexual wish' that subjects heterosexuals to eradication by murder – a murder that, no matter how vicariously, Iago as, specifically, a male homosexual takes great erotic pleasure in bringing about. The Iago that emerges from the interpretation that Saunders constructs in his essay is just as deviant and not at all normal (read: not heterosexual) as the Iago that Hyman constructs in his study. The heteronormative presumption that informs Saunders' essay is that straight males and their literary representations would never derive sexual enjoyment from the administration of an enema to themselves or any other person. Such satisfaction is something only gay or queer males who, like Iago, are deemed to be sick and perverted, are capable of experiencing. However, the point bears repeating: Iago is not evil because his erotic desires are non-heteronormative; he is evil simply because he is evil.

On the other side of the interpretive coin, Little and Robert Matz are two scholars whose criticism of *Othello* is arguably more nuanced as regards the play's repeated evocations of male same-sex queerness. Indeed, both Little and Matz read *Othello* without being heterosexist, to borrow again Sinfield's titular phrasing, and thus they part company with Hyman and Saunders. In his piece, Little uses the Freudian-psychoanalytic concept of the primal scene to interrogate the racial anxieties that pervade the dramatic text of *Othello*. These anxieties, he insists, are both reflected and refracted in the play's treatment of sexuality. Indeed, Little argues that the way *Othello* 'responds to and creates these anxieties is by mocking the sexual coupling of Othello and Desdemona and by associating it with other culturally horrifying scenes of sexuality, especially bestiality and homosexuality'.[19] Little makes a strong case for reading Iago/Cassio's dream as a description of a homosexual encounter between the ensign and the lieutenant. Thus the 'image hidden from, but being made visible for, Othello is supposedly of Desdemona and Cassio, while Iago presents a homoerotic scene involving the sexual interaction between Cassio and himself'.[20] Little adds that Othello's verbal reaction to Iago's account of Cassio's dream, which includes the doubly invoked adjective 'monstrous' (3.3.428), 'rather than missing the sex scene of Iago and Cassio, can be seen as immediately directed towards this sexual coupling'.[21] In other words, the term monstrous is used initially to characterize not Iago's homosexuality, but rather Cassio's heterosexuality. And it is monstrous in the same grotesque manner that would apply to the transgressions of bestiality (called to mind when, in 1.1, Iago crudely compares Othello and Desdemona to, respectively, a black ram and a white ewe) and adultery (the spectre of which Iago brings forth in his many implications that Cassio and Desdemona are having an affair that Othello knew nothing about before Iago's revealing it to him) that are instantiated concurrently as the dramatic action of *Othello* unfolds.[22] It is not therefore that bestiality, adultery or homosexuality in and of themselves are monstrous, but, rather, that the persons who would dare to engage in such transgressive acts at the expense of other 'normal or state/religiously sanctioned acts' are monstrous. Cassio is thus monstrous to Othello because of his alleged affair with Desdemona and not the fact that this expressly forbidden coupling is couched within the context of a homosexual dream narrative involving Cassio and Iago.

Meanwhile, how relationships of all kinds, but especially those between men, were policed during the early modern period in England is the larger subject of Matz's work. Where *Othello* is concerned, he notes that, 'in seeking to discredit Cassio, he [Iago] also seeks to displace Desdemona as Othello's "bedfellow",'[23] or, following Bray, as the person who is in the privileged position of sharing the most public and private intimacy possible with another individual of some influence. Since 'intimacy means access', for Matz, too, the relationship Iago seeks to (re)establish with Othello by removing Desdemona from the equation encompasses the homoerotic in addition to the homosocial.[24] Indeed, the 'supposed desire between Cassio and Desdemona substitutes even more clearly for the desire that Iago continually pursues and is pursuing in the dream' he relates about Othello's wife and his lieutenant, a dream that, for Matz, plainly evokes 'his [Iago's] own desire to win back Othello's love'.[25] Desdemona is then no more than the means to Iago's ultimate end: manifesting materially his intimate, erotic, exclusive and entirely self-serving (re)union with Othello.

III

As is perhaps obvious from the information presented above, interpretation of the text of *Othello* from a queer perspective has not yielded any kind of a consensus. Even so, such inquiry does provide a particular foundation from which to approach the study of how directors like Welles and Parker have dealt with the play's inherent queerness in the cinema. Starting with the first of these filmmakers, it can be noted that, although it was largely vilified when it premiered in Europe and later in

America, in the early and the mid-1950s, respectively, Welles's *Othello*[26] gained a great deal of both popular and critical currency when it was restored and re-released, largely through the efforts of the director's youngest daughter, Beatrice Welles-Smith, in 1992. The movie opens with an extreme close-up of a seemingly dark-skinned man, whose head is upside down to the viewer, lying in state; an insistent drumbeat and, very soon thereafter, sinister piano notes accompany this sobering image. Haunting choir music begins to sound as the body is lifted by hooded pallbearers who, underneath a blindingly bright sky, lead a funeral procession along the grounds of a vaguely medieval Moorish castle. Suddenly, across this tableau, a slight-looking man is led like a dog in chains and, before long, is thrown into a cage and hoisted high into the air for all to see him in his imprisonment. The man can do no more than look out through the iron bars on the somber memorial service taking place below, his expression grim but unrepentant. Thus Welles transforms and adapts the ending of Shakespeare's *Othello* into a compelling visual prologue to his cinematic adaptation of the play. Following a brief voiceover introduction to the major characters and the story that brings them together, the film proper begins. And though the production is not overtly homoerotic *per se*, it still yields insights that are worth considering from a queer perspective. It has, in fact, a noticeably queer ethos.

Critics from Michael Anderegg to Rothwell agree that Welles's *Othello* qualifies as an example of American film noir, a cinematic genre that finds its origins in the 1940s and 1950s. In fact, given the specificity of the director's emphasis on Iago's machinations in the production, the latter describes the movie as a 'foray into entrapment and fear [that] carries the movie into the realm of film noir, the Hollywood B movies that reflected the dark, paranoid side of America obscured by the genial fatuousness of the Eisenhower years'.[27] According to William Park, film noir is 'defined by a subject, a locale and a character. It consists of all three. Its subject is crime, almost always murder but sometimes a theft. Its locale is the contemporary world, usually a city at night. Its character is a fallible or tarnished man or woman'.[28] These elements are in turn complemented by 'expressionistic camera work' and 'narrative devices such as the voice over and flashback' to create the overall claustrophobic effect.[29] Where the subject of crime is concerned, because it both rearranges and extrapolates on the end of Shakespeare's original, Welles's *Othello* creates the uncanny effect of placing the viewer in the position of the detective or investigator who is trying to figure out what led to the deaths of Othello and Desdemona and, perhaps more importantly, who was responsible for such heinous acts. Welles's *Othello* does not lead, as in its source text, to the commission of these transgressions; rather, it begins with them, and thus it follows the traditional storytelling trajectory of film noir. As the costumes, the locations, which range all the way from Morocco to Venice and many points in between, and the cinematography make clear, the film is not set in a contemporary city at night but, rather, in Cyprus and at seemingly all hours. Arguably, though, the exotic look and feel of Welles's imagined Mediterranean world substitutes well as a stand-in for the sprawling and usually anonymous metropolis commonly found in film noir. In addition, if nothing else, Othello qualifies as a fallible film noir character around which the drama of a man who thinks he has been wronged by his wife and is seeking vengeance for that wrong swirls. These generic features are also punctuated by the two things that contribute to film noir's evocation of claustrophobia: expressionistic camera work – something perhaps most notable in Welles's penchant for staging his scenes from disorienting visual angles – and the incorporation of myriad jump-cuts, as well as the use of voiceover and flashback. Indeed, almost the whole of the movie is one long, extended flashback.

Welles's *Othello* is a queer Shakespeare film that also fits comfortably within the genre of film noir – or vice versa. Richard Dyer explains that among the 'first widely available images of homosexuality in our time were those provided by the

American film noir. Given the dearth of alternative images, it is reasonable to suppose that these had an important influence on both public ideas about homosexuality and, damagingly, gay self-images.'[30] As might be suspected, these images were not at all flattering; indeed, they can now be understood as stereotypical and reactionary despite, or perhaps because of, the fact that they were in accord with the prevailing heteronormative views of the time. Dyer goes so far as to label them 'aspects of the armoury of gay oppression'[31] many at the time used to disparage homosexuals and homosexuality. Interestingly, he proceeds to delineate the recurring iconography of gays' representation in film noir as follows: 'fastidious dress; crimped hair; perfume; manicured nails; love of art; bitchy wit; knowledge of clothes, jewellery; love of music; gaudy clothes; fussy hairstyles; love of fine cuisine'.[32] It is through this constellation of signifiers that in film noir '[g]ays are thus defined by everything but the very thing that makes us different' with that thing being, of course, sexual identity and the sexual desires that identity engenders, which could not be represented literally on the silver screen during the 1940s and 1950s because of censorship on the part of conservative regimes, particularly the Catholic Church and the cinema industry's resulting self-policing of its productions.[33] Based on these observations Dyer concludes that, in film noir, the

> ideological pairing of male homosexuality with luxury and decadence (with connotations of impotence and sterility) is of a piece with the commonplace [and misogynistic] linking of women with luxury (women as expensive things to win and keep, women as bearers of their husbands' wealth) and decadence (women as beings without sexuality save for the presence of men). The feeling that gay men are *like* women yet *not* women produces the 'perverse' tone of this mode of iconographic representation.[34]

Although, considering its somewhat troubled reception history it must have been a minor one compared to other more prominent examples of the genre, the role Welles's *Othello* played in this overarching dissemination of pop culture knowledge about gays and homosexuality through the medium of film noir is, queerly, apparent in retrospect.

Like all of the other male characters in Welles's *Othello* save the great Venetian general himself, Iago's (Micheál MacLiammóir) hair is shoulder-length rather than crimped, and always in a state of some disarray. What sets this Iago apart as far as this aspect of his appearance is that his hair always looks stringy and greasy. It is as if he does not care in the least about the image his coiffure presents to others. This unkempt as opposed to fussy hair quality contributes to the aura of the 'not quite right' (i.e. the 'not quite straight') that surrounds this Iago. Whether or not he has interests in perfume, manicured nails, fine dining, art and/or music, as Dyer's rubric suggests, is left to the viewer's speculation. Where clothes are concerned, on many occasions in the production, when he is not in the requisite tights the filmmakers' costume designers employ to mimic, more or less correctly, early modern male dress, Iago is pictured wearing a long flowing cloak complete with a willowy hood that frames his face like a veil. Not surprisingly, perhaps, this garment has the effect of muting his masculinity while heightening his non-heteronormative effeminacy (see Figure 20). Of course, the obvious symbolism of Iago's cloak ought not to be ignored; it is, after all, a piece of clothing that, given its specificity, suggests whomever is wearing it is hiding something sinister about himself from the rest of the world. This is apropos since Welles's Iago, following Shakespeare's original, *is* disguising his malevolent nature from one and all he associates with so that he can execute the vengeance he desires for having, he feels, been so wronged by Othello in being passed over for promotion to the rank of lieutenant. Not incidentally, the cloak also makes plain Dyer's point that in film noir – and the larger homophobic culture that gave birth to the genre – gay men are represented as *like* women, yet, at the same time, *not* women. Dressed as he is at a number of points in Welles's *Othello*,

FIGURE 20 *Iago (Micheál MacLiammóir) effeminately cloaked and hooded in* Othello, *dir. Orson Welles, 1952.*

Iago looks like a woman who is not actually a woman. Hence, from a reactionary heteronormative perspective, Iago is, in such garb, a perverse – a queer – mixture of the masculine and the feminine rather than being an obvious example of one or the other as he should be in accord with the usual gender, and their corresponding sexual, binaries. He is, to put it in slightly different terms, the ultimate horror: a gay man hiding in plain sight who has nefarious homoerotic designs on the straighter-than-straight hero whose honour and masculinity must be protected at all costs from such predators.

As portrayed by MacLiammóir, his Iago often gives voice to the bitchy wit Dyer claims is part and parcel of the film noir depiction of gay men. This is true even though most of his lines were supplied by Shakespeare and incorporated without much if any alteration by Welles into his screenplay for *Othello*. For instance, as the story proper gets underway and Iago is feigning commiseration with the inordinately besotted Roderigo (Robert Coote), the latter asks Iago what he should do now that the object of his desire, Desdemona

(Suzanne Clautier), is married to Othello (Welles) instead of himself. Iago responds by rolling his eyes behind Roderigo's back and telling the other man that he should 'go to bed and sleep' (1.3.305) in a tone dripping with exaggerated sarcasm. That Iago does not respect him in the least, and could not care less about his romantic misfortune, is completely lost on Roderigo who blurts out: 'I will incontinently drown myself' (1.3.306). With evident asperity, Iago proclaims, 'Oh villainous' (1.3.312) in response to Roderigo's assertion. But, of course, it is perfectly clear that Iago would shed no tears if Roderigo were to kill himself over Desdemona. Nevertheless, because he needs Roderigo's financial resources, Iago adds: 'Ere I would say I would drown myself for ... love ... I would change my humanity with a baboon' (1.3.315–17). MacLiammóir utters each word of this exchange with both admirable precision and a pronounced lisp that does everything to heighten the entirely caustic effect. Underneath the off-kilter humour, however, lies the bitter anger of someone who is deeply unhappy with how he has been treated by life and his fellow man, an experience not at all unfamiliar to queer folk the world over and, sometimes, dealt with by them in the same or similar passive-aggressive manner.

Though once again the words are Shakespeare's, it is difficult not to wonder if MacLiammóir's own homosexuality infuses his performance of Iago in this portion of *Othello* with the kind of bitchy wit – produced by the actor's idiosyncratic combination of inflection and gesture – demonstrated in the lines quoted above. It is Potter, among other critics, who calls attention to MacLiammóir's non-normative sexual identity in her extended analysis of Welles's film. In doing so she cites and interprets a key passage from the actor's published diary that details his involvements on and off set during the lengthy production of *Othello*, which extended from the end of January 1949 to the beginning of March 1950. At a dinner in Paris attended by MacLiammóir, Welles and a number of actresses, all of whom were, at the time, vying to play the role of Desdemona, Welles insisted that the character of Iago 'was in his opinion impotent' and that 'this secret malady was, in fact, to be the keystone of the actor's approach' to the role.³⁵ Moments later, with far more animation, the director went on: '"Impotent", he roared in (surely somewhat forced) rich bass baritone, "that's why he hates life so much – they always do".'³⁶ About this anecdote, Potter remarks that MacLiammóir could not have been unaware in these moments he recorded for posterity that Welles was 'taunting him in public' about his homosexuality and, furthermore, that the auteur was especially wary 'of the reality of the "all-male" persona being projected' into the cinematic narrative of *Othello* he was in the process of constructing.³⁷ However, it seems that such a reading ought to be tempered with additional thought.

If as Potter suggests Welles was openly 'taunting' MacLiammóir about his sexual proclivities, MacLiammóir does not say as much anywhere in *Put Money in Thy Purse*. Had he been offended by Welles's remarks it seems likely he would have expressed that feeling. Indeed, the overarching impression to be taken from *Put Money In Thy Purse* is that both Welles – who, after all, wrote a Foreword to the memoir that is equal parts praise for MacLiammóir and self-deprecation – and MacLiammóir had a great deal of professional and personal respect for one another. From the remove of nearly seventy years, Welles's words do come across as rather unkind and, perhaps more importantly, simultaneously evocative of then prevailing stereotypes, fuelled by misinformation and fear, about gay men who, from a strictly heteronormative perspective, were thought to be impotent because of their lack of 'normal' sexual desire for women. In relation to homosexuals and film noir, Dyer explains it this way: 'Such an image [i.e. of the impotent man] is amplified in the gay characters by the culturally widespread notion (reinforced by the non-sexuality of the gay iconography) that gays are intensely physical beings who cannot "do anything" physically and hence vibrate with frustrated twisted sexual energy.'³⁸ From this perspective, MacLiammóir's Iago cannot 'do anything' sexually with Othello because Othello is straight, thus Iago is little more than a dangerous bundle of sexual frustration that will eventually manifest itself in the form of bloody vengeance. The idea that two men could reciprocate romantic, affective and erotic – inclusive of the sexual – desire for each other was still a rather alien one to most of the general public of the time period and would remain so until at least the Stonewall Riots in 1969 in New York City, if not for a long while after that momentous event.

It is also difficult not to wish that Potter had expanded on her interpretation about Welles being wary of the 'reality' of the all-male ethos at the heart of his *Othello*. Presumably she means that Welles was concerned about the 'reality' of the homosexual/homoerotic aspects of the written text being more pronounced in cinematic form, particularly as regards the relationships Iago has with Roderigo, Cassio and Othello himself in the film. But as will be developed more fully below, the finished product does not bear out such a hypothesis, at least not in the most simplistic sense. For the moment it is sufficient to offer the reminder that Benshoff and Griffin note that one way to 'define queer film could be via its authorship: films might be considered queer when they are written, directed or produced by queer people or perhaps when they star lesbian, gay, or otherwise queer actors'.[39] In retrospect, then, knowledge of MacLiammóir's homosexuality, a fact 1950s European and American film audiences would have been unlikely to be aware of, allows queer and queer-allied twenty-first-century viewers of Welles's *Othello* to recoup a part of their heritage that had hitherto remained hidden from them. This understanding in turn activates another of Benshoff and Griffin's definitions of queer film: that 'all films might be potentially queer if read from a queer viewing position'.[40] Though not by any means heroic or admirable, the Iago that emerges under interpretive pressure of this type is queer kith and kin. Heteronormative audience members might well find MacLiammóir's Iago simply weird or odd in addition to being discomfiting; it is to be hoped that queer audiences, on the other hand, have the inherent ability to take a more nuanced view of the character. Their Iago may be one man in love with another (Othello) who has been deeply hurt because of that love – no matter how one-sided – and responds to that hurt in spectacular fashion.

The project of queering Welles's *Othello* can be continued in light of Daniel Juan Gil's fascinating work on the film in relation to the director's productions of, respectively, *Macbeth* (1948) and *Chimes at Midnight* (1965). In this analysis Gil argues that, where *Othello* is concerned, Welles effects an idiosyncratic visual grammar of sexuality. To accomplish this feat Welles uses a 'version of the shot/reverse shot technique' – the cinematic way of conveying the sense of two characters having a more or less private, back-and-forth conversation with each other – to represent 'a socially deviant form of sexualized bonding' as occurring between Iago and Othello.[49] As Gil explains it, in the first third of Welles's *Othello* Othello and Desdemona almost never appear in scenes that show them talking to one another in accord with the shot/reverse shot convention as might be expected of a newly married couple in the process of forging their just-begun marital relationship. Instead, they favour 'side-by-side, often non-linguistic [i.e. lacking dialogue], often public appearances' that can be read as a rather impersonal way of associating.[42] Of course, the same seems to apply to Othello and Iago; but that, Gil insists, only holds true until the precise moment when Iago begins to poison Othello's mind about Desdemona's sexual faithlessness. It is at this point that the conversationally intimate 'shot/reverse shot becomes the perfect visual emblem for Iago's inexplicable, antisocial scheming' against Othello.[43] Issue can be taken with Gil's use of the term 'inexplicable' here in his otherwise insightful analysis. In Welles's *Othello* Iago's motives for striking back at Othello are no more, nor less, inexplicable than they are in Shakespeare's original playtext. 'I hate the Moor' (1.3.385), Iago tells Roderigo as the two are standing at the back of the Venetian church in which Othello and Desdemona are bound in holy matrimony. Not long thereafter, Iago insists: 'I know my price, I am worth no worse a place' (1.1.10), giving voice to his complaint that the Florentine, Cassio, has been promoted to the position of lieutenant to Othello even though Iago, 'God bless the mark', is 'Othello's ensign' (1.1.32). Thus, contra Gil, it seems perfectly clear that Welles's Iago, like Shakespeare's original, is acting out of a lethal combination of jealousy, spite and malice at being so slighted.

But perhaps what Gil finds really inexplicable, like many *Othello* critics before him, is the excessiveness of Iago's desire for vengeance, which does, on the surface at least, appear completely out of proportion in comparison to the 'wrong' he thinks he has suffered. At the same time, however, Gil does seem to find an explanation for this immoderation in what he considers to be Iago's unrequited longing for Othello, which, in turn, becomes part and parcel of the visual grammar of sexuality evident in Welles's *Othello* that he takes such pains to delineate in his work. Of course, the spectre of Freud and the traditional heteronormative psychoanalytic understanding of male homosexuality haunts Gil's interpretation. Hence Iago's desire for Othello is sublimated, or 'impotent' as Welles put it, and only gains what can be characterized as a (homo)sexualized intelligibility as his all-consuming thirst for revenge, which is represented onscreen in accord with the visual grammar Gil anatomizes, inclusive as it is of the shot/reverse shot intimacy experienced by Othello and Iago as they, as a queer couple, spiral ever further into extreme anti-sociality. The homoeroticism at the core of these circumstances is thus perverted into something ugly and ultimately deadly. Iago's penetration of Othello is always only ever symbolic or figurative rather than literal; verbal rather than physical; suggestive rather than concrete. Still, it remains one man's penetration of another man nonetheless, and that penetration can be understood in, broadly speaking, queer, sexual and/or homoerotic terms. Gil's visual grammar of sexuality provides one means of mapping that penetration in a visceral and critical way that is particularly attuned to the language of Welles's film.

Despite its capaciousness, Gil's essay elides discussion of one part of Welles's *Othello* that seems to confirm, or at least to extend, his overall hypothesis regarding the visual grammar of sexuality the film evidences. This occurs approximately two thirds of the way into the production and involves the specificity of the fact that Welles chooses to set the scenes of Roderigo's unsuccessful attempt to murder Cassio, and that of Iago's later successful slaying of Roderigo, within the depths of an all-male sauna (see Figure 21). As the screen capture below makes clear, this is a place of decadence and opulence. It is also, not incidentally, the kind of location in which a homosexual like Iago would be expected to appear. Exposed male flesh is visible from the foreground to the background of the composition, though strategically placed white towels conceal both genitalia and buttocks. One of the men gathered here is being massaged by a grim-faced attendant while the entire company is being treated to the sounds of guitar music as they relax and unwind. Meanwhile, another man is lying

FIGURE 21 *Inside the Cypriot sauna, where, a short while later, Iago (Micheál MacLiammóir) will stab Roderigo (Robert Coote) to death in* Othello, *dir. Orson Welles, 1952.*

almost prone on a table in the lower left-hand corner of the shot; he seems to be in a deep conversation of some sort with the two other men who are very nearby. The whole aura of this setting is at once provocative and suggestive; this is particularly true for anyone with knowledge of gay and queer history. Saunas, also known as bathhouses in their more contemporary late twentieth- and early twenty-first-century American incarnations, have been relatively safe places where gay men have met each other for camaraderie and to have sexual relations for eons. Thus there can be no mistaking the connotations of such a place in relation to the character of Iago. No matter how platonic it may appear, a queer homoeroticism seethes just below the surface and around the edges of this space. It is perhaps not surprising then that Welles stages Iago's murder of Roderigo in the Cypriot sauna. After having failed to kill Cassio and sending everyone in the sauna into a panic, Roderigo makes the mistake of seeking Iago out. When the two are alone, Iago stabs Roderigo to death using a long sword. The Freudian/psychoanalytic reading of this action endorses the symbolic, homoerotic sexuality at the heart of this murder. In stabbing Roderigo, Iago has penetrated another man with his (substitute) phallus and has, thus, succeeded in having what can be considered the most perverse kind of sex possible with the unfortunate fop: near necrophilia. He has finally 'done something' with a member of his own gender and moved beyond the strictures of sublimation and impotence. The problem lies in the fact that he had to kill another human being to do so. He has thus become not just a criminal, but a criminal homosexual, who must be punished for his abhorrent behaviour.

As noted above, in a sentiment to which a provisional disagreement was ventured, Potter claims that Welles's *Othello* betrays the director's wariness of the film's all-male ethos. It demands arguing that, on the contrary, Welles exploits the homosociality and the homoeroticism inherent in his source material to a significant extent. In fact, it seems that rather than shying away from either Welles deliberately uses the potent combination of homosociality and homoeroticism bequeathed to him by Shakespeare to tell what amounts to a cautionary tale about homosexuals infused with homophobic conventions – at least for those who are able and willing to read his cinematic text from a queer perspective. That in so doing Welles manages to conflate homosexuality with murderous deviance is problematic because it fits a little too neatly with then prevalent ideas about homosexuals: that they are sad, lonely, angry people who will never be able to live life to the fullest because of their 'abnormality' and will, if pushed too far, kill in order to compensate for their normative failures. Yet in most quarters during the mid-twentieth century, this is exactly the kind of thinking that was commonplace. Welles's *Othello* thus stands as one important queer artefact from a thankfully bygone era in Western history.

IV

Starring Laurence Fishburne in the title role, Oliver Parker's *Othello*[44] begins in Venice and in the rather disturbing gloom of night. Gondolas furtively skirt the famed waterways of the darkened city, and Iago (Kenneth Branagh) is first encountered in the film with Roderigo (Michael Maloney) as they witness, in stealth – and in homage to Welles's *Othello* – Othello's marriage to Desdemona that takes place in a medieval Venetian church. After bride and groom kiss, Iago launches into his complaint about Othello's promotion of Michael Cassio (Nathaniel Parker) – instead of himself – to the position of lieutenant in the military organization in which they both serve the city-state of Venice: '[B]y the faith of man, / I know my price, I am worth no worse a place' (1.1.9–10). As spoken by Branagh, these words are filled with a potent mixture of bitterness and cynicism; they do a good job of explaining, at least initially, why Iago is so angry with Othello. But awareness of the homoerotic valence that inspires these sentiments, an awareness that, again following Benshoff and Griffin, informed queer Shakespeare spectators of Parker's *Othello* may bring to their experience of the film, renders Iago's feelings here somewhat more understandable rather than mysterious and abject.

At this juncture, two scenarios involving Iago and Othello emerge. The first is that the relationship between these two men has already – at some time in the past and, therefore, outside of the play/film proper – surpassed the platonic and the professional to include the physical and the sexual. For all intents then Othello's choosing of another man as his lieutenant could also signal to Iago that his superior has decided to end their affair and replace him in the bedroom with Cassio. No matter their sexual identity or preferences, not many people, male or female, would be able to respond with anything akin to equanimity in such circumstances. The second possibility is, of course, that Iago's deeper feelings for Othello have always been unrecognized and/or unrequited by the general and, with the out-of-the-blue promotion of Cassio, are destined to remain so. Although the latter seems more likely in regard to both the written and the cinematic *Othello*s under discussion here, in either case, the crucial point to understand is that Iago suffers the pain of what he considers to be an absolute rejection – and he lashes out accordingly. In terms of the visual representation of male homoeroticism, it proves significant that as part of this overall expository sequence, Parker also shows Cassio's promotion through the equivalent of Iago's mind's eye. The moment includes Othello's giving of an ornate knife as a gift to Cassio and, more significantly, the embrace of the two men as Cassio is welcomed into Othello's service. These images drive the point home that Iago has been set aside for another man. Iago's remembrance of Othello and Cassio's union here suggests that Iago understands he will likely never again experience such an intimacy with the general, unless he takes some kind of drastic action.

The queer nature of Iago's character becomes even more explicit as Parker's *Othello* continues. For instance, a portion of what corresponds to Shakespeare's 2.1, a scene that involves Iago and Roderigo, takes place underneath a large wooden cart at night during the riotous celebration of Othello and Desdemona's marriage on the island of Cyprus. Iago and Roderigo talk as they lie next to one another on the ground while a male and female couple enjoys rather energetic and noisy sexual relations in the cart directly above their heads. In reference to the relationship between Desdemona and Cassio he is in the process of fabricating to wreak his vengeance on Othello, as Iago speaks the suggestive line 'An index and obscure prologue to the history of lust and foul thoughts' (2.1.244–5), he moves his face slowly, and ever closer, to that of Roderigo. In fact, Iago's actions here become so intimate that it almost seems as if he is about to kiss the insensate Roderigo full on the lips. Alas, however, Iago does not kiss the other man; he merely continues his rhetorical exercise by saying with as much bawdy innuendo as possible: 'They met so near with their lips that their breaths embraced together. Villainous thoughts, Roderigo! When these mutualities so marshal the way, hard at hand comes the master and main exercise, th'incorporate conclusion' (2.1.245–8). Though he stops short of actually kissing Roderigo, it is nevertheless intriguing that Iago allows their 'breaths to mingle' just as he has intimated Desdemona's and Cassio's have done in their illicit coupling. Furthermore, when he says the words 'hard at hand' (in itself a bawdy pun on both male arousal and the frenetic nature of copulation), Iago slowly and deliberately places his right hand on Roderigo's thigh, then continues to move that hand until it cups Roderigo's penis. For his part, Roderigo is so distraught about the fact that Desdemona does not love him and, seemingly, prefers Cassio as a lover in addition to Othello as a husband who also makes love to her, that he fails to notice the touch and/or location of Iago's hand on his person. It is either that or being groped by another man in such a manner is so commonplace an occurrence for him that in and of itself the sensation no longer registers on his consciousness. Of course, in this case, the former idea is far more likely than the latter. Nevertheless, the homoeroticism Parker depicts here cannot be overlooked or dismissed – regardless of the fact that Iago is only ever using Roderigo for his own ends. That Iago just *might* consider Roderigo an extraneous sexual partner as well as his dupe only adds another layer to the overall opportunistic maliciousness of his character while simultaneously confirming the queer nature of his erotic desires.

As in Shakespeare's play itself the male homoeroticism reaches its peak in Parker's *Othello* during the depiction of Othello and Iago's bonding in 3.3. In the film this scene takes place upon the battlements of a medieval castle on Cyprus, and it includes the exchange of a blood vow between the two men, which is not, of course, an element in the source text. First, it is Othello who carves a gash into his palm with his knife; then, almost mesmerized, Iago follows suit immediately afterward. Then they clasp their bleeding hands together in complete solidarity with one another and Othello says, 'Now art though my lieutenant' (3.3.495). At this point both men are on their knees and, significantly, they embrace. First, this hug is seen from a distance, then the shot changes to a near close-up of Iago as he holds Othello and is in turn held in Othello's arms. As evidenced by the fact that his eyes are squeezed shut in an attempt to hold back his tears, the look on Iago's face is one of almost painful yet at the same time exquisite relief (see Figure 22). It is as if he cannot believe that he is, once again, allowed to be so close and intimate with his beloved Othello. 'I am your own forever' Iago says, and it is as if each word is being ripped from the very depths of his soul (3.3.496). The image presented here is redolent with emotion; it shows just how deeply one man may feel for another.

It is important, however, to take into account what occurs leading up to Othello and Iago's heartfelt embrace. After kneeling on the ground in front of Iago Othello says: 'Now, by yond marble heaven, / In the due reverence of a sacred vow / I here engage my words' (3.3.463–5). Iago then joins Othello on his knees and proceeds to say:

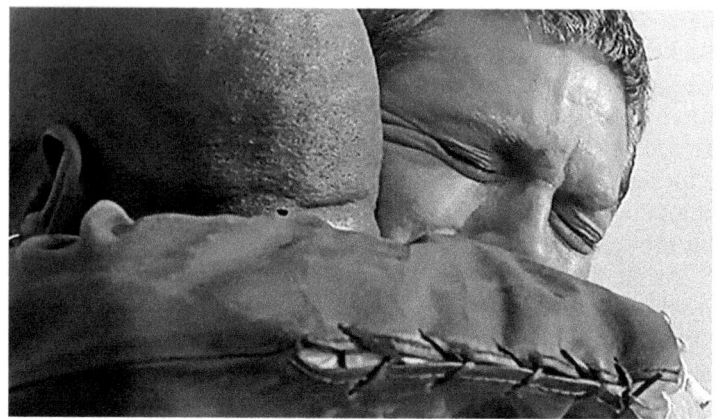

FIGURE 22 *Othello (Laurence Fishburne) and Iago (Kenneth Branagh) kneeling, swearing their vows to one another and embracing in 3.3 of* Othello, *dir. Oliver Parker, 1995.*

> Witness, you ever-burning lights above,
> You elements that clip us round about,
> Witness that here Iago doth give up
> The execution of his wit, hands, heart,
> To wronged Othello's service. Let him command,
> And to obey shall be in me remorse,
> What bloody business ever. (3.3.466–72)

Significantly at this point in the scene, Parker uses the intimate, conversational shot/reverse shot cinematic technique as Iago speaks and Othello hears these words – this swearing of their vows to one another. In his discussion of the written text, Smith describes this moment in *Othello* as a 'parody of a [heterosexual] marriage rite'.[45] Of course, Smith was writing in the days before same-sex marriage became a reality in the contemporary Western world and a Constitutional right in America. But disregarding – only momentarily and with specific purpose – the homicidal inflections the plot of *Othello* invokes, this passage, and the visual counterpart Parker presents of it, offers what can be considered a serious rendition of what a wedding ceremony between two men might well have been like if, as John Boswell and Alan A. Tulchin[46] have persuasively argued, such unions had been allowed to take place in early modern Europe. In any case, Parker's film both capitalizes on and makes vivid the male homoerotic potentiality inherent within this part of Shakespeare's play – and he manages to do so in a way that speaks volumes to the present moment of queer human history.

Interestingly, Parker offers one additional queerly homoerotic moment of note in his *Othello* that warrants attention. In the penultimate scene of the film, after the deaths Desdemona, Emilia and, finally, Othello himself, an angry Lodovico (Michael Sheen) forces Iago, who is on his knees and bleeding from several wounds, to gaze upon the heinous outcome of his deeds: 'Look on the tragic loading of this bed,' Lodovico orders him, 'This is thy work' (5.2.374–5). And Iago does turn his attention to the three lifeless bodies spread before him. But then, in complete and utter silence, Iago forces himself upward, on to the bed, and lays his head in the crook of Othello's leg (see Figure 23). Though undeniably grotesque, this singular action of Iago's reveals nothing if not the fact that his queer attachment to the general, his beloved Othello, lingers, even in the chaos of destruction and the finality of death.

VI

According to Stephen Greenblatt, in early modern England 'there were both selves and a sense that they could be fashioned'; furthermore, this self-fashioning involved the 'power to impose a shape upon oneself [that] is an aspect of the more general power to control [one's] identity', and it signalled a 'characteristic address to the world, a consistent mode of perceiving and behaving' subjects manifested in the material world.[47] So reads the overarching claim of *Renaissance Self-Fashioning: From More to Shakespeare*, the

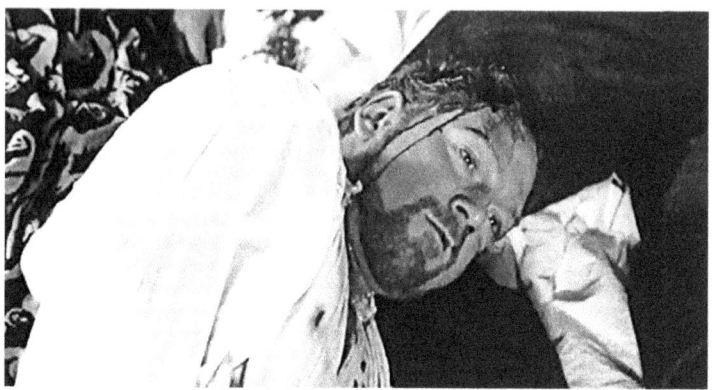

FIGURE 23 *Iago (Kenneth Branagh) lying in the crook of Othello's (Laurence Fishburne) leg at the conclusion of* Othello, *dir. Oliver Parker, 1995.*

brilliant study that marked the advent of New Historicism as a mode of literary criticism that continues, in the main, to dominate the field of Shakespeare studies. As would be expected from a critical practice like new historicism, with its unwavering commitment to the notion that individuals can only ever be the products of their times and, therefore, ought to be studied as such as opposed to through the lenses of any of the concerns of the present in which a critic is situated, self-fashioning always already occurs within a matrix of historically situated forces, including prevalent social customs, government policies, economic circumstances, religious doctrines, gender conventions, educational opportunities, familial and national traditions, and the like. The self that results from this kind of fashioning is very much a response – or a set of responses – to the larger cultural influences that surround it and which human beings must navigate in life.

Shakespeare's Iago is a fictionalized representation that epitomizes the self-fashioned English Renaissance man. He is also what Greenblatt characterizes in his work as an improviser *par excellence*. Key to Iago's improvisational success is his ability to empathize. Drawing on the work of Daniel Lerner, Greenblatt initially defines empathy as the 'capacity to see oneself in the other fellow's situation'.[48] Though empathy is often a force for good, Iago uses it for the opposite purpose. Since Iago can, all too easily it seems, see himself in others' situations, his empathy allows him to take advantage of them and to do real damage to them, as evidenced by the thorough destruction he effects on Othello, Desdemona, Emilia, Cassio and Roderigo. Thus Greenblatt claims that '[w]hat Professor Lerner calls "empathy," Shakespeare calls "Iago".'[49] Taking this idea one step further, what Lerner calls empathy, and what Shakespeare calls Iago, is called queer in this chapter. In this context, one of the indications of Iago's queerness is his steadfast determination to wreak evil rather than good using his capacity to see himself in others' circumstances. For instance, since he, without specific evidence of any kind, suspects that Othello has cuckolded him by having sex with his wife Emilia, Iago can imagine what Othello would feel like if it turned out that Desdemona was cuckolding him by having sex with Cassio (1.3.381–403). Though there is no truth whatsoever to the idea of Desdemona's unfaithfulness, Iago is able to improvise his way through to convincing Othello that the idea is a certainty and, thus, must be dealt with accordingly – by punishing Desdemona and Cassio with death. Here, Iago's rhetorical success can be read queerly; as a man, he has managed to penetrate another man in a way that is analogous to the kind of homosexual penetration that occurs during male same-sex intercourse. Indeed, on this point, Greenblatt notes that Iago 'is as intensely preoccupied [as Othello] with adultery, while his anxiety about his own sexuality may be gauged from the fact that he conceives of his very invention [of Desdemona's mythical infidelity], as the images of engendering suggest, as a kind of demonic semen that will bring forth monsters'.[50] And so it does as the drama of *Othello* unfolds.

Greenblatt contends – in keeping with one of the key precepts of self-fashioning, that it is subject to the cultural forces at work in any given subject's particular historical situation – that Iago's success at making Othello believe Desdemona is an unfaithful wife is grounded in the wholly repressive views – views that pervaded the thinking and behaviour of people everywhere in early modern Europe – of the church on sexuality in any form. Put bluntly, to the church, sex was almost always bad, even when it occurred within the confines of marriage. Greenblatt explains that 'there are four motives for conjugal intercourse: to conceive offspring; to render the marital debt to one's partner so that he or she might avoid incontinency; to avoid fornication oneself; and to satisfy desire'.[51] He goes on to add that the 'first two motives are without sin and excuse intercourse; the third is a venial sin; the fourth – to satisfy desire – is mortal. Among the many causes that underlie this institutional hostility to desire is the tenacious existence, in various forms, of the belief that pleasure constitutes a legitimate release from dogma and constraint' that the church simply could not countenance.[52] The moment in 1.3 of the play when, summoned to speak before the Venetian Senate, Desdemona makes it plain to one and all that she has a passionate love – a passionate desire – for Othello, Desdemona falls afoul of the sexual prohibitions of the church that Christians had accepted whole cloth. 'This moment of erotic intensity,' Greenblatt writes, 'this frank acceptance of pleasure and submission to her spouse's pleasure is ... as much as Iago's slander the cause of Desdemona's death, for it awakens the deep current of sexual anxiety in Othello, anxiety that with Iago's help expresses itself in quite orthodox fashion as the perception of adultery.'[53] What Iago accomplishes by painting Desdemona as false to Othello, then, is Othello's sexual arousal – a queer arousal that has been engendered by another man; an arousal that will have devastating consequences for all concerned as it reaches its climax.

The textual queer self-fashioning of Iago elaborated on here is made strikingly apparent in the two films of *Othello* considered earlier in this chapter. Spanning a period of a little less than forty-five years, or the bulk of the second half of the twentieth century, these movies also evidence specific ways of dealing cinematically with the queer male homoeroticism embedded by Shakespeare into his play. By treating Iago, even in highly coded form, as a gay/queer villain within an overarching noir structure, Welles's production manages to conflate homosexuality and psychology in a way that makes it seem as if Iago is the evil character he is because of his non-normative desires; this Iago is a sick individual who will stop at nothing – including the murder of innocents – to secure the kind of same-sex love he, being caught in the throes of sublimation, does not even realize is his prime motivation. This is a portrayal that fits then commonplace normative notions of homosexuals and homosexuality that were informed by fear and paranoia rather than understanding or compassion. Parker's *Othello*, on the other hand, is the only cinematic production of the play that, it can be argued, gets all things right as far as race and male homoeroticism are concerned. Not only is the title character, in the figure of an actor with the stature and countenance of Laurence Fishburne, sufficient to quell any stereotypical notions about race and sexuality, but Kenneth Branagh's Iago is a masculine – as opposed to an effeminate (like Micheál MacLiammóir's Iago) – antagonist who succeeds at being evil simply because he is evil and not because he also happens to be homosexual or, at the very least, bisexual in terms of his erotic desires. Of both, then, it is Parker's production that registers most fully what seems to be the cinema's increasing comfort and sophistication with representations of queerness in the Shakespeare film that, arguably, became more common – at least in terms of intelligibility – in the 1990s, especially when compared to the 1930s and films like Reinhardt and Dieterle's *Midsummer* and Cukor's *Romeo and Juliet*, than ever before in the history of the medium.

CONCLUSION: QUEERING THE SHAKESPEARE FILM IN THE EARLY TWENTY-FIRST CENTURY

In order to draw conclusions about queering the Shakespeare film during the period covered in this book, which ranges from 1935 and Max Reinhardt and William Dieterle's *A Midsummer Night's Dream* to 2011 and Alan Brown's *Private Romeo*, it proves helpful to begin by calling to mind the idea of cinema being a capitalistic industry that produced entertainment for the masses from the moment of its inception. Although based on the specifics (i.e. plots, characters, themes, directors, actors, producers, musicians, set designers, cinematographers and so on) analysed in the myriad studies of film available in the archive it may seem otherwise, filmmakers did not have free reign to present any kind of content they wished in their movies. Nevertheless, Gregory D. Black points out that 'most film history is written as if the code and the PCA did not exist',[1] fostering the idea that anything was possible in the realm of cinematic representation. That, however, was not the case in the beginning, nor is it the case now in the early twenty-first century. The difference between the two eras can be, at least in part, understood in relation to the presence and then the absence of the PCA and its code detailing what was acceptable and what was not acceptable for film as a public medium.

PCA is an acronym for the Production Code Administration, a no-longer-extant semi-autonomous agency within the Motion Picture Producers and Distributors of America (MPPDA) – later to become the Motion Picture Association of America (MPAA) – trade association that was, as of 1930, empowered to regulate the content of any film made and/or screened in the United States. The code Black refers to is known as the Motion Picture Production Code, or, more colloquially, as the Hays Code, so named after one of the early heads of the PCA, William Harrison Hays. Once in place, studios from MGM to Warner Brothers had to ensure that every one of their productions conformed to the dictates of the Hays Code from 1930 until the end of the 1960s. The production code, and all those who enforced it either tacitly or explicitly, embodied the overarching conviction – written into the preamble of the code itself – that the 'MORAL IMPORTANCE of entertainment is something which has been universally recognized. It enters intimately into the lives of men and women ... it occupies their minds and affections during leisure hours; and ultimately touches the whole of their lives. A man may be judged by his standard of entertainment as easily as by the standard of his work.'[2] The code's particular applications addressed such items as crimes against the law, vulgarity, obscenity, profanity, costume, dances, religion, locations, national feelings, titles, repellant subjects and, of course, sex. The last category features two proscriptions that are of interest here. The first of these states that the 'sanctity of the institution of marriage and the home shall be upheld. Pictures shall not infer that low forms of sex relationship are the accepted or common thing', while the second insists that '[s]*ex perversion* or any inference to it is forbidden' in film.[3] There is no doubt that homosexuality qualified as one type of 'sex perversion', or as a specific kind of 'low form of sex relationship', that the Hays Code prohibited depictions of in the cinema for four decades.

In a number of respects the Hays Code betrays a rather Platonic ethos. Just like for Plato poetry had to contribute to the benefit of the state and the moral and ethical well-being of its citizens or it risked being banished from the ideal republic, film, at least during the reign of the production code in the United States, had to engender tangible, wholly positive effects as regards the presumed morals and ethics of its viewers. If film failed to uphold these lofty ideals, it too risked censorship at the hands of those who had deemed themselves the highest authorities on such matters – conservative factions of the American government that were, in turn, backed by vocal higher-ups in the Catholic Church, both of which succeeded in forcing Hollywood into policing itself and its productions under the auspices of the PCA.

The historical circumstances detailed above are those from which Reinhardt and Dieterle's *Midsummer* (1935) and George Cukor's *Romeo and Juliet* (1936) emerged. Given the censoriousness of this period in film history, especially where matters of (homo)sexuality were concerned, it is unsurprising that neither production comes across as blatantly queer, especially if the concept of queerness is limited to only a well-defined and unambiguously recognizable set of (homo)sexual acts. But as was demonstrated in Chapter 1 and the first part of Chapter 2 of this study, under the pressure of critical interpretation queerness reveals itself in Reinhardt and Dieterle's *Midsummer* through misogyny, gender trouble, bigamy, implied incest and bestiality and male effeminacy, and in Cukor's *Romeo and Juliet* through, among other things, the older actors and actresses cast in the key roles of Romeo, Juliet, Mercutio, Tybalt and Benvolio, and its gay director (Cukor), writer (Shakespeare), set designer (Oliver Messel) and music composer (Tchaikovsky), all of whom can be said to have endowed the film with a latent queer spirit that only wanted for the kind of sensitive, informed and enlightening reading done by Richard Burt nearly two decades ago and also attempted here, hopefully with similar success.

Though it grew out of the multiple countercultural forces at work in the United States by the mid-twentieth century, the Sexual Revolution can be said to have begun in earnest when the pill was approved by the Food and Drug Administration as a safe and effective contraceptive in 1960. It was in that moment, in fact, when sexual permissiveness and experimentation – for everyone, not just straight, white males – became generally acceptable. Indeed, at this point in time sexuality was, at least ostensibly, no longer in thrall to ignorance, fear, religion, repression, the demands of heteronormativity or patriarchal control. By 1968, when Franco Zeffirelli's *Romeo and Juliet* made its debut to near universal acclaim, the Sexual Revolution was well underway. It is, quite simply, impossible to imagine a film like Zeffirelli's *Romeo and Juliet* even being produced much less screened to such rousing success prior to the wholesale change in thinking about sexual matters the 1960s brought about in a huge swath of the world. As was detailed in the second part of Chapter 2, Zeffirelli's film incorporated the queer via, in particular, the male homoerotic. Indeed, never before in Shakespearean cinema had a director lavished such specific attention on the male form, creating what Renata Adler described as 'the softly homosexual cast over the film'. William Van Watson, on the other hand, went so far as to claim that Zeffirelli used a 'homosexual camera' in his filming of *Romeo and Juliet*. Arguably, that homosexual camera is most apparent in the aubade scene in which the nude Leonard Whiting's Romeo is placed in the *to be looked at* position – a position that, according to Laura Mulvey and others, is most often occupied by women in film instead of men, making Zeffirelli's treatment of Romeo and Juliet's 'morning after' effectively queer – for all of the film's viewers to appreciate, female and male alike, no matter where they fall on the sexual identity spectrum.

The birth of the modern gay rights movement would follow the premiere of Zeffirelli's *Romeo and Juliet* by a little more than seven months when the Stonewall Riots erupted on the streets of New York City in June 1969. Since then, GLBTQQIA (gay, lesbian, bisexual, transgender/sexual, queer, questioning, intersex, and asexual) people have fought for (and won more than a measure of) acceptance, tolerance and, perhaps above all, the freedom to live their lives with the kind of understanding, dignity and respect that all human beings deserve. Though in mainstream Shakespearean film the struggles of the gay rights movement have not yet been depicted, some of the results of those struggles have appeared on screen. These effects are perhaps most prominent in the discussions of gender trouble in Trevor Nunn's *Twelfth Night*, Baz Luhrmann's *Romeo + Juliet* and Michael Hoffman's *William Shakespeare's A Midsummer Night's Dream*, and male homoeroticism in Michael Radford's *The Merchant of Venice* and Nunn's *Twelfth Night* found in Chapters 3 and 4. The fact that gender is a problem because, as Judith Butler revealed at the very beginning of the 1990s, it is always a performance of being and appearing in the world rather than a natural given based on one's biological sex, is brought to life in the Shakespeare films of Nunn, Luhrmann and Hoffman through their representations of, respectively, a woman (Viola) dressed up as a male youth (Cesario) that another man (Orsino) and woman (Olivia) fall in love with; a drag queen Mercutio besotted with a Romeo who is equally besotted with Juliet rather than his friend; and a Francis Flute who refuses to stay in character as Thisbe as she/he laments the death of her/his beloved Pyramus. Nunn and Radford, meanwhile, treat the fact that the two Antonios in *Twelfth Night* and *Merchant* are in love with their friends Sebastian and Bassanio as a matter of course. Radford even goes so far as to show *Merchant*'s Bassanio kissing Antonio who, significantly, returns the kiss with equal feeling. Each of these representations, redolent with gender trouble and male homoeroticism as they are, may be considered queer because they can, as is done in this study, be understood as discrete critiques of proscriptive heteronormativity.

Of course, as was made clear in the latter part of Chapter 4, both Nunn and Radford end their films of *Twelfth Night* and *Merchant* on an insistently heteronormative note. Each makes it a point to include scenes that show both of the Antonios being left behind as their friends/lovers, Sebastian and Bassanio respectively, enthusiastically embrace married life with their spouses Olivia and Portia. It seems that with this representational strategy, Nunn and Radford are trying to overcompensate for the screen time they gave to depicting the male homoeroticism of the relationships between Antonio and Sebastian and Antonio and Bassanio. However, the fact that Shakespeare's original playtexts of *Twelfth Night* or *Merchant* conclude with neither of the two Antonios being banished from Illyria or Belmont suggests the very real possibility that the marriages of Sebastian and Bassanio do not automatically preclude the continuation of the relationships they have with their respective friends/lovers. That makes the directorial choices of Nunn and Radford as regards the ends of their films all the more questionable from a queer perspective. It warrants pointing out too that, historically speaking, it would be more accurate for the relationships between Antonio and Sebastian and Antonio and Bassanio to remain in place following the marriages of the two Antonios given the staunchly male homosocial ethos that held sway in the early modern world.

Perhaps because Iago is and always has been such a queer character, *Othello* is and always has been a queer play. That queerness is evident in both of the twentieth-century film productions of *Othello* explored in Chapter 5. In contrast to Samuel Taylor Coleridge's assertion that Iago chooses to act the way that he does in the aftermath of Othello's promoting Cassio his lieutenant out of a 'motiveless malignancy', the productions of Welles and Parker – in tandem with Shakespeare's original playtext – make it clear that Iago's motivation is simply a powerful sense of betrayal. They also make it equally clear that Iago's feelings for Othello cross the line that separates the homosocial from the homoerotic and the homosexual; his feelings for the general are therefore queer. That queerness, furthermore, is not dependent on nor is it a result of Iago's intrinsic evil. As Shakespeare and, in turn, Welles and Parker present the character, Iago is evil regardless of whether or not his sexual inclinations tend toward the homo-, the hetero- or the bisexual. Nevertheless, what adds to the disquieting nature of *Othello* in its dramatic and cinematic forms is the fact that, for too long, queerness was automatically equated with evil. Arguably, the character of Iago – on the stage and on the screen – renders such a judgement invalid, at least as far as *Othello* is concerned, and that is a possibility that only queer theory as applied to Shakespeare studies could bring to light.

The overall summation of this book is one that is intuitive: the arc of queering the Shakespeare film seems to follow more or less the arc of history. As Western society became more knowledgeable about and less fearful of, more accepting and less condemnatory of, queerness in the twentieth and early twenty-first centuries – particularly queerness in its homosexual forms – the Shakespeare film followed suit. The highly coded and difficult to discern representations of the queer in productions from the 1930s like Reinhardt and Dieterle's *Midsummer* and Cukor's *Romeo and Juliet* have in the 2000s, in large part because of the queer depictions featured in the Shakespeare films of Zeffirelli, Welles, Parker, Luhrmann, Nunn, Hoffmann and Radford that preceded them, given way to unabashedly queer film productions of Shakespeare like Brown's *Private Romeo*, which features an all-male cast that retells the story of Romeo and Juliet complete with a happy ending for the two young men who fall in love with one another as they play the parts of Shakespeare's immortal 'pair of star-crossed lovers'. That such a queer subversion – exemplified in particular by the triumph, rather than the destruction, of the gay male couple – is now a reality in the Shakespeare film is a remarkable development.

Furthermore, given the limitations of its scope – it is not encyclopaedic and, as such, it examines only a comparatively small subset of mainstream and independent Anglophone Shakespeare films from the sound era – this book ends with a hopeful glance into the future. It looks forward to the other critical interventions in queering the Shakespeare film that may follow and direct attention to, for example, those films that could not be covered in this volume: the silent Shakespeare film; the television Shakespeare production; the teen Shakespeare film; and the world Shakespeare film. It is in fact a 'consummation devoutly to be wished' that the project of queering the Shakespeare film is only just beginning.

NOTES

Introduction: The presence of the queer in the Shakespeare film

1 Judith Buchanan, *Shakespeare on Silent Film: An Excellent Dumb Discourse* (Cambridge and New York: Cambridge University Press, 2007), 59.

2 Ibid., 60. See also Kenneth S. Rothwell's discussion of the 1899 *King John* in *A History of Shakespeare on Screen: A Century of Film and Television*, 2nd edn (Cambridge and New York: Cambridge University Press, 2004), 1–3.

3 Russell Jackson, *The Cambridge Companion to Shakespeare on Film*, 2nd edn (Cambridge and New York: Cambridge University Press, 2007), 2.

4 Ibid.

5 Ibid., 3.

6 Ibid.

7 Kate Chedgzoy, '"The Past is Our Mirror": Marlowe, Shakespeare, Jarman', Ch. 5 of *Shakespeare's Queer Children: Sexual Politics and Contemporary Culture* (Manchester and New York: Manchester University Press, 1995), 177–221, esp. 181.

8 Richard Burt, 'The Love That Dare Not Speak Shakespeare's Name: New Shakesqueer Cinema', Ch. 1 of *Unspeakable ShaXXXspeares: Queer Theory and American Kiddie Culture* (New York: St Martin's Press, 1998), 29–75, esp. 35.

9 Helen Moore, 'Present and Correct?' Rev. of *Shakespeare, Race and Colonialism*, *Shakespeare in the Present*, *The Sound of Shakespeare* and *Shakespeare's Perfume: Sodomy and Sublimity in the Sonnets, Wilde, Freud and Lacan*. Times Literary

Supplement (*TLS*) 5237 (15 August 2003): 22. Feminism, gay and lesbian studies and queer theory have all been thoroughly contextualized and historicized elsewhere. On Presentism in relation to Shakespeare, see 'Introduction', Terence Hawkes, *Shakespeare in the Present* (London and New York: Routledge, 2002), 1–5; Ewan Fernie, 'Shakespeare and the Prospect of Presentism', *Shakespeare Survey* 58: 169–84; 'Introduction', Hugh Grady and Terence Hawkes, eds, *Presentist Shakespeares* (London and New York: Routledge, 2007), 1–5; 'The Presence of the Past', Evelyn Gajowski, ed., *Presentism, Gender, and Sexuality in Shakespeare* (Basingstoke and New York: Palgrave Macmillan, 2009), 1–22; James O'Rourke, 'Introduction: Retheorizing Shakespeare', *Retheorizing Shakespeare Through Presentist Readings* (New York and London: Routledge, 2012), 1–7; as well as 'Introduction', 'Ch. 1' and 'Ch. 2' in Cary DiPietro and Hugh Grady, eds, *Shakespeare and the Urgency of Now: Criticism and Theory in the 21st Century* (Basingstoke and New York: Palgrave Macmillan, 2013), 1–59.

1: Max Reinhardt and William Dieterle's *A Midsummer Night's Dream* and the queer problematics of gender, sodomy, marriage and masculinity

1 *A Midsummer Night's Dream*, DVD, directed by Max Reinhardt and William Dieterle (1935; Burbank, CA: Warner Home Video, 2007). All references to Reinhardt and Dieterle's *Midsummer* are to this edition of the production.

2 Critics in the British press were particularly hard on Rooney and Puck. One described the actor as 'an offensive little American boy of the most impudent and irritating kind'; another claimed the character of 'Puck was unbearable ("an urchin, a guttersnipe")'. See Russell Jackson, *Shakespeare Films in the Making: Vision, Production and Reception* (Cambridge and New York: Cambridge University Press, 2007), 65–6.

3 Though they generally found Mickey Rooney's Puck to be intolerable, at least one British critic claimed that the 'youth and the "zeal and intelligence" of Cagney's performance were refreshing'. See ibid., 66.
4 Ibid., 59–69. Scott MacQueen surveys similar ground in 'Midsummer Dream, Midwinter Nightmare: Max Reinhardt and Shakespeare Versus the Warner Bros.', *The Moving Image* 9.2 (2009): 30–103, esp. 87–92.
5 Jack J. Jorgens, *Shakespeare on Film* (Lanham, MD: University Press of America, 1991), 50.
6 MacQueen, 'Midsummer Dream, Midwinter Nightmare', 30–103, esp. 31, 32.
7 Madhavi Menon, 'Introduction', *Shakesqueer: A Queer Companion to the Complete Works of Shakespeare*, ed. Madhavi Menon (Durham and London: Duke University Press, 2011), 4.
8 Ibid.
9 Ibid. Queerness in relation to temporality in relation to Shakespeare is also the theoretical starting point of Menon's *Unhistorical Shakespeare: Queer Theory in Shakespearean Literature and Film* (Basingstoke and New York: Palgrave Macmillan, 2008), esp. 1–25.
10 William Shakespeare, *Macbeth*, ed. Kenneth Muir, *The Arden Shakespeare, Second Series* (London and Cambridge, MA: Methuen and Harvard University Press, 1951), 5.1.41ff. On the larger implications of the change in gender to which Lady Macbeth alludes, see Bruce R. Smith, 'Resexing Lady Macbeth's Gender – and Ours', Ch. 1 of *Presentism, Gender, and Sexuality in Shakespeare*, ed. Evelyn Gajowski, (Basingstoke and New York: Palgrave Macmillan, 2009), 25–48.
11 The standard work on this subject is Suzanne W. Hull's *Chaste, Silent and Obedient: English Books for Women, 1475–1640* (San Marino, CA: Huntington Library, 1981), which has informed the work of countless other scholars since the early 1980s.
12 This quartet includes cinema and television productions of *Midsummer* by the following directors: Peter Hall (1968),

Joan Kemp-Welch (1964), Elijah Moshinsky (1981) and Max Reinhardt and William Dieterle (1935).

13 C. W. Griffin, 'Hippolyta's Dress and Undress: Subtext and Scopophilia in *A Midsummer Night's Dream*', *Shakespeare Bulletin* 12.2 (1994): 43.

14 Ibid., 44.

15 All textual references to *A Midsummer Night's Dream* are keyed to the Arden 2 edition of the play edited by Harold F. Brooks (London: Methuen/Thomson Learning, 1979); they are detailed in the standard act, scene and line number format. Any changes to the text made in the screenplay of Reinhardt and Dieterle's *Midsummer* are noted in brackets in the individual citations.

16 A. B. Taylor, 'Ovid's Myths and the Unsmooth Course of Love in *A Midsummer Night's Dream*', in *Shakespeare and the Classics*, eds Charles Martindale and A. B. Taylor (Cambridge and New York: Cambridge University Press, 2004), 49.

17 Tom Clayton, '"So Quick Bright Things Come to Confusion": or, What Else Was *A Midsummer Night's Dream* About?', *Shakespeare: Text and Theater: Essays in Honor of Jay L. Halio*, eds Lois Potter and Arthur F. Kinney (Newark: University of Delaware Press and London: Associated University Presses, 1999), 64.

18 Ibid., 66–7.

19 Griffin, 'Hippolyta's Dress and Undress', 44.

20 David M. Halperin, *Saint Foucault: Towards a Gay Hagiography* (Oxford and New York: Oxford University Press, 1995), 61–2, italics in the original.

21 Adrienne Rich, 'Compulsory Heterosexuality and Lesbian Existence', in *Feminism in our Time: The Essential Writings, World War II to the Present*, ed. Miriam Schneir (New York: Vintage, 1994), 310–28.

22 Griffin, 'Hippolyta's Dress and Undress', 44.

23 Ibid.

24 Ibid.

25 Archival evidence exists that reveals Reinhardt and Dieterle's *Midsummer* was supposed to contain scenes at the beginning

that dramatized Theseus's conquering of the Amazons and his taking of Hippolyta as his betrothed prisoner back to Athens. This sequence was omitted from the shooting script because of costs and because of the thought that it did nothing to advance the story itself. It is nevertheless fascinating – and queer – to ponder what such depictions would have contributed to the repeated representations of Hippolyta's initial resistance to Theseus and the strictures of compulsory heterosexuality that are still evident in the first part of the film. See Jackson, *Shakespeare Films in the Making*, 28 and MacQueen, 'Midsummer Dream, Midwinter Nightmare', 43.

26 Clayton, 'So Quick Bright Things Come to Confusion', 70.

27 Montrose, '*A Midsummer Night's Dream* and the Shaping Fantasies of Elizabethan Culture', 77.

28 Peter Holland, 'Theseus' Shadows in *A Midsummer Night's Dream*', *Shakespeare Survey* 47 (1995): 143.

29 Ibid.

30 Thanks in part to the extant dramas of Euripides and Seneca, it is known that Hippolytus became the subject of the insistent amorous attentions of his stepmother, Phaedra – the woman Theseus, in some versions of the story, abandoned Hippolyta for. When Hippolytus spurned Phaedra's advances, she claimed to Theseus that Hippolytus had attempted to rape her. An enraged Theseus turned for vengeance to the gods, who saw to it that Hippolytus, though he was innocent, was slain, most likely by being trampled by his own horses.

31 Richard Rambuss, 'Shakespeare's Ass Play', in *Shakesqueer*, ed. Menon, 236.

32 Shirley Nelson Garner, '*A Midsummer Night's Dream*: "Jack shall have Jill; / Nought shall go ill"', *Women's Studies* 9 (1981): 48–9.

33 Clayton, 'So Quick Bright Things Come to Confusion', 71.

34 Garner, '*A Midsummer Night's Dream*', 49.

35 *Oxford English Dictionary Online*, s.v. 'Erotic'.

36 MacQueen recounts how the role of the Indian boy was originally supposed to be played by a youth named Bobby Kolb, but Sheila Brown took on the role by the time actual

filming began in late 1934. Ironically given the context of *Queering the Shakespeare Film*, queer filmmaker Kenneth Anger would claim, from the 1960s onward, that he was the one who had, in fact, played the Indian boy. Other than for attention, what spurred Anger to put forth such a story remains a mystery. See 'Midsummer Dream, Midwinter Nightmare', 50. Interestingly, Bruce Babbington's article 'Shakespeare Meets Warner Brothers: Reinhardt and Dieterle's *A Midsummer Night's Dream* (1935)', Ch. 18 of *Shakespearean Continuities: Essays in Honour of E. A. J. Honigmann*, eds John Batchelor, Tom Cain and Claire Lamont (Basingstoke: Macmillan Press and New York: St Martin's Press, 1997), 259–74, features on 264, a still from the film of the Indian prince with the child actor's name labelled, incorrectly, as Kenneth Anger, rather than Sheila Brown.

37 Babbington, 'Shakespeare Meets the Warner Brothers', 267.

38 Ibid.

39 Sigmund Freud, *Three Essays on the Theory of Sexuality* (excerpt), in *The Freud Reader*, ed. Peter Gay (New York and London: W. W. Norton, 1995), 291.

40 Aranye Fradenburg, 'Momma's Boys', in *Shakesqueer*, ed. Menon, 320.

41 Clayton, 'So Quick Bright Things Come to Confusion', 71.

42 Christy Desmet, 'Disfiguring Women with Masculine Tropes: A Rhetorical Reading of *A Midsummer Night's Dream*', in *A Midsummer Night's Dream: Critical Essays*, ed. Dorothea Kehler (New York and London: Routledge, 2001), 309.

43 Stephen Greenblatt, ed., *A Midsummer Night's Dream*, in *The Norton Shakespeare: Based on the Oxford Edition*, 2nd edn, eds Stephen Greenblatt et al (New York and London: W. W. Norton, 2008), 878.

44 Jan Kott, 'Titania and the Ass's Head', excerpted from 'Shakespeare our Contemporary', in Kehler, ed., *A Midsummer Night's Dream*, 118.

45 Ibid.

46 Taylor, 'Ovid's Myths', 60.

47 25 Henry VIII, 'The Law in England, 1290–1885', Fordham

University, http://www.fordham.edu/halsall/pwh/englaw.asp (accessed 1 October 2014).
48 Ibid., n.p.
49 Bruce Thomas Boehrer, 'Bestial Buggery in *A Midsummer Night's Dream*', in *The Production of English Renaissance Culture*, eds David Lee Miller, Sharon O'Dair and Harold Weber (Ithaca and London: Cornell University Press, 1994), 132.
50 Ibid.
51 In a discussion of sodomy in *Homosexual Desire in Shakespeare's England: A Cultural Poetics* (Chicago and London: The University of Chicago Press, 1991), Bruce R. Smith explains that, in the mid-to-late sixteenth century, 'indictments for bestiality in the Home Counties outnumber indictments for sodomy six to one. Once indicted for bestiality, a person was three times likelier to be convicted and executed than a person indicted for sodomy' (49). This information speaks to Boehrer's caveat about actual people being prosecuted for bestiality even though, in his view, bestiality itself was something more talked about than a lived reality at this time in English history.
52 Alan Bray, *Homosexuality in Renaissance England* (New York: Columbia University Press, 1982, 1995), 13.
53 Ibid., 3–14.
54 Alan Bray, 'Homosexuality and the Signs of Male Friendship in Elizabethan England', in *Queering the Renaissance*, ed. Jonathan Goldberg (Durham and London: Duke University Press, 1994), 41.
55 Ibid.
56 Michel Foucault, *The History of Sexuality, Volume I: An Introduction*, trans. Robert Hurley (New York: Vintage, 1978, 1990), 101.
57 Boehrer, 'Bestial Buggery in *A Midsummer Night's Dream*', 123.
58 Ibid.
59 In many respects, Titania's amorous physicality toward Bottom in this scene mirrors the amorous physicality Theseus inflicted on Hippolyta in the early part of Reinhardt and Dieterle's *Midsummer*.

60 Michael P. Jensen, '*A Midsummer Night's Dream*: How German Expressionism Dominated this Classical 1935 Fantasy!', *Filmfax* 106 (2005): 110–11.

61 Jan Kott, 'Titania and the Ass's Head', 119. Italics added. Note that A. D. Nuttall takes serious issue with Kott's assertions here: 'His [Kott's] notorious description of Titania as longing for animal love (as if Titania were Pasiphae) is simply ludicrous. Has he not noticed that Titania is deluded? She is attracted by what she sees as a wise and beautiful being. She cannot see the grotesque half-donkey available to the rest of us.' See Nuttall's '*A Midsummer Night's Dream*: Comedy as Apotrope of Myth', *Shakespeare Survey* 53 (2000): 51.

62 Gail Kern Paster, *The Body Embarrassed: Drama and the Disciplines of Shame in Early Modern England* (Ithaca: Cornell University Press, 1993), 141.

63 Jensen, '*A Midsummer Night's Dream*', 111.

64 Arthur L. Little, Jr, '"A Local Habitation and a Name": Presence, Witnessing, and Queer Marriage in Shakespeare's Romantic Comedies', in Gajowski, ed., *Presentism, Gender, and Sexuality in Shakespeare*, 218.

65 Deborah Wyrick, 'The Ass Motif in *The Comedy of Errors* and *A Midsummer Night's Dream*', *Shakespeare Quarterly* 33 (1982): 444. Cited in Boehrer, 'Bestial Buggery in *A Midsummer Night's Dream*', n.1, 123.

66 Joseph H. Summers, *Dreams of Love and Power: On Shakespeare's Plays* (Oxford: Clarendon Press, 1984), 11. Cited in Boehrer, 'Bestial Buggery in *A Midsummer Night's Dream*', n.1, 123–4.

67 Garner, '*A Midsummer Night's Dream*', 50.

68 Rambuss, 'Shakespeare's Ass Play', 234.

69 Boehrer, 'Bestial Buggery in *A Midsummer Night's Dream*', 140.

70 Stephen Orgel, *Impersonations: The Performance of Gender in Shakespeare's England* (Cambridge and New York: Cambridge University Press, 1996), 20.

71 Ibid.

72 Ibid.

73 Ibid.
74 Ibid., 25.
75 Ibid.
76 Ibid.
77 In her analysis of *Troilus and Cressida*, a play rife with fears associated with effeminacy, Laura Lavine notes that 'if anxieties of effeminization are not particular to one figure or camp' in the play, 'what they do share is that they are all associated with love, heterosexual or homoerotic'. See Levine, *Men in Women's Clothing: Anti-Theatricality and Effeminization, 1579–1642* (Cambridge and New York: Cambridge University Press, 1994), 37. Within the realm of *Troilus and Cressida* at least, this suggests that the gender of the love object does not matter as far as effeminacy is concerned; love itself is the actual problem. By suggesting such a scenario in his play, Shakespeare could be indicating that the culture at large of which he was a part thought along similar lines.
78 Babbington, 'Shakespeare Meets the Warner Brothers', 270.
79 Robert F. Willson, Jr, *Shakespeare in Hollywood, 1929–1956* (Madison/Teaneck, NJ and London: Fairleigh Dickinson University Press and Associated University Presses, 2000), 43.
80 Jack J. Jorgens, *Shakespeare on Film* (Lanham, MD: University Press of America, 1991), 41.
81 Ibid.
82 Ibid., 43.
83 Ibid.

2: The queer director, gay spectatorship, and three cinematic productions of Shakespeare's 'straightest' play – *Romeo and Juliet*

1 Kenneth S. Rothwell, *A History of Shakespeare on Screen: A*

Century of Film and Television, 2nd edn (Cambridge and New York: Cambridge University Press, 2004), 356–8.

2 For reasons made clear there, director Baz Lurhmann's *Romeo + Juliet* (1996) is dealt with in the next chapter rather than this one.

3 *Romeo and Juliet*, DVD, directed by George Cukor (1936; Burbank, CA: Warner Home Video, 2007). All references to Cukor's *Romeo and Juliet* are to this edition of the production.

4 Ibid., 42.

5 Courtney Lehmann, *Screen Adaptations, Shakespeare's Romeo and Juliet: The Relationship Between Text and Film* (London: Methuen Drama, 2010), 87.

6 Ibid., 87–8.

7 Ibid., 88.

8 Stephen Orgel, 'Shakespeare Illustrated', in *The Cambridge Companion to Shakespeare and Popular Culture*, ed. Robert Shaughnessy (Cambridge and New York: Cambridge University Press, 2007), 91.

9 Richard Burt, 'No Holes Bard: Homonormativity and the Gay and Lesbian Romance with *Romeo and Juliet*', in *Shakespeare Without Class: Misappropriations of Cultural Capital* (New York: Palgrave, 2000), 165.

10 Harry M. Benshoff and Sean Griffin, *Queer Images: A History of Gay and Lesbian Film in America* (Lanham, MD: Rowman & Littlefield, 2006), 10.

11 Patrick McGilligan, *George Cukor: A Double Life* (New York: St Martin's Press, 1991), 114.

12 Ibid., 115.

13 Ibid.

14 Ibid.

15 Emmanuel Levy, *George Cukor: Master of Elegance: Hollywood's Legendary Director and His Stars* (New York: William Morrow, 1994), 16.

16 Ibid.

17 Burt, 'No Holes Bard', 164.

18 Ibid., 165.
19 Ibid.
20 McGilligan, *George Cukor*, 105.
21 Ibid.
22 Levy, *George Cukor*, 91.
23 McGilligan, *George Cukor*, 106.
24 Jackson, *Shakespeare Films in the Making*, 137.
25 Ibid.
26 Burt, 'No Holes Bard', 165.
27 Shirley Bury, 'Preface', *Earrings: From Antiquity to the Present*, eds Daniela Mascetti and Amanda Triossi (London: Thames & Hudson, 1990), 7.
28 Ibid.
29 Ibid.
30 Ronald D. Steinbach, *The Fashionable Ear: A History of Ear-Piercing Trends for Men and Women* (New York: Vantage Press, 1995), 228.
31 Ibid., 250–7.
32 Joseph A. Porter, *Shakespeare's Mercutio: His History and Drama* (Chapel Hill, NC and London: The University of North Carolina Press, 1988), 189–90.
33 Burt, 'No Holes Bard', 166.
34 See Jonathan Dollimore, *Sexual Dissidence: Augustine to Wilde, Freud to Foucault* (Oxford and New York: Oxford University Press, 1991).
35 *Romeo and Juliet*, DVD, directed by Franco Zeffirelli (1968; Hollywood, CA: Paramount Pictures, 2013). All references to Zeffirelli's *Romeo and Juliet* are to this edition of the production. For an in-depth account of the production of this film, see 'Shakespeare's "Dream of Italy" and the Generation Gap: Franco Zeffirelli's *Romeo and Juliet*, 1968', Ch. 3.3 of Jackson, *Shakespeare Films in the Making*, 191–221.
36 Rothwell, *A History of Shakespeare on Screen*, 123.
37 Peter S. Donaldson in '"Let Lips Do What Hands Do": Male Bonding, Eros and Loss in Zeffirelli's *Romeo and Juliet*',

Ch. 6 of his *Shakespearean Films/Shakespearean Directors* (Boston: Unwin Hyman, 1990), discusses Zeffirelli's sexuality and speculates on how it relates to *Romeo and Juliet*; see esp. 145–52.

38 Ibid., 145.

39 Renata Adler, 'Romeo and Juliet', rev. of *Romeo and Juliet* (1968), dir. Franco Zeffirelli, *The New York Times*, 9 October 1968, n.p.

40 Ibid.

41 Ibid.

42 Indeed, the *Times*'s long-running motto is: 'All the News That's Fit to Print'. It was first used in 1897 and appears on the newspaper's masthead to this day.

43 Donaldson, 'Let Lips Do What Hands Do', 145.

44 Ibid., 145–6.

45 Ibid., 146.

46 Franco Zeffirelli, *Zeffirelli: The Autobiography of Franco Zeffirelli* (New York: Weidenfeld & Nicolson, 1986), 228.

47 Donaldson, 'Let Lips Do What Hands Do', 154.

48 Laura Mulvey, 'Visual Pleasure and Narrative Cinema', in *The Film Theory Reader: Debates and Arguments*, ed. Marc Furstenau (London and New York: Routledge, 2010), 202.

49 Ibid.

50 Ibid., 203.

51 Ibid., 204.

52 Brett Farmer, *Spectacular Passions: Cinema, Fantasy, Gay Male Spectatorships* (Durham, NC and London: Duke University Press, 2000), 199.

53 Ibid., 199–200.

54 Ibid., 200.

55 Ibid., 11.

56 William Van Watson, 'Shakespeare, Zeffirelli, and the Homosexual Gaze', in *Shakespeare and Gender: A History*, eds Deborah Barker and Ivo Kamps (London and New York: Verso, 1995), 249.

57 Farmer, *Spectacular Passions*, 203.

58 Ibid.

59 Ibid., 205.

60 Ibid.

61 Ibid.

62 Ibid., 206.

63 Ibid.

64 Marjorie Garber, *Vested Interests: Cross-Dressing and Cultural Anxiety* (New York: Routledge, 1997), 122.

65 Will Fisher, *Materializing Gender in Early Modern English Literature and Culture* (Cambridge and New York: Cambridge University Press, 2006), 59.

66 Ibid., 62.

67 Ibid., 64–7.

68 Ibid., 69.

69 Ibid., 82.

70 Van Watson, 'Shakespeare, Zeffirelli, and the Homosexual Gaze', 249.

71 Ibid.

72 All textual references to *Romeo and Juliet* are keyed to the Arden 3 edition of the play edited by René Weis (London: Methuen Drama/Bloomsbury, 2012); they are noted in the standard act, scene and line number format.

73 Christine Varnado, '"Invisible Sex!": What Looks Like the Act in Early Modern Drama', in *Sex Before Sex: Figuring the Act in Early Modern England*, eds James M. Bromley and Will Stockton (Minneapolis and London: University of Minnesota Press, 2013), 34.

74 Ibid., 34–5.

75 Ibid., 32.

76 Ibid.

77 Ibid.

78 Ibid.

79 Jack J. Jorgens, *Shakespeare on Film* (Lanham, MD: University Press of America, Inc., 1991), 84.

80 Porter, *Shakespeare's Mercutio*, 154.

81 Gavin Lambert, *On Cukor*, ed. Robert Trachtenberg (New York: Rizzoli International Publications, 2000), 86.

82 Ibid., 84.

83 *Private Romeo*, DVD, directed by Alan Brown (2011; San Jose, CA: Wolfe Video, 2011). All references to Brown's *Private Romeo* are to this edition of the production.

84 See www.privateromeothemovie.com (last accessed 1 February 2016). The site was still live as of this writing.

85 Eve Kosofsky Sedgwick, *Between Men: English Literature and Male Homosocial Desire* (New York: Columbia University Press, 1985), 1.

86 Ibid.

87 Judith Butler, 'Imitation and Gender Insubordination', in *Feminist Literary Theory and Criticism: A Reader*, eds Sandra M. Gilbert and Susan Gubar (New York and London: W. W. Norton, 2007), 716, italics in the original.

88 Ibid.

89 See Ch. 14, Part II of Coleridge's *Biographia Literaria*, where he writes: 'In this idea originated the plan of the "Lyrical Ballads"; in which it was agreed, that my endeavours should be directed to persons and characters supernatural, or at least romantic; yet so as to transfer from our inward nature a human interest and a semblance of truth sufficient to procure for these shadows of imagination that willing suspension of disbelief for the moment, which constitutes poetic faith' (677).

90 See *The History of Sexuality, Volume I: An Introduction*: 'As defined by the ancient civil or canonical codes, sodomy was a category of forbidden acts, their perpetrator was nothing more than the juridical subject of them. The nineteenth-century homosexual became a personage, a past, a case history, and a childhood, in addition to being a type of life, a life form, and a morphology, with an indiscreet anatomy and possibly a mysterious physiology' (43).

91 Burt, 'No Holes Bard', 154.
92 Ibid.
93 Ibid., 156.
94 Ibid., 156–7.
95 Ibid., 157.

3: The visual poetics of gender trouble in Trevor Nunn's *Twelfth Night*, Baz Luhrmann's *Romeo + Juliet* and Michael Hoffman's *William Shakespeare's A Midsummer Night's Dream*

1 Keir Elam, ed., 'Introduction', *Twelfth Night, Or What You Will*, The Arden Shakespeare, Third Series (London: Arden Shakespeare, 2008), 146–53.

2 Kenneth S. Rothwell, *A History of Shakespeare on Screen: A Century of Film and Television* (Cambridge: Cambridge University Press, 2004), 364–5.

3 H. R. Coursen, *Shakespeare: The Two Traditions* (Madison, NJ: Fairleigh Dickinson University Press and London: Associated University Presses, 1999), 199–200.

4 Ibid., 202.

5 *Twelfth Night*, DVD, directed by Trevor Nunn (1996; Burbank, CA: Warner Home Video, 1996). All references to Nunn's *Twelfth Night* are to this edition of the production. Unless otherwise noted, all textual references to *Twelfth Night* are keyed to the Arden 3 edition of the play edited by Keir Elam (London: Arden Shakespeare, 2008); they are noted in the standard act, scene and line number format.

6 Rothwell, *A History of Shakespeare on Screen*, 227.

7 Since there are sometimes significant differences between the

two, Nunn's published screenplay is, where clear alterations have been made, cross-referenced with the act, scene and line numbers from Elam's Arden 3 edition of *Twelfth Night* from this point forward in the chapter. See Trevor Nunn, *William Shakespeare's Twelfth Night: A Screenplay* (London: Methuen Drama, 1996).

8 Phyllis Rackin, 'Androgyny, Mimesis, and the Marriage of the Boy Heroine on the English Renaissance Stage', *PMLA* 102.1 (1987): 29–41, esp. 29.

9 Judith Butler, *Gender Trouble: Feminism and the Subversion of Identity* (New York: Routledge, 1990, 2007), 43–4.

10 Maria F. Magro and Mark Douglas, 'Reflections on Sex, Shakespeare and Nostalgia in Trevor Nunn's *Twelfth Night*', in *Retrovisions: Reinventing the Past in Film and Fiction*, eds Deborah Cartmell, I.Q. Hunter and Imelda Whelan (London and Sterling, VA: Pluto Press, 2001), 41–58, esp. 53.

11 Coursen, *Shakespeare: The Two Traditions*, 203.

12 Rothwell, *A History of Shakespeare on Screen*, 227.

13 David Schalkwyk, *Shakespeare, Love and Service* (Cambridge and New York: Cambridge University Press, 2008), 19.

14 Ibid., 21.

15 Curtis Perry, *Literature and Favoritism in Early Modern England* (Cambridge and New York: Cambridge University Press, 2006), 131.

16 Alan Sinfield, 'How to Read *The Merchant of Venice* Without Being Heterosexist', Ch. 4 of his monograph *Shakespeare, Authority, Sexuality: Unfinished Business in Cultural Materialism* (London and New York: Routledge, 2006), 29.

17 Jean E. Howard, 'Crossdressing, the Theatre, and Gender Struggle in Early Modern England', *Shakespeare Quarterly* 39.4 (1988): 418–40, esp. 432.

18 Bruce R. Smith, *Shakespeare and Masculinity* (Oxford and New York: Oxford University Press, 2000), 122–3.

19 See Act 4, scene 6 of *King Henry V*, The Arden Shakespeare, Third Series, ed. T. W. Craik (Thompson Learning: London, 1995, 2005).

20 Smith, *Shakespeare and Masculinity*, 123.
21 Schalkwyk, *Shakespeare, Love and Service*, 125.
22 *Romeo + Juliet*, DVD, directed by Baz Luhrmann (1996; Los Angeles, CA: 20th Century Fox, 1996). All references to Lurhmann's *Romeo + Juliet* are to this edition of the production.
23 Rothwell, *A History of Shakespeare on Screen*, 229.
24 Ibid., 229–30.
25 Nicholas F. Radel, 'The Ethiop's Ear: Race, Sexuality, and Baz Luhrmann's *William Shakespeare's Romeo + Juliet*', *Upstart Crow* 28 (2009): 17–34, esp. 17.
26 Rothwell, *A History of Shakespeare on Screen*, 231–2.
27 Ibid., 232.
28 James N. Loehlin, ed., *Romeo and Juliet*, Shakespeare in Production (Cambridge and New York: Cambridge University Press, 2002), 127.
29 Courtney Lehmann, *Screen Adaptations, Shakespeare's Romeo and Juliet: The Relationship Between Text and Film* (London: Methuen Drama, 2010), 173.
30 Radel, 'The Ethiop's Ear', 19.
31 Ibid., 23.
32 Ibid.
33 Richard Burt, *Unspeakable ShaXXXspeares: Queer Theory and American Kiddie Culture* (New York: St Martin's Press, 1998), 159.
34 Butler, *Gender Trouble*, 179, italics in the original.
35 Marjorie Garber, *Vested Interests: Cross-Dressing and Cultural Anxiety* (New York: Routledge, 1997), 130.
36 Ibid.
37 Ibid., italics in the original.
38 Radel, 'The Ethiop's Ear', 23.
39 Butler, *Gender Trouble*, 178.
40 All textual references to *Romeo and Juliet* are keyed to the Arden 3 edition of the play edited by René Weis (London:

Methuen Drama/Bloomsbury Publishing, 2012); they are noted in the standard act, scene and line number format.

41 Ibid., 235.

42 Craig Pearce and Baz Luhrmann, *William Shakespeare's Romeo and Juliet, The Contemporary Film and the Classic Play* (New York: Bantam Doubleday Dell, 1996), 97.

43 *Oxford English Dictionary Online*, s.v. 'Blow'.

44 Radel, 'The Ethiop's Ear', 21.

45 *William Shakespeare's A Midsummer Night's Dream*, DVD, directed by Michael Hoffman (1999; Los Angeles, CA: Fox Searchlight Pictures, 1999). All references to Hoffman's *Midsummer* are to this edition of the production.

46 All textual references to *A Midsummer Night's Dream* are keyed to the Arden 2 edition of the play edited by Harold F. Brooks (London: Methuen/Thomson Learning, 1979); they are detailed in the standard act, scene and line number format.

47 Edward Berry, 'Laughing at "Others"', in *The Cambridge Companion to Shakespearean Comedy*, ed. Alexander Leggatt (Cambridge and New York: Cambridge University Press, 2002), 123.

48 Ibid.

49 Ibid.

50 Ibid., 124.

51 Ibid.

52 Ibid.

53 Garber, *Vested Interests*, 130, italics in the original.

54 Michael Hoffman, *William Shakespeare's A Midsummer Night's Dream* (New York: Harper Paperbacks, 1999), 107–8.

55 Samuel Crowl, *Shakespeare at the Cineplex: The Kenneth Branagh Era* (Athens, OH: Ohio University Press, 2003), 186.

4: Screening the male homoerotics of Shakespearean romantic comedy on film in Michael Radford's *The Merchant of Venice* and Trevor Nunn's *Twelfth Night*

1 The articles are: Joseph Pequigney, 'The Two Antonios and Same-Sex Love in *Twelfth Night* and *The Merchant of Venice*', in *Shakespeare and Gender: A History* eds Deborah E. Barker and Ivo Kamps (London and New York: Verso, 1995), 178–95; and Valerie Traub, 'The Homoerotics of Shakespearean Comedy (*As You Like It, Twelfth Night*)', Ch. 5 of *Desire and Anxiety: Circulations of Sexuality in Shakespearean Drama* (London and New York: Routledge, 1992), 117–44.

2 Pequigney, 'The Two Antonios', 191.

3 Portions of what follows have appeared in slightly different form in other publications. See Anthony Guy Patricia, '"Through the Eyes of the Present": Screening the Male Homoerotics of Shakespearean Drama', in *Presentism, Gender, and Sexuality in Shakespeare*, ed. Evelyn Gajowski (Basingstoke and New York: Palgrave Macmillan, 2009), 157–78; and Anthony Guy Patricia, '"Say How I Loved You": Queering the Emotion of Male Same-Sex Love in *The Merchant of Venice*', in *Shakespeare and Emotions: Inheritances, Enactments, Legacies*, eds R. S. White, Mark Houlahan and Katrina O'Loughlin (Basingstoke and New York: Palgrave Macmillan, 2015), 116–23.

4 *William Shakespeare's The Merchant of Venice*, DVD, directed by Michael Radford (2004; Culver City, CA: Sony Pictures Home Entertainment, 2004). All references to Radford's *Merchant* are to this edition of the production.

5 Kenneth S. Rothwell, *A History of Shakespeare on Screen: A Century of Film and Television*, Second Edition (Cambridge and New York: Cambridge University Press, 2004), 274 and 351 respectively. Here, Rothwell lists a thirteenth production of *Merchant* as being in progress at the time of the publication

of the second edition of his book, though it seems never to have been completed. Apparently, it would have starred Ian McKellen and Patrick Stewart.

6 All citations from *The Merchant of Venice* are keyed to John Drakakis's The Arden Shakespeare Series 3 edition of the play (London: Methuen Drama/A&C Black, 2010); they are noted in the standard act, scene and line number format.

7 Arthur L. Little, Jr, 'The Rites of Queer Marriage in *The Merchant of Venice*', in *Shakesqueer: A Queer Companion to the Complete Works of Shakespeare*, ed. Madhavi Menon (Durham and London: Duke University Press, 2011), 216–24, esp. 217.

8 Ibid., 216.

9 Janet Adelman, 'Male Bonding in Shakespeare's Comedies', in *Shakespeare's 'Rough Magic': Renaissance Essays in Honor of C. L. Barber*, eds Peter Erickson and Coppélia Kahn (Newark: University of Delaware Press, and London and Toronto: Associated University Presses, 1985), 73–103, esp. 75.

10 Coppélia Kahn, 'The Cuckoo's Note: Male Friendship and Cuckoldry in *The Merchant of Venice*', in *Shakespeare's 'Rough Magic*, eds Erickson and Kahn, 104–12, esp. 106.

11 Laury Magnus, 'Michael Radford's *The Merchant of Venice* and the Vexed Question of Performance', *Literature/Film Quarterly* 35.2 (2007): 108–20, esp. 111.

12 Ibid., 111.

13 Ibid.

14 See the *Oxford English Dictionary Online*, s.v. 'Bedroom'. Interestingly, the *OED Online* defines 'bedroom' as a 'room used or intended to contain a bed or beds; a sleeping apartment' (Def. 2.). Thus its editors would have readers believe that the term did not acquire specifically sexual connotations until the early twentieth century. But to support the definition of bedroom as a place for nothing more than rest, the editors cite a line spoken by the character of Lysander to his girlfriend/fiancée Hermia, having lost their way and therefore preparing to spend the night in the forest outside Athens, in Shakespeare's *Midsummer*: 'Then by your side, no bed-roome

me deny'. The irony of this citation is that Lysander is trying to get Hermia to sleep – as in have sex – with him in their outdoor bedroom. It is left to Hermia to school the randy Lysander in the kinds of behaviour appropriate for a virtuous bachelor and a maid like themselves to engage in if they are to remain as chaste as they should be until they are married.

15 Seymour Kleinberg, '*The Merchant of Venice*: The Homosexual as Anti-Semite in Nascent Capitalism', in *Essays on Gay Literature*, ed. Stuart Kellogg (New York and Binghamton: Harrington Park Press, 1985), 113–26, esp. 116.

16 Magnus, 'Michael Radford's *The Merchant of Venice* and the Vexed Question of Performance', 114.

17 Alan Bray, 'Homosexuality and the Signs of Male Friendship in Elizabethan England', in *Queering the Renaissance*, ed. Jonathan Goldberg (Durham and London: Duke University Press, 1994), 40–61, esp. 43, 42.

18 '*The Merchant of Venice*: Shakespeare Through the Lens', *William Shakespeare's The Merchant of Venice*, dir. Michael Radford, Sony Home Pictures Entertainment, 2004, DVD.

19 *Shakespeare's Sonnets*, Katherine Duncan-Jones, ed., The Arden Shakespeare Third Series Revised Edition (Methuen Drama/A&C Black, 1997, 2010), 255.

20 Alan Sinfield, *Shakespeare, Authority, Sexuality: Unfinished Business in Cultural Materialism* (London and New York: Routledge, 2006), 62.

21 Trevor Nunn, *William Shakespeare's Twelfth Night: A Screenplay* (London: Methuen Drama, 1996).

22 The 'Introduction' to Nunn's screenplay of *Twelfth Night* is not paginated.

23 *Twelfth Night*, DVD, directed by Trevor Nunn (1996; Burbank, CA: Warner Home Video, 1996). All references to Nunn's *Twelfth Night* are to this edition of the production. Unless otherwise noted, all textual references to *Twelfth Night* are keyed to the Arden 3 edition of the play edited by Keir Elam (London: Arden Shakespeare, 2008); they are noted in the standard act, scene and line number format.

24 Since there are sometimes significant differences between the

two, Nunn's published screenplay is, where clear alterations have been made, cross-referenced with the act, scene and line numbers from Elam's Arden 3 edition of *Twelfth Night* from this point forward in the chapter. See Trevor Nunn, *William Shakespeare's Twelfth Night: A Screenplay* (London: Methuen Drama, 1996).

25 Pequigney, 'The Two Antonios', 179.
26 David Schalkwyk, *Shakespeare, Love and Service* (Cambridge and New York: Cambridge University Press, 2008), 128.
27 Rothwell, *A History of Shakespeare on Screen*, 227.
28 Cynthia Lewis, *Particular Saints: Shakespeare's Four Antonios, Their Contexts, and Their Plays* (Newark, DE: University of Delaware Press, and London and Cranbury, NJ: Associated University Presses, 1997), 92, 93.
29 When the bawdy sense of 'purse' is taken into account – it refers to a man's scrotum – the homoeroticism of the Antonio/Sebastian relationship is even more pronounced.
30 Pequigney, 'The Two Antonios', 204.
31 Ungerer's essay is entitled 'My Lady's a Catayan, We are Politicians, and Malvolio's a Peg-a-Ramsie' and it appears in *Shakespeare Survey* 32 (1979), 85–104.
32 Yu Jin Ko, *Mutability and Division on Shakespeare's Stage* (Newark: University of Delaware Press, 2004), 71. In his consideration of what kind of a place the Elephant could be in *Twelfth Night*, Ko, like Elam, also references Ungerer's essay. Unlike Elam, however, Ko uses Ungerer's alternate spelling of Oliphant instead of Elephant.
33 See *Othello*, The Arden Shakespeare, Third Series, ed. E. A. J. Honigmann (London: Thomson Learning, 1997), esp. 1.2.63–80, 1.3.59–64, 1.3.94–106.
34 See Honigmann's *Othello*, esp. 1.3.76–94, 127–68.
35 Rothwell, *A History of Shakespeare on Screen*, 229.
36 H. R. Coursen, *Shakespeare: The Two Traditions*, (Madison, NJ: Fairleigh Dickinson University Press and London: Associated University Presses, 1999), 204.
37 Maria F. Magro and Mark Douglas, 'Reflections on Sex,

Shakespeare and Nostalgia in Trevor Nunn's *Twelfth Night*', in *Retrovisions: Reinventing the Past in Film and Fiction*, eds Deborah Cartmell, I. Q. Hunter and Imelda Whelan (London and Sterling, VA: Pluto Press, 2001), 41–58, esp. 55.

38 Ibid.

39 Sinfield, *Shakespeare, Authority, Sexuality*, 65–6. See also Pequigney, 'The Two Antonios', 182.

40 Bruce R. Smith, *Homosexual Desire in Shakespeare's England* (Chicago and London: The University of Chicago Press, 1991, 1994), 72.

41 Arthur L. Little, Jr, '"A Local Habitation and a Name": Presence, Witnessing, and Queer Marriage in Shakespeare's Romantic Comedies', in *Presentism, Gender, and Sexuality in Shakespeare*, ed. Evelyn Gajowski (Houndmills and New York: Palgrave Macmillan, 2009), 207–36, esp. 211.

5: 'I am your own forever': Iago, queer self-fashioning and the cinematic *Othellos* of Orson Welles and Oliver Parker

1 On either side, many would consider the most celebrated Shakespearean tragedy to be *Hamlet*; the most disturbing, *Titus Andronicus*.

2 Lois Potter, *Shakespeare in Performance: Othello* (Manchester and New York: Manchester University Press, 2002), 6.

3 Ibid.

4 In particular, see 2.1.99–180. All citations from *Othello* are keyed to E. A. J. Honigmann's *The Arden Shakespeare* Series 3 edition of the play (London: Thomson Learning, 1997); they are noted in the standard act, scene and line number format.

5 Kenneth S. Rothwell, *A History of Shakespeare on Screen: A Century of Film and Television*, Second Edition (Cambridge and New York: Cambridge University Press, 1999, 2004), 352–4.

6 Stanley Edgar Hyman, *Iago: Some Approaches to the Illusion of his Motivation* (New York: Atheneum, 1970), 101.
7 Ibid.
8 Ibid., 102.
9 Ibid., 104, 107.
10 Ibid., 114.
11 Ibid., 117.
12 Ben Saunders, 'Iago's Clyster: Purgation, Anality, and the Civilizing Process', *Shakespeare Quarterly* 55.2 (Summer 2004): 148–76, esp. 151.
13 Ibid.
14 Saunders's logic here is rather difficult to follow. Based on Iago's dream of sleeping with him that he relates to Othello in 3.3, readers are left to assume that the anus in question belongs to Cassio. However, the incident related in 2.1 that Saunders directs critical attention to suggests that the anus is Desdemona's. But in this formulation, symbolically, the referent will always be the object of Iago's sublimated homosexual desire. As such, Desdemona, Cassio and even Othello are conflated into the matrix.
15 Saunders, 'Iago's Clyster', 148–76, esp. 150.
16 Ibid., 154.
17 Ibid., 175.
18 Ibid., 175–6.
19 Arthur L. Little, Jr, '"An Essence That's Not Seen": The Primal Scene of Racism in *Othello*'. *Shakespeare Quarterly* 44.3 (Autumn 1993): 304–24, esp. 306.
20 Ibid., 317.
21 Ibid., 318.
22 Ibid.
23 Robert Matz, 'Slander, Renaissance Discourses of Sodomy, and *Othello*', *ELH* 66.2 (Summer 1999): 261–76, esp. 264.
24 Ibid., 264–5.
25 Ibid., 265.

26 *Othello*, DVD, directed by Orson Welles (1952; New York: Castle Hill Productions and BWE Video, 2003). All references to Welles's *Othello* are to this edition of the production.
27 Rothwell, *A History of Shakespeare on Screen*, 77.
28 William Park, *What is Film Noir?* (Lewisburg, PA: Bucknell University Press, 2011), 25.
29 Ibid., 26.
30 Richard Dyer, *The Matter of Images: Essays on Representations* (London and New York: Routledge, 1993, 2002), 52.
31 Ibid.
32 Ibid., 60.
33 Ibid., 61.
34 Ibid., 65.
35 Micheál MacLiammóir, *Put Money in Thy Purse: The Diary of the Film of Othello* (London: Methuen, 1952), 26.
36 Ibid.
37 Potter, *Shakespeare in Performance: Othello*, 143.
38 Dyer, *The Matter of Images*, 68.
39 Harry M. Benshoff and Sean Griffin, *Queer Images: A History of Gay and Lesbian Film in America* (Lanham, MD: Rowman & Littlefield, 2006), 10.
40 Ibid.
41 Daniel Juan Gil, 'Avant-garde Technique and the Visual Grammar of Sexuality in Orson Welles's Shakespeare Films', *Borrowers and Lenders: The Journal of Shakespeare and Appropriation* 1.2 (Fall/Winter 2005): n.p., http://www.borrowers.uga.edu/781447/display (accessed 1 February 2016).
42 Ibid.
43 Ibid.
44 *Othello*, DVD, directed by Oliver Parker (1995; Burbank, CA: Warner Home Video, 1995). All references to Parker's *Othello* are to this edition of the production.
45 Bruce R. Smith, *Homosexual Desire in Shakespeare's England* (Chicago and London: The University of Chicago Press, 1991, 1994), 63.

46 See John Boswell, *Same-Sex Unions in Premodern Europe* (New York: Villard, 1994); Alan A. Tulchin, 'Same-Sex Couples Creating Households in Old Regime France: The Uses of the Affrèrement', *Journal of Modern History* 79.3 (September 2007): 613–47.

47 Stephen Greenblatt, *Renaissance Self-Fashioning: From More to Shakespeare* (Chicago: University of Chicago Press, 1980 and 1984), 1–2.

48 Lerner is quoted in ibid., 225.

49 Ibid., 225.

50 Ibid., 251.

51 Ibid., 248.

52 Ibid.

53 Ibid., 250.

Conclusion: Queering the Shakespeare film in the early twenty-first century

1 Gregory D. Black, 'Who Controls What We See? Censorship and the Attack on Hollywood "Immorality"', Ch. 4 of *Movies and American Society*, ed. Steven J. Ross (Oxford and Malden, MA: Blackwell, 2002), 98–127, esp. 100. Black's assertion that 'most film history is written as if the code and the PCA did not exist' may be quibbled with as far as gay and lesbian and, later, queer film history is concerned. Histories of film that encompass the gay and lesbian – and, later, the queer – perspective, either in terms of subject matter, author affiliation or, in many cases, both, have directed a great deal of attention to the PCA and the production code. For example, Vito Russo, who published the first contemporary history of gay and lesbian cinema, *The Celluloid Closet: Homosexuality in the Movies*, in 1981, deals repeatedly with the PCA and the production code as he charts the widespread and all-too-often negative impact of both on the (re)presentation of homosexuality in American film.

Others, such as Benshoff and Griffin, authors of the more recent volume *Queer Images: A History of Gay and Lesbian Film in America*, also comment often on the PCA and its code as they extend and update the work of Russo, taking it forward from the early 1980s to the early 2000s. What Russo, Benshoff and Griffin and others have brought to light in their works is that which has been previously hidden from 'official' film history as regards homosexuality and queerness in the cinema.

2 'The Production Code', in *Movies and Mass Culture*, ed. John Belton (New Brunswick, NJ: Rutgers University Press, 1996), 135–52, esp. 142; all capitals appear in the original text.

3 Ibid., 139, 140; italics in the original.

BIBLIOGRAPHY

A Midsummer Night's Dream. DVD. Directed by Max Reinhardt and William Dieterle. 1935; Burbank, CA: Warner Home Video, 2007.

Adelman, Janet. 'Male Bonding in Shakespeare's Comedies'. In *Shakespeare's "Rough Magic": Renaissance Essays in Honor of C. L. Barber*, eds Peter Erickson and Coppélia Kahn. Newark: University of Delaware Press and London and Toronto: Associated University Presses, 1985, 73–103.

Adler, Renata. 'Romeo and Juliet'. Rev. of *Romeo and Juliet* (1968), dir. Franco Zeffirelli. *The New York Times* 9 October, 1968: n.p.

Babbington, Bruce. 'Shakespeare Meets the Warner Brothers: Reinhardt and Dieterle's *A Midsummer Night's Dream* (1935)'. In *Shakespearean Continuities: Essays in Honour of E. A. J. Honigmann*, eds John Batchelor, Tom Cain and Claire Lamont. Basingstoke and New York: Macmillan/St Martin's Press, 1997, 259–74.

Benshoff, Harry M. and Sean Griffin. *Queer Images: A History of Gay and Lesbian Film in America*. Lanham, MD: Rowman & Littlefield, 2006.

Berry, Edward. 'Laughing at "Others"'. In *The Cambridge Companion to Shakespearean Comedy*, ed. Alexander Leggatt. Cambridge and New York: Cambridge University Press, 2002.

Black, Gregory D. 'Who Controls What We See? Censorship and the Attack on Hollywood "Immorality"'. In *Movies and American Society*, ed. Steven J. Ross. Oxford and Malden, MA: Blackwell, 2002, Ch. 4, 98–127.

Boehrer, Bruce Thomas. 'Bestial Buggery in *A Midsummer Night's Dream*'. In *The Production of English Renaissance Culture*, eds David Lee Miller, Sharon O'Dair and Harold Weber. Ithaca and London: Cornell University Press, 1994, 123–50.

Bray, Alan. *Homosexuality in Renaissance England*. New York: Columbia University Press, 1982, 1995.

Bray, Alan. 'Homosexuality and the Signs of Male Friendship in Elizabethan England'. In *Queering the Renaissance*, ed. Jonathan Goldberg. Durham and London: Duke University Press, 1994.

Buchanan, Judith. *Shakespeare on Silent Film: An Excellent Dumb Discourse*. Cambridge and New York: Cambridge University Press, 2007.

Burt, Richard. 'No Holes Bard: Homonormativity and the Gay and Lesbian Romance with *Romeo and Juliet*'. In *Shakespeare Without Class: Misappropriations of Cultural Capital*, eds Donald Hedrick and Bryan Reynolds. New York: Palgrave, 2000, 153–86.

Burt, Richard. 'The Love That Dare Not Speak Shakespeare's Name: New Shakesqueer Cinema'. In *Unspeakable ShaXXXspeares: Queer Theory and American Kiddie Culture*. New York: St Martin's Press, 1998, Ch. 1, 29–75.

Burt, Richard. *Unspeakable ShaXXXspeares: Queer Theory and American Kiddie Culture*. New York: St Martin's Press, 1998.

Bury, Shirley. 'Preface'. *Earrings: From Antiquity to the Present*, Daniela Mascetti and Amanda Triossi. London: Thames & Hudson, 1990, 7–8.

Butler, Judith. *Gender Trouble: Feminism and the Subversion of Identity*. New York: Routledge, 1990, 2007.

Butler, Judith. 'Imitation and Gender Insubordination'. In *Feminist Literary Theory and Criticism: A Norton Reader*, eds Sandra M. Gilbert and Susan Gubar. New York and London: W. W. Norton, 2007. 708–22.

Chedgzoy, Kate. '"The Past is Our Mirror": Marlowe, Shakespeare, Jarman'. In *Shakespeare's Queer Children: Sexual Politics and Contemporary Culture*. Manchester and New York: Manchester University Press, 1995, Ch. 5, 177–221.

Clayton, Tom. '"So Quick Bright Things Come to Confusion": Or, What Else Was *A Midsummer Night's Dream* About?' In *Shakespeare: Text and Theater: Essays in Honor of Jay L. Halio*, eds Lois Potter and Arthur F. Kinney. Newark: University of Delaware Press and London: Associated University Presses, 1999, 62–91.

Coleridge, Samuel Taylor. *Biographia Literaria*. In *The Norton Anthology of Theory and Criticism*, Vincent B. Leitch, General Editor. New York and London: W. W. Norton, 2001, 668–82.

Coursen, H. R. *Shakespeare: The Two Traditions*. Madison, NJ: Fairleigh Dickinson University Press and London: Associated University Presses, 1999.

Crowl, Samuel. *Shakespeare at the Cineplex: The Kenneth Branagh Era*. Athens, OH: Ohio University Press, 2003.

Desmet, Christy. 'Disfiguring Women with Masculine Tropes: A Rhetorical Reading of *A Midsummer Night's Dream*'. In *A Midsummer Night's Dream: Critical Essays*, ed. Dorothea Kehler. New York and London: Routledge, 2001, 299–329.

Dollimore, Jonathan. *Sexual Dissidence: Augustine to Wilde, Freud to Foucault*. Oxford and New York: Oxford University Press, 1991.

Donaldson, Peter S. '"Let Lips Do What Hands Do": Male Bonding, Eros and Loss in Zeffirelli's *Romeo and Juliet*'. In *Shakespearean Films/Shakespearean Directors*. Boston: Unwin Hyman, 1990, Ch. 6, 145–88.

Dyer, Richard. *The Matter of Images: Essays on Representations*. London and New York: Routledge, 1993, 2002.

Elam, Keir, ed. 'Introduction'. *Twelfth Night, Or What You Will*. The Arden Shakespeare. Third Series. London: Arden Shakespeare, 2008.

Farmer, Brett. *Spectacular Passions: Cinema, Fantasy, Gay Male Spectatorships*. Durham, NC and London: Duke University Press, 2000.

Fisher, Will. *Materializing Gender in Early Modern English Literature and Culture*. Cambridge and New York: Cambridge University Press, 2006.

Foucault, Michel. *The History of Sexuality, Volume I: An Introduction*. Trans. Robert Hurley. New York: Vintage, 1978, 1990.

Fradenburg, Aranye. 'Momma's Boys'. In *Shakesqueer: A Queer Companion to the Complete Works of Shakespeare*, ed. Madhavi Menon. Durham, NC and London: Duke University Press, 2011, 319–27.

Freud, Sigmund. *Three Essays on the Theory of Sexuality* (excerpt). In *The Freud Reader*, ed. Peter Gay. New York and London: W. W. Norton, 1995, 239–92.

Garber, Marjorie. *Vested Interests: Cross-Dressing and Cultural Anxiety*. New York: Routledge, 1997.

Garner, Shirley Nelson. '*A Midsummer Night's Dream*: "Jack shall have Jill; / Nought shall go ill"'. *Women's Studies* 9 (1981): 47–63.

Gil, Daniel Juan. 'Avant-garde Technique and the Visual Grammar of Sexuality in Orson Welles's Shakespeare Films'. *Borrowers and Lenders: The Journal of Shakespeare and Appropriation* 1.2 (Fall/Winter 2005): n.p. http://www.borrowers.uga.edu/781447/display (accessed 1 February 2016).

Greenblatt, Stephen. *Renaissance Self-Fashioning: From More to Shakespeare*. Chicago: The University of Chicago Press, 1980, 1984.

Greenblatt, Stephen, ed. *A Midsummer Night's Dream*. In *The Norton Shakespeare: Based on the Oxford Edition*, second edition, eds Stephen Greenblatt et al. New York and London: W. W. Norton, 2008. 839–96.

Griffin, C. W. 'Hippolyta's Dress and Undress: Subtext and Scopophilia in *A Midsummer Night's Dream*'. *Shakespeare Bulletin* 12.2 (1994): 43–4.

Halperin, David M. *Saint Foucault: Towards a Gay Hagiography*. Oxford and New York: Oxford University Press, 1995.

Hoffman, Michael. *William Shakespeare's A Midsummer Night's Dream*. New York: Harper Paperbacks, 1999.

Holland, Peter. 'Theseus' Shadows in *A Midsummer Night's Dream*'. *Shakespeare Survey* 47 (1995): 139–51.

Howard, Jean E. 'Crossdressing, the Theatre, and Gender Struggle in Early Modern England'. *Shakespeare Quarterly* 39.4 (1988): 418–40.

Hyman, Stanley Edgar. *Iago: Some Approaches to the Illusion of his Motivation*. New York: Atheneum, 1970.

Jackson, Russell. *Shakespeare Films in the Making: Vision, Production and Reception*. Cambridge and New York: Cambridge University Press, 2007.

Jackson, Russell. *The Cambridge Companion to Shakespeare on Film*, 2nd edn. Cambridge and New York: Cambridge University Press, 2004.

Jensen, Michael P. '*A Midsummer Night's Dream*: How German Expressionism Dominated this Classical 1935 Fantasy!'. *Filmfax* 106 (2005): 104–12, 122.

Jorgens, Jack J. *Shakespeare on Film*. Lanham, MD, London and New York: University Press of America, 1991.

Kahn, Coppélia. 'The Cuckoo's Note: Male Friendship and

Cuckoldry in *The Merchant of Venice*'. In *Shakespeare's 'Rough Magic': Renaissance Essays in Honor of C. L. Barber*, eds Peter Erickson and Coppélia Kahn. Newark: University of Delaware Press, and London and Toronto: Associated University Presses, 1985, 104–12.
Kleinberg, Seymour. '*The Merchant of Venice*: The Homosexual as Anti-Semite in Nascent Capitalism'. In *Essays on Gay Literature*, ed. Stuart Kellogg. New York and Binghamton: Harrington Park Press, 1985, 113–26.
Ko, Yu Jin. *Mutability and Division on Shakespeare's Stage*. Newark: University of Delaware Press, 2004.
Kott, Jan. 'Titania and the Ass's Head'. Excerpted from *Shakespeare our Contemporary*. In *A Midsummer Night's Dream: Critical Essays*, ed. Dorothea Kehler. New York and London: Routledge, 2001, 107–25.
Lambert, Gavin. *On Cukor*, ed. Robert Trachtenberg. New York: Rizzoli International Publications, 2000.
'Law in England, 1290–1885, The'. 25 Henry VIII. C6. Fordham University. Accessed 1 October 2014. http://www.fordham.edu/halsall/pwh/englaw.asp (accessed 1 February 2016).
Lehmann, Courtney. *Screen Adaptations, Shakespeare's Romeo and Juliet: The Relationship Between Text and Film*. London: Methuen Drama, 2010.
Levine, Laura. *Men in Women's Clothing: Anti-Theatricality and Effeminization, 1579–1642*. Cambridge and New York: Cambridge University Press, 1994.
Levy, Emanuel. *George Cukor: Master of Elegance: Hollywood's Legendary Director and His Stars*. New York: William Morrow, 1994.
Lewis, Cynthia. *Particular Saints: Shakespeare's Four Antonios, Their Contexts, and Their Plays*. Newark, DE: University of Delaware Press, and London and Cranbury, NJ: Associated University Presses, 1997.
Little, Arthur L., Jr. '"An Essence That's Not Seen": The Primal Scene of Racism in *Othello*'. *Shakespeare Quarterly* 44.3 (Autumn 1993): 304–24.
Little, Arthur L., Jr. 'The Rites of Queer Marriage in *The Merchant of Venice*'. In *Shakesqueer: A Queer Companion to the Complete Works of Shakespeare*, ed. Madhavi Menon. Durham, NC and London: Duke University Press, 2011, 216–24.

Little, Arthur L., Jr. '"A Local Habitation and a Name": Presence, Witnessing, and Queer Marriage in Shakespeare's Romantic Comedies'. In *Presentism, Gender, and Sexuality in Shakespeare*, ed. Evelyn Gajowski. Houndmills and New York: Palgrave Macmillan, 2009. 207–36.

Loehlin, James N., ed. *Romeo and Juliet, Shakespeare in Production*. Cambridge and New York: Cambridge University Press, 2002.

MacLiammóir, Micheál. *Put Money in Thy Purse: The Diary of the Film of Othello*. London: Methuen, 1952.

MacQueen, Scott. 'Midsummer Dream, Midwinter Nightmare: Max Reinhardt and Shakespeare Versus the Warner Bros'. *The Moving Image* 9.2 (2009): 30–103.

Magnus, Laury. 'Michael Radford's *The Merchant of Venice* and the Vexed Question of Performance'. *Literature/Film Quarterly* 35.2 (2007): 108–20.

Magro, Maria F. and Mark Douglas. 'Reflections on Sex, Shakespeare and Nostalgia in Trevor Nunn's *Twelfth Night*'. In *Retrovisions: Reinventing the Past in Film and Fiction*, eds Deborah Cartmell, I.Q. Hunter and Imelda Whelan. London and Sterling, VA: Pluto Press, 2001, 41–58.

Matz, Robert. 'Slander, Renaissance Discourses of Sodomy, and *Othello*'. *ELH* 66.2 (Summer 1999): 261–76.

McGilligan, Patrick. *George Cukor: A Double Life*. New York: St Martin's Press, 1991.

Menon, Madhavi. 'Introduction'. *Shakesqueer: A Queer Companion to the Complete Works of Shakespeare,* ed. Madhavi Menon. Durham and London: Duke University Press, 2011.

Menon, Madhavi. *Unhistorical Shakespeare: Queer Theory in Shakespearean Literature and Film*. New York: Palgrave Macmillan, 2008.

Montrose, Louis Adrian. '*A Midsummer Night's Dream* and the Shaping Fantasies of Elizabethan Culture: Gender, Power, Form'. In *Rewriting the Renaissance: The Discourses of Sexual Difference in Early Modern Europe*, eds Margaret W. Ferguson, Maureen Quilligan and Nancy J. Vickers. Chicago and London: University of Chicago Press, 1986, 65–87.

Moore, Helen. "Present and Correct?" Rev. of *Shakespeare, Race and Colonialism, Shakespeare in the Present, The Sound of*

Shakespeare, and *Shakespeare's Perfume: Sodomy and Sublimity in the Sonnets, Wilde, Freud and Lacan*. Times Literary Supplement *(TLS)* 5237 (15 August 2003): 22.

Mulvey, Laura. 'Visual Pleasure and Narrative Cinema'. In *The Film Theory Reader: Debates and Arguments*, ed. Marc Furstenau. London and New York: Routledge, 2010, 200–8.

Nunn, Trevor. *William Shakespeare's Twelfth Night: A Screenplay*. London: Methuen Drama, 1996.

Nuttall, A. D. '*A Midsummer Night's Dream*: Comedy as Apotrope of Myth'. *Shakespeare Survey* 53 (2000): 49–59.

Orgel, Stephen. 'Shakespeare Illustrated'. In *The Cambridge Companion to Shakespeare and Popular Culture*, ed. Robert Shaughnessy. Cambridge and New York: Cambridge University Press, 2007, 67–92.

Orgel, Stephen. *Impersonations: The Performance of Gender in Shakespeare's England*. Cambridge and New York: Cambridge University Press, 1996.

Othello. DVD. Directed by Orson Welles. 1952; New York: Castle Hill Productions and BWE Video, 2003.

Othello. DVD. Directed by Oliver Parker. 1995; Burbank, CA: Warner Home Video, 1995.

Park, William. *What is Film Noir?* Lewisburg, PA: Bucknell University Press, 2011.

Paster, Gail Kern. *The Body Embarrassed: Drama and the Disciplines of Shame in Early Modern England*. Ithaca: Cornell University Press, 1993.

Patricia, Anthony Guy. '"Say how I loved you": Queering the Emotion of Male Same-Sex Love in *The Merchant of Venice*'. In *Shakespeare and Emotions: Inheritances, Enactments, Legacies*, eds R. S. White, Mark Houlahan and Katrina O'Loughlin. Basingstoke and New York: Palgrave Macmillan, 2015, 116–23.

Patricia, Anthony Guy. '"Through the Eyes of the Present": Screening the Male Homoerotics of Shakespearean Drama'. In *Presentism, Gender, and Sexuality in Shakespeare*, ed. Evelyn Gajowski. Basingstoke and New York: Palgrave Macmillan, 2009, 157–78.

Pearce, Craig and Baz Luhrmann. *William Shakespeare's Romeo and Juliet, The Contemporary Film and the Classic Play*. New York: Bantam Doubleday Dell, 1996.

Pequigney, Joseph. 'The Two Antonios and Same-Sex Love in

Twelfth Night and *The Merchant of Venice'*. In *Shakespeare and Gender: A History*, eds Deborah E. Barker and Ivo Kamps. London and New York: Verso, 1995, 178–95.

Perry, Curtis. *Literature and Favoritism in Early Modern England*. Cambridge and New York: Cambridge University Press, 2006.

Porter, Joseph A. *Shakespeare's Mercutio: His History and Drama*. Chapel Hill, NC and London: The University of North Carolina Press, 1988.

Potter, Lois. *Shakespeare in Performance: Othello*. Manchester and New York: Manchester University Press, 2002.

Private Romeo. DVD. Directed by Alan Brown. 2011; San Jose, CA: Wolfe Video, 2011.

Rackin, Phyllis. 'Androgyny, Mimesis, and the Marriage of the Boy Heroine on the English Renaissance Stage'. *PMLA* 102.1 (1987): 29–41.

Radel, Nicholas F. 'The Ethiop's Ear: Race, Sexuality, and Baz Luhrmann's *William Shakespeare's Romeo + Juliet'*. *Upstart Crow* 28 *(2009):* 17–34.

Radford, Michael, dir. *William Shakespeare's The Merchant of Venice*. Sony Pictures Classics, 2004. DVD.

Rambuss, Richard. 'Shakespeare's Ass Play'. In *Shakesqueer: A Queer Companion to the Complete Works of Shakespeare*, ed. Madhavi Menon. Durham and London: Duke University Press, 2011, 234–44.

Rich, Adrienne. 'Compulsory Heterosexuality and Lesbian Existence'. In *Feminism in our Time: The Essential Writings, World War II to the Present*, ed. Miriam Schneir. New York: Vintage, 1994, 310–28.

Romeo + Juliet. DVD. Directed by Baz Luhrmann. 1996; Los Angeles, CA: 20th Century Fox, 1996.

Romeo and Juliet. DVD. Directed by George Cukor. 1936; Burbank, CA: Warner Home Video, 2007.

Romeo and Juliet. DVD. Directed by Franco Zeffirelli. 1968; Hollywood, CA: Paramount Pictures, 2013.

Rothwell, Kenneth S. *A History of Shakespeare on Screen: A Century of Film and Television*, 2nd edn. Cambridge and New York: Cambridge University Press, 2004.

Saunders, Ben. 'Iago's Clyster: Purgation, Anality, and the Civilizing Process'. *Shakespeare Quarterly* 55.2 (Summer 2004): 148–76.

Schalkwyk, David. *Shakespeare, Love and Service*. Cambridge and New York: Cambridge University Press, 2008.

Sedgwick, Eve Kosofsky. *Between Men: English Literature and Male Homosocial Desire*. New York: Columbia University Press, 1985.

Shakespeare, William. *Romeo and Juliet*. The Arden Shakespeare. Third Series, ed. René Weis. London: Methuen Drama/Bloomsbury, 2012.

Shakespeare, William. *Shakespeare's Sonnets*, 2nd rev. edn. The Arden Shakespeare. Third Series, ed. Katherine Duncan-Jones. Methuen Drama/A&C Black 1997, 2010.

Shakespeare, William. *The Merchant of Venice*. The Arden Shakespeare. Third Series, ed. John Drakakis. London: Methuen Drama/A&C Black, 2010.

Shakespeare, William. *Twelfth Night, Or What You Will*. The Arden Shakespeare. Third Series, ed. Keir Elam. London: Arden Shakespeare, 2008.

Shakespeare, William. *King Henry V*. The Arden Shakespeare. Third Series, ed. T. W. Craik. Thompson Learning: London, 1995, 2005.

Shakespeare, William. *Othello*. The Arden Shakespeare. Third Series, ed. E. A. J. Honigmann. London: Thomson Learning, 1997.

Shakespeare, William. *A Midsummer Night's Dream. The Arden Shakespeare*. Second series, ed. Harold F. Brooks. London: Thomson Learning, 1979.

Shakespeare, William. *Macbeth. The Arden Shakespeare*. Second series, ed. Kenneth Muir. London and Cambridge, MA: Methuen and Harvard University Press, 1951.

Sinfield, Alan. 'How to Read *The Merchant of Venice* Without Being Heterosexist'. In *Shakespeare, Authority, Sexuality: Unfinished Business in Cultural Materialism*. London and New York: Routledge, 2006, Ch. 4.

Smith, Bruce R. *Shakespeare and Masculinity*. Oxford and New York: Oxford University Press, 2000.

Smith, Bruce R. *Homosexual Desire in Shakespeare's England: A Cultural Poetics*. Chicago and London: The University of Chicago Press, 1991.

Steinbach, Ronald D. *The Fashionable Ear: A History of Ear-Piercing Trends for Men and Women*. New York: Vantage Press, 1995.

Summers, Joseph H. *Dreams of Love and Power: On Shakespeare's Plays*. Oxford: Clarendon Press, 1984.
Taylor, A. B. 'Ovid's Myths and the Unsmooth Course of Love in *A Midsummer Night's Dream*'. In *Shakespeare and the Classics*, eds Charles Martindale and A. B. Taylor. Cambridge and New York: Cambridge University Press, 2004, 49–65.
'*The Merchant of Venice:* Shakespeare Through the Lens'. *William Shakespeare's The Merchant of Venice*. DVD. Director Michael Radford. Sony Home Pictures Entertainment, 2004.
'The Production Code'. In *Movies and Mass Culture*, ed. John Belton. New Brunswick, NJ: Rutgers University Press, 1996, 135–52.
Traub, Valerie. 'The Homoerotics of Shakespearean Comedy (*As You Like It, Twelfth Night*)'. Ch. 5 of *Desire and Anxiety: Circulations of Sexuality in Shakespearean Drama*. London and New York: Routledge, 1992. 117–44.
Twelfth Night. DVD. Directed by Trevor Nunn. 1996; Burbank, CA: Warner Home Video, 1996.
Van Watson, William. 'Shakespeare, Zeffirelli, and the Homosexual Gaze'. In *Shakespeare and Gender: A History*, eds Deborah Barker and Ivo Kamps. London and New York: Verso, 1995, 235–62.
Varnado, Christine. '"Invisible Sex!": What Looks Like the Act in Early Modern Drama'. In *Sex Before Sex: Figuring the Act in Early Modern England*, eds James M. Bromley and Will Stockton. Minneapolis and London: University of Minnesota Press, 2013.
William Shakespeare's A Midsummer Night's Dream. DVD. Directed by Michael Hoffman. 1999; Los Angeles, CA: Fox Searchlight Pictures, 1999.
William Shakespeare's The Merchant of Venice. DVD. Directed by Michael Radford. 2004; Culver City, CA: Sony Pictures Home Entertainment, 2004.
Willson, Jr, Robert F. *Shakespeare in Hollywood, 1929–1956*. Madison/Teaneck, NJ and London: Fairleigh Dickinson University Press and Associated University Presses, 2000.
Wyrick, Deborah. 'The Ass Motif in *The Comedy of Errors* and *A Midsummer Night's Dream*'. *Shakespeare Quarterly* 33 (1982): 432–48.
Zeffirelli, Franco. *Zeffirelli: The Autobiography of Franco Zeffirelli*. New York: Weidenfeld & Nicolson, 1986.

INDEX

a word and a blow (*William Shakespeare's Romeo + Juliet*) 115
abnormal/ity 8, 45, 202
Achilles 117
active 58, 60, 63, 66
adaptation/s xx–xxi, xxvii, 2, 4, 9, 25, 30, 37, 43, 54, 56, 68, 82, 84–5, 90, 109, 138, 174, 182, 190, 230 n.5, 237 n.29, 253
Adelman, Janet 140, 240 n.9, 249
Adler, Renata 55, 216, 232 n.39, 249
adult/child eroticism 29–30
adulterous 28
adultery 188, 209–10
Adventures of Priscilla, Queen of the Desert, The (Film, dir. Stephan Elliot, 1994) 110
affection/s/ate 36, 56, 70–1, 81, 113, 142, 144, 148, 151, 165, 171, 214
affective/ly 45, 155, 165–6, 170, 177, 197
agency 65, 138, 214
albatross 113
Alexander, Ross (Demetrius; *A Midsummer Night's Dream*; 1935) ix, 32, 34

all-male (sauna) xxiv, 74–5, 87, 97, 185, 196–7, 200–1, 219
Amazon/ian/s 3, 6, 32, 225 n.25
America/n xiv–xv, xvii, xxi, 1, 73, 90, 190, 192, 197, 201, 206, 214, 215, 221 n.8, 222 n.2, 230 n.10, 237 n.33, 245 n.39, 246 n.1, 247, 249, 250
anachronism 68, 115, 186
anal penetration 63
anality 30, 63, 66–7, 244 n.12, 256
anal-retentive 186
anatomizes 199
Ancient Assyria 50
Anderegg, Michael 190
androgynous 161
Anger, Kenneth 226 n.36
Anglophone xxii, 28, 219
anthropomorphic 21
antiquity 21, 119, 131, 231 n.27, 250
anti-Semitism 138
antisocial 198
Antonio (character; *The Merchant of Venice*) xxv, 135–7, 139–42, 144–6, 153–60, 217–18, 239

n.1, 242 n.30, 243 n.39, 253, 255
Antonio (character, *Twelfth Night*) xxv, 135–7, 160–74, 176–7, 217–18, 239 nn.1–2, 242 nn.25, 28–30, 243 n.39, 253, 255
Antonio (Jeremy Irons; *The Merchant of Venice*, 2004) x–xi, xxvi, 137, 139, 140–60, 178, 179, 217, 218
Antonio (Nicholas Farrell; *Twelfth Night*, 1996) xi, xxvi, 103, 137, 160–77, 217–18, 242 n.29
anus 63, 186, 244 n.14
apes 21
Appleman, Hale (Cadet Neff; *Private Romeo*, 2011) 77
art/ful/ist/istic 2, 42–4, 49, 56, 73, 119, 186, 192
artificial construction 95
As You Like It (Play) 125, 136, 239 n.1
Ashurnasirpal II (883–859 BC) 50
ass xxiii, 16, 21, 23, 25–8, 30, 38, 225 n.31, 226 n.44, 228 nn.61, 65, 68, 253, 256, 258
Athenian/s xxv, 4, 10, 11, 124
Athens xxiii, 4–6, 10, 14, 18, 31–2, 119, 123, 130, 131, 225 n.25, 240 n.14
aubade 56, 68, 81, 216
audience/s ix, xx, 1, 2, 5, 8, 10, 14, 19, 25, 29, 31, 46, 48, 52, 53, 57, 61, 62, 67–71, 73, 77, 81–2, 85–6, 90–2, 95, 98, 100, 103, 113, 118–19, 122, 124–30, 132, 142, 149, 155, 159, 162, 166, 175, 177, 178, 182, 197
Aurora 18, 19
auteur 196

Babbington, Bruce 14, 37, 38, 226 nn.36–7, 229 n.78, 249
Baedeker Guidebook to Illyria 167
Bakhtin, Mikhail 124
Bale, Christian (Demetrius; *A Midsummer Night's Dream*, 1999) 128
Balthazar (Keith Skinner; *Romeo and Juliet*, 1968) 57
Balthazar (Lynn Collins; *William Shakespeare's The Merchant of Venice*, 2004) 157, 159
Barrymore, John (Mercutio; *Romeo and Juliet*; 1936) ix, 43, 44, 48, 50, 51, 52
Bassanio (character, *The Merchant of Venice*) xxv, 136, 139–42, 144–7, 149–60, 179, 217–18
Bassanio (Joseph Fiennes; *The Merchant of Venice*, 2004) x–xi, xxv–xxvi, 139–60, 177–9, 217–18
Batchelor, John 226 n.36

bathhouse/s 201
bawdy 115, 204, 242
bears 21
beast 21, 22
Belmont 145, 146, 147, 149, 150, 152, 153, 154, 156, 177, 179, 218
Belton, John 247, 258
Benshoff, Harry M. 44, 197, 203, 230 n.10, 245 n.39, 247 n.1, 249
Benvolio (Bruce Robinson; *Romeo and Juliet*, 1968) 66, 86
Benvolio (Dash Mihok; *Romeo + Juliet*, 1996) 114
Benvolio (Reginald Denny; *Romeo and Juliet*; 1936) ix, 48, 49, 215
Benvolio/Gus Sanchez (Sean Hudock; *Private Romeo*, 2011) 77
Berry, Edward 124, 125, 130, 238, 249
best friend/s x, 108, 109, 117, 118
bestial/ity xxiii, 21–5, 28–9, 30, 39, 188, 215, 227 nn.49, 51, 57, 228 nn.65, 66, 69, 249
betrothal/ed 152, 154, 225 n.25
Big Bad Wolf 112
big death 72
bigamist/ous/y 28, 30, 215
biological sex/es 75, 89, 94, 111, 132, 217
Birdcage, The (Film, dir. Mike Nichols, 1996) 110
bisexual/ity xxiii, 18, 24, 55, 111, 113, 116, 151, 211, 219
bitchy wit 192, 194, 195
black (ram) ix, xix, 4, 5, 6, 39, 54, 61, 93, 107, 109, 110, 157, 161, 163, 170, 178, 188
Black, Gregory D. 213, 214, 246 n.1, 249
blood vow 205
blow/s 149, 238 n.43
BMBC (British Mutoscope and Biograph Company) xvii
boars 21
Boehrer, Bruce Thomas 22–4, 28–30, 227 nn.49, 51, 57, 228 nn.65, 66, 249
Bollywood xxi
Boston Globe 48
Boswell, John 207, 246 n.46
Bottom (character, *A Midsummer Night's Dream*) xxiii, 25–9, 37–8
Bottom/Pyramus (James Cagney; *A Midsummer Night's Dream*, 1935) 2, 16, 20–9, 38–9, 227 n.59
Bottom/Pyramus (Kevin Kline; *A Midsummer Night's Dream*, 1999) 119–23, 129, 131–2
Bottom's Wife (Heather Elizabeth Parisi; *A Midsummer Night's Dream*, 1999) 119
boy actor/s xix, 93, 94, 124, 125, 131
boys 17, 19, 94, 226 n.40, 251
Branagh, Kenneth (Iago;

Othello, 1995) xi, xviii,
  131, 202, 206, 208, 211,
  238 n.55, 251
Bray, Alan 23–4, 28, 142, 149,
  151, 154, 171, 189, 227
  nn.52, 54, 241 n.17,
  249, 250
Brindisi 119
British Museum 50
British Mutoscope and
  Biograph Company
  (BMBC) xvii
Brooks, Harold F. 224 n.15,
  238 n.46, 257
brothel/s 171
Brown, Alan (dir. *Private
  Romeo*, 2011) ix–x, xxiv,
  42, 73–8, 80–4, 87, 213,
  219, 234 n.83, 256
Brown, Sheila (Changeling Boy;
  *A Midsummer Night's
  Dream*, 1935) 14, 226
  n.36
Buchanan, Judith xvii, 221 n.1,
  250
bugger/y 22–4, 28, 227 nn.49,
  57, 228 nn.65, 66, 69, 249
Buggery Act 21–3
Buhler, Stephen M. xx
bulls 21
Burnett, Mark Thornton xx
Burt, Richard xix, xxi, 43–6,
  49, 52, 84–7, 109, 215,
  221 n.8, 230 nn.9, 17,
  231 nn.26, 33, 235 n.91,
  237 n.33, 250
Burton, Richard 53
Bury, Shirley 49, 50, 231 n.27,
  250
Busby Berkeley 107

Butler, Judith 75–6, 95, 111,
  114, 217, 234, 236, 237
  nn.34, 39, 250
buttocks 69

Cadet Neff (Hale Appleman;
  Private Romeo, 2011) 77
Cagney, James (Bottom/
  Pyramus; *A Midsummer
  Night's Dream*, 1935) 2,
  223 n.3
Caliban (character, *The
  Tempest*) 125
Captain (Sid Livingstone;
  Twelfth Night, 1996)
  91–3, 96
Capulet Ball 77, 107, 110
Capulet's Wife (character,
  Romeo and Juliet) 76
Carlei, Carlo 41
Carter, Helena Bonham
  (Countess Olivia; *Twelfth
  Night*, 1996) 92, 175
Cassio (character, *Othello*)
  183, 185–9, 197, 199,
  218, 244 n.14
Cassio (Michael Laurence;
  Othello, 1955) 200–1,
  218
Cassio (Nathaniel Parker;
  Othello, 1995) 202–4,
  209, 218
Cassio's dream 185, 188
castration 63
catamite 23
Catholic Church 192, 215
cats 21
*Celluloid Closet:
  Homosexuality in the
  Movies, The* 246 n.1

Cephalus 18–19
changeling boy (character, *A Midsummer Night's Dream*) 12–14, 18–19, 20
changeling boy (Sheila Brown; *A Midsummer Night's Dream*, 1935) 14–16, 19–20, 25, 30, 38–9
Chedgzoy, Kate xix–xx, 221 n.7, 250
child abusive 28
child-love 30
Chimes at Midnight (dir. Orson Welles, 1965) 198
Christ 167
Christian/s 4, 22, 125, 138, 167, 186, 210
cinaedus 23
cinematography 2, 192, 213
Cinthio 183–4
classical 6, 11, 23, 70, 228 n.60, 252
claustrophobic 191
Clautier, Suzanne (Desdemona; *Othello*, 1952) 195
Clayton, Tom 6–7, 12, 17, 224 n.17, 225 nn.26, 33, 226 n.41, 250
clyster-pipes 186–7
codpiece 61, 64–6, 69
Coleridge, Samuel Taylor 76, 218, 234 n.89, 250
Collins, Lynn (Portia; *The Merchant of Venice*, 2004) 139
Columbine 182
Come Away Death 101
compulsory heterosexuality xx, xxii, 8–10, 118, 138, 224 n.21, 225 n.25, 256

Constitutional 206
contained/ment 11, 118, 126
continuum 2, 74
Coote, Robert (Roderigo; *Othello*, 1952) xi, 194, 200
Cordelia (character, *King Lear*) 83
costume/s 4, 9, 43, 45, 47, 51, 54, 91, 94, 122, 127, 191, 193, 214
Count Orsino's court 165
Countess Olivia (Helena Bonham Carter; *Twelfth Night*, 1996) xxiv, xxvi, 92, 97, 100–1, 172, 175
Coursen, H. R. 91, 96, 174, 175, 235 n.3, 236 n.11, 242 n.36, 251
Cox, Charlie (Lorenzo; *The Merchant of Venice*, 2004) 142
Craik, T. W. 236 n.19, 257
crime/s xxiii, 22–4, 28, 190–1, 214
Cromwell, Thomas 21–3
cross-dress/es 78, 107
crossdressing 233 n.64, 237 n.35, 251
Crowl, Samuel 131, 132, 238 n.55, 251
Crying Game, The (Film, dir. Neil Jordan, 1992) 110
cuckold/ed/ing/ry 187, 209, 240 n.10, 253
Cukor, George (dir. *Romeo and Juliet*, 1936) ix, xxiii–xxiv, 42–55, 72–4, 85–7, 106–7, 211, 215, 219, 230–1, 234, 253–4, 256

Cypriot xi, 200, 201
Cyprus 181, 186, 191, 204–5

damsel 172
debauchery 24
decadence 192, 200
deconstruction 60, 75, 132
Demetrius (Christian Bale; *A Midsummer Night's Dream*, 1999) 128, 130
Demetrius (Ross Alexander; *A Midsummer Night's Dream*, 1935) ix, xxiii, 10, 31–6
demonic semen 209
Denny, Reginald (Benvolio; *Romeo and Juliet*; 1936) ix, 48–9
Desdemona (character, *Othello*) 174, 183, 185–9, 209, 210, 244 n.14
Desdemona (Irène Jacob; *Othello*, 1995) 202, 204, 207
Desdemona (Suzanne Clautier; *Othello*, 1952) 191, 194–5, 198
Desmet, Christy 18, 226 n.42, 251
detritus 186
deviant/s 34, 112, 137, 149, 187, 198
DiCaprio, Leonardo (Romeo; *Romeo + Juliet*, 1996) x, 107, 118
Dieterle, William (dir. *A Midsummer Night's Dream*, 1935) vii, ix, xxii, xxiii, 1–5, 8–12, 14–16, 18–21, 23–5, 27–30, 32–9, 42, 123–5, 130–1, 211, 213, 215, 219, 222 n.1, 224 nn.12, 15, 25, 226 n.36, 227 n.59, 249
DiPietro, Cary 222 n.9
discordant 4, 9
disidentification 68
displace/d/ment 20, 106, 114, 140, 189
distrust of elders 55
Dollimore, Jonathan 53, 231 n.34, 251
Donaldson, Peter S. xx, 55, 56, 57, 58, 59, 231 n.37, 232 nn.43, 47, 251
Douglas, Mark xxi, 95, 176, 236 n.10, 242 n.37, 254
Doyle, Matt (Glenn Mangan/ Juliet; *Private Romeo*, 2011) ix, x, 77, 80, 83
drag 127
drag queen xxiv, 107, 110, 112, 124, 217
Drakakis, John 240 n.6, 257
duchess 10, 119, 126–7
duke 6, 10, 33, 92
Duke of Exeter (character, *Henry V*) 104
Duke of York (character, *Henry V*) 104
Duke Orsino (Toby Stephens; *Twelfth Night*, 1996) x, 93, 95–103, 105, 157, 165, 167, 173
Duke Theseus (David Strathairn; *William Shakespeare's A Midsummer Night's Dream*, 1999) 119, 126–7, 156

Duncan-Jones, Katherine 241 n.19, 257
dupe 205
Dyer, Richard 191–4, 196, 245 nn.30, 38, 251
dysfunctional episode 69

Earl of Suffolk (character, *Henry V*) 104
earring(s) ix, 49–51, 231 n.27, 250
economic circumstances 208
Edgar (character, *King Lear*) 83
educational opportunities 208
effeminacy 36, 52, 116, 193, 215, 229 n.77
effeminate/ly/s xi, xxiii, 32, 34–7, 52, 117, 194, 211
Egeus (Grant Mitchell; *A Midsummer Night's Dream*, 1935) 31–3
Eisenhower 190
Elam, Keir 90, 92, 98, 99, 100, 103, 104, 105, 162, 163, 164, 165, 166, 167, 168, 169, 170, 171, 172, 173, 235 nn.1, 5, 236 n.7, 241 n.23, 242 nn.24, 32, 251, 257
Elephant, The 170–2, 242 n.32
Elizabethan 5, 24–5, 28, 41, 54, 106, 115, 149, 155, 171, 182, 225 n.27, 227 n.54, 241 n.17, 250, 254
Ellis, Havelock 36
Ellis, Jim xix
Emilia (Anna Patrick; *Othello*, 1995) 207, 209
Emilia (character, *Othello*) 185, 209

empathy 209
enema tubes 186
enforced marriage 8
engaged 152
ensign 188, 199
Erickson, Peter 240 nn.9, 10, 249, 253
eros xx, 96, 231 n.37, 251
erotic/ally/ises/ized 13–16, 18, 21, 30, 37–9, 45, 58–63, 65–6, 68–9, 74, 81, 98, 112, 144, 148, 153, 155, 163, 177, 187, 189, 197, 205, 210–11, 225 n.35
eroticism xxiii, 12, 13, 20, 29, 30, 37, 38, 39, 160
Euripides 225 n.30
Europe/an 22, 50, 189, 197, 207, 210, 246 n.46, 254
evil 186–7, 209, 211, 218–19
exhibitionist 58–9
expressionistic camera work 191
extreme means 156, 158

Fabian (Peter Gunn; *Twelfth Night*, 1996) 172–3
fag hags 52
Fairy in Titania's Service (Nina Theilade; *A Midsummer Night's Dream*, 1935) 14
fairy king/dom xxiii, 12, 16, 18–20, 29–30, 33, 39
fairy queen 12, 14–16, 18, 25, 28, 30
falsetto 32, 34, 37, 115, 122, 127, 129
Falstaff (character, *The Merry Wives of Windsor*, *Henry IV Parts 1 and 2*) 125

fantasmatic 60–3, 65, 67–8
Farmer, Brett 59–60, 62–3, 232 n.52, 233 n.57, 251
Farrell, Nicholas (Antonio; *Twelfth Night*, 1996) xi, 103, 160, 163–4, 168
fellatio 115–16
Fellowes, Julian 41
feminine gender 94
feminism xxii, 132, 182, 222 n.9, 224 n.21, 236 n.9, 250, 256
Fernie, Ewan 222 n.9
Feste (Ben Kingsley; *Twelfth Night*, 1996) 101, 103, 161, 175
fetish/ization/ized/izes 12, 65, 111
Fiennes, Joseph (Bassanio; *The Merchant of Venice*, 2004) x, xi, 139, 148, 150, 160
film noir xxvii, 190–4, 196, 245 n.28, 255
fine dining 193
First Duke of Buckingham (George Villiers) 51
First Folio 91
Fishburne, Laurence (Othello; *Othello*, 1995) xi, 202, 206, 208, 211
Fisher, Gregor (Solanio; *The Merchant of Venice*, 2004) 159
Fisher, Will 64, 233 n.65, 251
flashback 191
Flockhart, Calista (Helena; *A Midsummer Night's Dream*, 1999) 119, 128
Florentine 199

Food and Drug Administration (United States) 216
forbidden love 47, 86
Foucauldian 112
Foucault, Michel 24, 34, 76, 184, 224 n.20, 227 n.56, 231 n.34, 251–2
Fradenburg, Aranye 15–16, 226 n.40, 251
Francis Flute/Thisbe (Sam Rockwell; *A Midsummer Night's Dream*, 1999) x, xxv, 120–1, 217
Freud, Sigmund xxvii, 15, 26, 38, 199, 222 n.9, 226 n.39, 231 n.34, 251, 255
Freudian xxvi, 63, 184, 186, 188, 201
Friar Laurence (Adam Barrie; *Private Romeo*, 2011) 83
Friar Laurence (Milo O'Shea; *Romeo and Juliet*, 1968) 67
Friedman, Michael D. xx
Friel, Anna (Hermia; *A Midsummer Night's Dream*, 1999) 128

G/ganymede 18, 23
Gajowski, Evelyn v, xiii, xv, 222 n.9, 223 n.10, 228 n.64, 239 n.3, 243 n.41, 254–5
Galen 35
gangsta rap 106
Garber, Marjorie 64, 111–13, 126, 233 n.64, 237 n.35, 238 n.53, 251
Garner, Shirley Nelson 12, 13,

20, 29, 225 nn.32, 34, 228 n.67, 251
gay xxiii–xxiv, 3, 18, 24, 44–6, 52, 54, 59–61, 65, 67, 69, 82, 84–5, 87, 104, 109, 111–14, 116, 126, 139, 150–1, 171, 178, 187, 192–4, 196–7, 201, 211, 219, 224 n.20, 230 nn.9, 10, 241 n.15, 245 n.39, 246 n.1, 247 n.1, 249–50, 252–3
gay and lesbian studies xxiii–xxiv, 132, 222 n.9
gay desire 52, 85
gay director 73, 215
gay drag queen 107
gay film spectatorship iii, vii, xxii, xxiv, 41, 60, 61, 62, 63, 229, 232 n.52, 251
gay male crossdresser 110
gay male fantasmatic 60, 61, 67
gay male gaze 66, 67
gay male subjectivities 60
gay oppression 192
gay pornography 65
gay rights movement 51, 73, 216, 217
gay sex xx, 85
gay spectatorship 66
gay subject 62, 63, 65
gay utopian fantasy 84, 87
gay writer 73
gayness 43, 44, 45, 46, 52
gaze xxi, 52, 58–9, 61, 66–7, 69–70, 79, 141, 207, 232 n.56, 233 n.70, 258
gender vii, xv, xxii, xxiv, 1, 3–4, 35–6, 39, 44, 49, 51, 56, 60–1, 64, 75–6, 78–9, 85, 87, 89, 91, 94–5, 100, 102, 105, 107, 110–12, 114, 122, 126, 129, 130, 132–3, 148, 160, 182–4, 194, 201, 217, 222, 222 n.9, 223 n.10, 228 nn.64, 70, 229 n.77, 232 n.56, 233 n.65, 234 n.87, 236 n.17, 237 nn.34, 39, 239 nn.1, 3, 243 n.41, 250–6, 258
gender bending 132, 161
gender conventions 208
gender identity 57, 95, 132
gender trouble iii, vii, xxii, xxiv–xxv, 89, 90, 91, 96, 97, 99, 108, 109, 118, 120, 126, 132, 215, 217, 235, 236 n.9
gender undecidability 64
gendered 20, 111
gendered self 111
generosity 154
genital homosexuality 3
genital/s 13, 35, 36, 48, 64, 92
genitalia 200
George Villiers (First Duke of Buckingham) 51
Gibson, Mel 54
Gil, Daniel Juan xxi, 198–200, 245 n.41, 252
Glenn Mangan/Juliet (Matt Doyle; *Private Romeo*, 2011) ix–x, 77–83
Goldberg, Jonathan xix, 227 n.54, 241 n.17, 250
government policies 208
Grady, Hugh 222 n.9
Grant, Richard E. (Sir Andrew

Aguecheek; *Twelfth Night*, 1996) 172
Graziano (Kris Marshall; *The Merchant of Venice*, 2004) 141, 153–4, 178
Greek etymology 13
Greek mythology 11
Greek warrior 31
Greenblatt, Stephen 18, 183, 207–10, 226 n.43, 252
Griffin, C. W. 4, 6, 8–9, 224 nn.13, 19, 22, 252
Griffin, Sean 44, 46, 197, 203, 230 n.10, 245 n.39, 247 n.1, 249
grotesque xx, 38, 188, 207, 228 n.61
Gunn, Peter (Fabian; *Twelfth Night*, 1996) 172
Gus Sanchez/Benvolio (Sean Hudock; *Private Romeo*, 2011) 77

Hall, Peter 123–5, 130, 224 n.12
Hall, Savannah v
Halperin, David M. 8, 38, 224 n.20, 252
Hamlet (Film, dir. Franco Zeffirelli, 1990) 54
Hamlet (Play) 181, 243 n.1
Harlow, Jean 107
Havilland, Olivia de (Hermia; *A Midsummer Night's Dream*, 1935) 60
Hawkes, Terence 222 n.9
Hawthorne, Nathaniel 4
Hawthorne, Nigel (Malvolio; *Twelfth Night*, 1996) 175

Hays Code 214–15
Hays, William Harrison 214
Hecatomithi 183
Hector 117
hegemonic 112, 184
Helena (Calista Flockhart; *A Midsummer Night's Dream*, 1999) 128, 130
Helena (Jean Muir; *A Midsummer Night's Dream*, 1935) 10, 31–3
Henry V (Play) xix, 104, 236 n.19, 257
heritage 119, 197
Hermia (Anna Friel; *A Midsummer Night's Dream*, 1999) 127, 130
Hermia (character, *A Midsummer Night's Dream*) 240 n.14
Hermia (Olivia de Havilland; *A Midsummer Night's Dream*, 1935) 10, 32, 33, 37
Hermione (character, *The Winter's Tale*) 124
Hester Prynne (character; Hawthorne novel, *The Scarlet Letter*) 4
heterocentric 8
heteroerotic 95
heteronormative xxiv, xxvi, 28–9, 62, 66, 68–9, 79, 84–7, 100–1, 114, 122, 124, 126, 132, 137, 142, 177, 179, 187, 192–6, 217
heteronormative imaginary 130
heteronormative utopia 136

heteronormativity xxi, 73, 85, 139–41, 151, 216–17
heterosexist 34, 69, 71, 76, 78, 188, 236 n.16, 257
heterosexual marriage 140
heterosexual marriage rite 206
heterosexual/ity/ized/ly xx, xxii–xxiii, xxvi–xxvii, 8–10, 19, 28, 30, 38–9, 42, 49, 52, 56, 58–9, 62–3, 69, 75, 79, 82, 84–6, 107, 109, 112–14, 118, 121, 125–6, 130, 138, 140, 144, 149, 176–8, 184–8, 224 n.21, 225 n.25, 229 n.77, 256
hiphop 106
Hippolyta (character, *A Midsummer Night's Dream*) 6, 9, 11, 31
Hippolyta (Sophie Marceau; *A Midsummer Night's Dream*, 1999) 120
Hippolyta (Verree Teasdale; *A Midsummer Night's Dream*; 1935) ix, xxiii, 3–11, 31, 39, 224 nn.13, 19, 22, 225 nn.25, 30, 227 n.59, 252
Hippolytus 11, 225 n.30
historical situation 210
History of Sexuality, The (Foucault) 184, 227 n.56, 234 n.90, 251
Hobbes, Thomas 124
Hobbesian 124–5
Holland, Peter 11, 225 n.28, 252
Hollywood B movies 190

Holocaust 138
Homer 117
homoerotic/ism/izing/s iii, viii, xv, xx–xxvi, 29–30, 48–9, 56, 59, 61, 67, 69, 70–4, 86, 91, 95–6, 98–9, 100–5, 107–9, 114, 116–18, 120, 129–32, 135–79, 185, 188–90, 194, 197, 199, 201–3, 205, 207, 211, 216–18, 229 n.77, 239, 239 nn.1, 3, 242 n.29, 255
homonormativity 84–5, 230 n.9, 250
homophobia/ic/ically xxv, 45, 58, 113–14, 116, 148, 186, 193, 202
homosexual/ity/s xx, xxi, xxiii, xxvi–xxvii, 3, 23–4, 34, 36, 42, 44–5, 47, 49, 51, 54–6, 59–61, 63, 71, 74–5, 77, 84, 86, 112–15, 126, 148, 151, 171, 176, 183–97, 199–202, 209, 211, 214, 216, 218–19, 227 nn.51, 52, 54, 232 n.56, 233 n.70, 234 n.90, 241 nn.15, 17, 243 n.40, 244 n.14, 245 n.45, 246 n.1, 247 n.1, 249, 250, 253, 257–8
homosocial/ity/ly xix, 66, 70–1, 74, 95, 107, 116–17, 146, 151, 155, 170, 189, 201–2, 218, 234 n.85, 257
Honigmann, E. A. J. 226 n.36,

242 nn.33, 34, 243 n.4, 249, 257
Houlahan, Mark xv, 239 n.3, 255
Howard, Jean E. 64, 103, 236 n.17, 252
Howard, Leslie (Romeo; *Romeo and Juliet*; 1936) ix, 43, 48, 85
Howard's End (Film, dir. James Ivory, 1992) 119
Hull, Suzanne W. 223 n.11
Hunter, Ian (Theseus; *A Midsummer Night's Dream*, 1935) 4
Hussey, Olivia (Juliet; *Romeo and Juliet*, 1968) ix, 53, 67
Hyman, Stanley Edgar 183–8, 244 n.6, 252
hyper-masculine 2, 62

Iago (character, *Othello*) viii, xxvi, 181, 183–9, 208–11, 218–19, 243, 244 nn.6, 12, 14, 15, 252, 256
Iago (Kenneth Branagh; *Othello*, 1995) xi, xxvi–xxvii, 202–8
Iago (Micheál MacLiammóir; *Othello*, 1952) xi, xxvi–xxvii, 190, 193–201
iconography 192, 196
idealizing incorporation 62
identification 14, 54, 60, 63, 68
identity 34, 51, 57, 63, 79, 87, 111–12, 116, 126, 132, 140, 186, 192, 195, 203, 207, 216, 236 n.9, 250
Iliad, The 117

Illyria/n xi, 91–3, 97–8, 166–71, 173, 218
impossible penetration 69
impotence 192, 201
Indian king (character, *A Midsummer Night's Dream*) 12, 14
Indian prince (character, *A Midsummer Night's Dream*) 12, 226 n.36
infidelity 209
ingle 23
Inns of Court 90
institution of marriage 214
international youth movement 55
interpolation 92, 177
intertextually 18, 84
intimate/ly 20, 56, 71, 78, 95, 97–8, 101–2, 116–17, 140–1, 144–5, 165, 167, 182, 189, 198, 204–6, 214
Introduction (*Twelfth Night*, 1996; screenplay) 160, 241 n.22
Irons, Jeremy (*The Merchant of Venice*, 2004) x–xi, 139, 148, 150–1, 160
Irwin, Bill (Snout; *A Midsummer Night's Dream*, 1999) 120
Italy 119, 231 n.35

Jackson, Russell xviii, 2, 47–9, 52, 221 n.3, 222 n.2, 225 n.25, 231 nn.24, 35, 252
Jacobean 54, 115, 149, 155, 182
Jacques (character, *As You Like It*) 125

INDEX

Jarman, Derek xix–xxi, 221 n.7, 250
Jbara, Gregory (Snug; *A Midsummer Night's Dream*, 1999) 120
Jennings, Talbot 42
Jensen, Michael P. 26–7, 228 nn.60, 63, 252
Jews 138
jockstrap 65
Jorgens, Jack J. 2, 38–9, 70, 223 n.5, 229 n.80, 234 n.79, 252
Jory, Victor (Oberon; *A Midsummer Night's Dream*, 1935) 16
Jove 18
joyful 174
Juliet (character, *Romeo and Juliet*) 43, 44, 68–9, 76–7, 82, 85, 104, 114, 117–18, 131, 215–17
Juliet (Norma Shearer; *Romeo and Juliet*, 1936) 46, 72, 85
Juliet (Olivia Hussey; *Romeo and Juliet*, 1968) ix, 67–70, 216
Juliet/Glenn (Matt Doyle; *Private Romeo*, 2011) ix–x, 77–83, 219
jump-cuts 191
Jun, Joon-Taek xix

Kahn, Coppélia 140, 240 nn.9, 10, 249, 252–3
Katherina 124–5
Kehler, Dorothea 226 nn.42, 44, 251, 253
Kemp-Welch, Joan 224 n.12

King Charles I 51
King Henry VIII 22, 65
King James I 51, 97
King John (Film), BMBC, 1899 xvii–xviii, 221 n.2
King Lear (character, *King Lear*) 83
King Lear (Play) 83
Kingsley, Ben (Feste; *Twelfth Night*, 1996) 101, 161, 175
Kinney, Arthur F. 224 n.17, 250
Kleinberg, Seymour 146, 176, 241 n.15, 253
Kline, Kevin (Bottom/Pyramus; *A Midsummer Night's Dream*, 1999) x, 119, 128, 132
knight in shining armor 172
Ko, Yu Jin 171, 242 n.32, 253
Kolb, Bobby 225 n.36
Korngold, Erich Wolfgang 26
Kott, Jan 21, 26, 226 n.44, 228 n.61, 253
Kristeva, Julia 15

Lady Macbeth (character, *Macbeth*) 4, 124, 223 n.10
Lamont, Claire 226 n.36
'Law in England, The, 1290–1885' 226 n.47
Leggatt, Alexander 238 n.47, 249
Lehmann, Courtney 42–3, 52, 107, 230 n.5, 237 n.29, 253
leopards 21
Lerner, Daniel 209, 246 n.48
Levine, Laura 253

Levy, Emanuel 45–7, 230 n.15, 231 n.22, 253
Lewis, Cynthia 167, 242 n.28, 253
lieutenant 188–9, 193, 199, 202–3, 205, 218
lions 21
little death 72
Little, Jr., Arthur L. xiii, 27, 139–40, 146, 178, 187–8, 228 n.64, 240 n.7, 243 n.41, 244 n.19, 253–4
Livingstone, Sid (Captain; *Twelfth Night*, 1996) 91
Lobrutto, Vincent xx
Lodovico (Michael Sheen; *Othello*, 1995) 207
Loehlin, James N. 107, 113, 237 n.28, 254
Loncraine, Richard xx–xxi
London xvii, xix, 41, 90, 131, 138, 171, 181
Lorenzo (Charlie Cox; *The Merchant of Venice*, 2004) 142, 153
Louise, Anita (Titania; *A Midsummer Night's Dream*, 1935) 14
Luhrmann, Baz (dir. *William Shakespeare's Romeo + Juliet*, 1996) vii, x, xviii–xix, 89–90, 106–18, 132–3, 217, 219, 235, 237 nn.22, 25, 238 n.42, 255–6
lynxes 21
Lysander (character, *A Midsummer Night's Dream*) 240 n.14

Lysander (Dick Powell; *A Midsummer Night's Dream*; 1935) ix, xxiii, 10, 31–6
Lysander (Dominic West; *A Midsummer Night's Dream*, 1999) 127, 130

Macbeth (dir. Orson Welles, 1948) 198
Macbeth (Play) 223 n.10, 257
Mackintosh, Stephen (Sebastian; *Twelfth Night*, 1996) xi, 92, 160, 164, 168
MacLiammóir, Micheál (Iago; *Othello*, 1952) xi, 193–7, 200, 211, 245 n.35, 254
MacQueen, Scott 2, 223 nn.4, 6, 225 nn.25, 36, 254
Magnus, Laury xxi, 142, 148, 240 n.11, 241 n.16, 254
Magro, Maria F. xxi, 95, 176, 236 n.10, 242 n.37, 254
male arousal 204
male body 47, 49, 86
male friendship/s 142, 155, 177, 227 n.54, 240 n.10, 241, 250, 252
male same-sex kiss 103
male spectator/s/ship 58, 62, 232 n.52, 251
male-male desire 186
Maloney, Michael (Roderigo; *Othello*, 1995) 202
Malvolio (character, *Twelfth Night*) 125, 242 n.31
Malvolio (Nigel Hawthorne; *Twelfth Night*, 1996) 175

manicured nails 192–3
Maria (Imelda Staunton; *Twelfth Night*, 1996) 175
marriage/s vii, ix, xxii, xxvi, 1, 3, 6, 8, 9, 11, 21, 27–8, 30, 65, 67–8, 82–3, 90, 117, 136, 138, 140, 146, 152, 154–5, 159, 176, 178, 182, 184, 202, 204, 206, 210, 214, 218, 222, 228 n.64, 236 n.8, 240 n.7, 243 n.41, 253, 256
married same-sex couple 82
Marshall, Kris (Graziano; *The Merchant of Venice*, 2004) 142
masculinity vii, xxii, 1, 3, 14, 17, 30, 32, 35–6, 51, 60, 63–7, 76, 114, 117–18, 130, 193–4, 222, 236 n.18, 237 n.20, 257
matrimony 6, 27, 95, 154, 184, 198
Matz, Robert 187–9, 244 n.23, 254
Maurice (Film, dir. James Ivory, 1987) 119
Mazell, Kym 110
McEnery, John (Mercutio; *Romeo and Juliet*, 1968) 70
McGilligan, Patrick 44–7, 230 n.11, 231 nn.20, 23, 254
McKellen, Ian xx–xxi, 240 n.5
McKinley Military Academy 74, 77, 81–2
McRuer, Robert xx
Mediterranean 72, 191

melancholy xxvi, 66, 97, 101, 146, 160, 174, 176
Mendelssohn, Felix 27, 38, 119
Menon, Madhavi xix–xxi, 3, 223 nn.7, 9, 225 n.31, 226 n.40, 240 n.7, 251, 253–4, 256
mercenary 171
Merchant of Venice, The (Play) xv, xxii, 125, 135, 160, 236 n.16, 239 n.1, 240 nn.6, 7, 10, 241 n.15, 253, 255–8
'*Merchant of Venice, The*: Shakespeare through the Lens' 150, 241 n.18, 258
Mercutio (character, *Romeo and Juliet*) 71, 231 n.32, 234 n.80, 256
Mercutio (Harold Perrineau; *Romeo + Juliet*, 1996) x, xxiv–xxv, 107–18, 132, 217
Mercutio (John Barrymore; *Romeo and Juliet*; 1936) ix, xxiii, 43, 48–52, 215
Mercutio (John McEnery; *Romeo and Juliet*, 1968) 67, 70–2, 86, 109
Merry Wives of Windsor, The 125
Messaline 161, 163, 177
Messel, Oliver 46, 85, 215
Metro-Goldwyn-Mayer (MGM) 42
Middle Temple 90
Midsummer Night's Dream (Film, A dir. Max Reinhardt and William Dieterle, 1935) vii, ix,

xxii, 1, 5, 34, 213, 222,
222 n.1, 249, 252–5,
257–8
*Midsummer Night's Dream,
A* (Play) xxii, 27, 224
nn.13, 15, 16, 17, 225
nn.27, 28, 32, 34, 226
nn.36, 42, 43, 44, 227
nn.49, 57, 228 nn.60,
61, 63, 65, 66, 67, 69,
238 nn.45, 46, 250–2
minstrels 116
mirthful 174
mise-en-scene xxvi, 2, 74
misogynistic/y 8, 12, 58, 182,
192, 215
moneylender 156, 159
monkeys 21
monstrous birth 187
montage xxvi, 92, 108, 177,
179
Monte Athena 119–20, 131
Montrose, Louis Adrian 11,
17–19, 225 n.27, 254
Moonlight and Night (*A
Midsummer Night's
Dream*, 1935) 38–9
Moor/ish 186, 190, 198
Moore, Helen 221 n.9, 254
moral/ists/s xvii, 22, 114, 138,
214, 215
morning-after-the-wedding-
night/morning after 56,
216
Morning's love 18
Morocco 191
Moshinsky, Elijah 123, 224
n.12
'Most Lamentable Comedy and
Cruel Death of Pyramus
and Thisbe, The' 2, 10,
120, 127, 128–9, 131
Motion Picture Association of
America (MPAA) 214
Motion Picture Producers and
Distributors of America
(MPPDA) 214
Motion Picture Production
Code 214
motiveless malignancy 218
Mrs. Doubtfire (Film, dir. Chris
Columbus, 1993) 110
MTV (Music Television) 106,
110
Muir, Jean (Helena; *A
Midsummer Night's
Dream*, 1935) 32
Muir, Kenneth 223 n.10, 257
Mulvey, Laura 57–61, 66, 69,
216, 232 n.48, 255
murderous 38, 202
music/al/s xxiii, 2, 26, 43, 46,
66, 73, 81, 85, 92, 101,
110, 190, 192–3, 200,
215
My Own Private Idaho (Film,
dir. Gus Van Sant, 1991)
xix–xxi

narrative cinema 59, 61, 69,
232 n.48, 255
national traditions 208
necrophilia 201
Nelson, Tim Blake (dir. '*O*',
2001) 182
New Historicism/t 18, 208
New York City 73, 197, 216
New York Times, The 55, 232
n.39, 249
Noble, Adrian 123–4, 130

non-gay 111
non-genital 13
non-heteronormative 100, 126, 137, 187, 193
non-transvestite 111
normal/ally/ity/ized xxii, 8, 21, 30, 34, 38, 85–7, 126, 129, 148, 187–8, 196
Norton Shakespeare, The 18, 226 n.43, 252
Numrich, Seth (Sam Singleton/Romeo; *Private Romeo*, 2011) ix–x, 77, 80, 83
Nurse (character, *Romeo and Juliet*) 76
Nuttall, A. D. 228 n.61, 255

Oberon (character, *A Midsummer Night's Dream*) xxiii, 12–14, 17–21, 29–30
Oberon (Victor Jory; *A Midsummer Night's Dream*, 1935) 12, 14, 16–21, 27–8, 30–3, 38–9
obscenity 23, 214
OED (*Oxford English Dictionary*) 13, 115, 240 n.14
Oedipal 14, 38, 62
Old Testament 22
Oliphant 171, 242 n.32
Olivier, Laurence xviii
O'Loughlin, Katrina xv, 239 n.3, 255
ontological/ly 60, 75
Orgel, Stephen 35, 36, 43, 52, 228 n.70, 230 n.8, 255
O'Rourke, James 222 n.9

O'Shea, Milo (Friar Laurence; *Romeo and Juliet*, 1968) 67
Otello (Verdi), 1986 54
Othello (character, *Othello*) 174, 183, 185, 209, 210, 218, 244 n.14
Othello (Film, dir. Oliver Parker, 1995) viii, xi, xxvi–xxvii, 181–2, 186–9, 202–3, 205–8, 210–11, 218–19, 243, 245 n.44, 255
Othello (Film, dir. Orson Welles, 1952) viii, xi, xxvi, 181–2, 190–1, 193–202, 210, 218–19, 243, 245 nn.26, 35, 37, 254–5
Othello (Laurence Fishburne; *Othello*, 1995) xi, 202–8
Othello (Orson Welles; *Othello*, 1952) 191–9
Othello (Play) xxii, xxvi, 174, 181–3, 185–9, 209, 218–19, 242 nn.33, 34, 243 nn.2, 4, 244 nn.19, 23, 254, 256–7
Other/s 112, 125, 184, 238 n.47, 249
Overture to *A Midsummer Night's Dream* 119
Ovid/ian 18, 224n.16, 226 n.46, 258

P/platonic 13, 62, 136, 142, 145, 147, 201, 203, 215
pacifism 55, 117
Pacino, Al (Shylock; *The Merchant of Venice*, 2004) 138

page 95, 100
palazzo 139, 178
parent–child eroticism xxiii
Paris is Burning (Film, dir.
    Jennie Livingston, 1990)
    107
Parisi, Heather Elizabeth
    (Bottom's Wife; *A
    Midsummer Night's
    Dream*, 1999) 119
Park, William 190, 245 n.28,
    255
Parker, Nathaniel (Cassio;
    Othello, 1995) 202
Parker, Oliver (dir. *Othello*,
    1995) viii, xi, xxvi–xxvii,
    181–2, 189, 202–3,
    205–8, 211, 218–19,
    243, 245 n.44, 255
passive/ly 58, 60, 62, 63, 66,
    179
passive-aggressive 195
Paster, Gail Kern 26, 228 n.62,
    255
pathic 23
patriarchal xxiii, 4–5, 11, 17,
    28–9, 31, 56, 58–9, 63,
    69, 71, 78, 82, 86, 138,
    184, 186, 216
Patricia, Anthony Guy iii–iv,
    xxi, 239 n.3, 255
Patricia, Margaret v, xiii
Patricia, Richard v, xiii
PCA (Production Code
    Administration) 213,
    214, 246 n.1
Pearce, Craig 115, 238 n.42,
    255
penetrability 63
penetrated 201

penetration 63, 69, 72, 199,
    209
penis/es 36, 49, 61, 63, 68, 204
Pequigney, Joseph xix, 135–8,
    163, 166, 170, 176, 239
    nn.1, 2, 242 nn.25, 30,
    243 n.39, 255
performative acts 111
perfume 192–3, 221 n.9, 255
Perrineau, Harold (Mercutio;
    Romeo + Juliet, 1996)
    x, 107, 108, 113, 115,
    118
Perry, Curtis 98, 236 n.15,
    256
perverse/sion/sity/ed 26–7, 109,
    187, 192, 194, 199, 201,
    214
Peter Quince (Roger Rees;
    *William Shakespeare's
    A Midsummer Night's
    Dream*, 1999) x, xxv,
    120–1, 123
Pfeiffer, Michelle (Titania;
    *William Shakespeare's
    A Midsummer Night's
    Dream*, 1999) 119
Phaedra 11, 225 n.30
phallic 60, 62–3, 66–7
phallocentric 63, 69, 82
phallus 21, 201
Philostrate (John Sessions;
    *William Shakespeare's
    A Midsummer Night's
    Dream*, 1999) 123
physical beauty 174
play-within-a-film xxv, 130,
    131
play-within-a-play 119
poison 83, 185, 198

pop culture 193
Porter, Joseph A. 52, 55, 71, 109, 231 n.32, 234 n.80, 256
Portia (Lynn Collins; *The Merchant of Venice*, 2004) xxvi, 145–7, 149, 151–5, 157–9, 177–9, 218
post-classical 6
postcolonial/ism 182–3
postmodern xix, 13, 106
Potter, Lois 181, 195–7, 201, 224 n.17, 243 n.2, 245 n.37, 250, 256
Powell, Dick (Lysander; *A Midsummer Night's Dream*; 1935) ix, 32, 34
predatory 171
premature climax 69
presentism/ist xv, xxii, 19, 222 n.9, 223 n.10, 228 n.64, 239 n.3, 243 n.41, 253, 255
Prince Escalus (character, *Romeo and Juliet*) 108
Private Romeo (Film, dir. Alan Brown, 2011) ix–x, xxiv, 42, 73–8, 80–4, 87, 213, 219, 234 n.83, 256
profanity 214
projection 68
prologue (*Twelfth Night*, dir. Trevor Nunn, 1996) 160, 163, 166, 177, 190
promotion (*Othello*) 193, 202–3
proscriptive heteronormativity xxi, 217
psychoanalysis xix, 38
psychoanalytic theory 13, 58

psychological 19, 30, 45, 60, 124, 140
psychopath(s) 185
Puck (Mickey Rooney; *A Midsummer Night's Dream*, 1935) 2, 12, 14, 18, 20, 21, 27, 33, 222 n.2, 223 n.3
purge 187
Puritans 76
purse 144, 156, 158, 170–1, 173, 242 n.29
Put Money In Thy Purse 196, 245 n.35, 254

Queen Elizabeth I 22
Queen Mab 70–1, 107
Queen Mary 22
queer audience/s 8, 69, 103, 175, 177, 197
queer character 218
queer desire/s xxvii, 18, 178
queer marriage 27, 178, 228 n.64, 240 n.7, 243 n.41, 253
queer primal scene 27
queer problematics vii, 1, 222
queer self-fashioning xxii, xxvi, 181, 183, 210, 243
queer subversion 219
queer theory xxi
queer/ed/er/est/ly/s vii–viii, xvii, xix–xxvii, 1, 3, 8, 10–13, 16, 18–21, 24, 27, 30–1, 34, 37, 41–2, 44, 46–7, 49, 52–3, 55–6, 59, 61–2, 65–72, 75, 78–9, 82, 85–6, 90–1, 101, 103–5, 108, 111–13, 116, 119, 126,

132, 137, 139, 149, 151, 157, 160, 166, 173, 175–9, 181, 183, 186–7, 189, 199, 201–3, 205, 207, 209–11, 215–19, 221, 222 n.9, 223 nn.7, 9, 225 n.25, 226 n.35, 228 n.64, 229, 230 n.10, 237 n.33, 240 n.7, 243 n.41, 245 n.39, 249–51, 253–4
queer-allied 52, 105, 197
queering i–iii, viii, xv, xxi, 2, 47, 70, 73, 84, 100, 107, 177, 179, 198, 213, 219–20, 239 n.3, 241 n.17, 246 n.1, 247 n.1, 250, 255–6
queerness xxi, xxiii, 3, 8–9, 12, 18, 28, 38, 43–4, 51–2, 64, 74, 81, 85, 87, 182–3, 188–91, 193–5, 197, 209, 211, 215, 218–19, 223 n.9, 226 n.35, 227 n.54, 247 n.1

R/romance xviii, 4, 55, 82, 84–5, 87, 95, 165, 230, 250
race 106, 182, 211, 221 n.9, 237 n.25, 254, 256
Rackin, Phyllis 64, 93, 236 n.8, 256
Radel, Nicholas F. 106, 107, 109, 114, 117, 237 n.25, 237 nn.30, 38, 238 n.44, 256
Radford, Michael (dir. *William Shakespeare's The Merchant of Venice*, 2004) viii, x–xi, xxi, xxv–xxvi, 135, 137–45, 148–51, 154–5, 159–60, 177–9, 217–19, 239, 239 n.4, 240 n.11, 241 n.16, 241 n.18, 254, 256, 258
Rambuss, Richard 12, 30, 225 n.31, 228 n.68, 256
Rathbone, Basil (Tybalt; *Romeo and Juliet*; 1936) ix, 43, 48
Rees, Roger (Peter Quince; *A Midsummer Night's Dream*, 1999) x, 120–1
refashioning 87
Reinhardt, Max (dir. *A Midsummer Night's Dream*, 1935) vii, ix, xxii–xxiii, 1–5, 8–12, 14–16, 18–21, 23–5, 27–30, 32–9, 42, 123–5, 130–1, 211, 213, 215, 219, 222 n.1, 224 nn.12, 15, 25, 226 n.36, 227 n.59, 249, 254
religious doctrines 208
Renaissance 3, 6, 21–2, 35, 37, 54, 61, 65, 119, 124, 142, 186, 208, 227 n.49, 227 nn.52, 54, 236 n.8, 240 n.9, 241 n.17, 244 n.23, 246 n.47, 249–50, 252–4, 256, 258
Renaissance Self-Fashioning: From More to Shakespeare 207
repellant subjects 214
representational strategy xxvii, 218

requited/unrequited 75, 97, 101, 117, 136, 176, 199, 203
resistance 4, 8–10, 225 n.25
rich golden shaft 100
Rich, Adrienne 8, 224 n.21, 256
Richard III (Film, dir. Richard Loncraine, 1995) xx, xxi
Robin Starveling (Max Wright; *William Shakespeare's A Midsummer Night's Dream*, 1999) 120
Rockwell, Sam (Francis Flute/Thisbe; *William Shakespeare's A Midsummer Night's Dream*, x, 120–1, 128–9, 131–2
Roderigo (character, *Othello*) 209
Roderigo (Michael Maloney; *Othello*, 1995) 202, 204–5
Roderigo (Robert Coote; *Othello*, 1952) xi, 194–5, 197–8, 200–1
Román, David xix
romantic/ally vii, 13, 21, 36, 44–5, 51–2, 66, 73, 77, 90, 96, 98, 103, 109, 112–13, 132, 135–7, 142, 145–6, 148–9, 151, 165–6, 169–70, 172, 178, 195, 197, 228 n.64, 234 n.89, 239, 243 n.41, 253
Romeo (character, *Romeo and Juliet*) 104
Romeo (Leonard Whiting; *Romeo and Juliet*; 1936) ix, xxiv, 56–7, 61, 66–72, 81, 86, 215–16
Romeo (Leonardo DiCaprio; *Romeo + Juliet*, 1996) x, xxiv, 107–10, 113–14, 116–18, 217
Romeo (Leslie Howard; *Romeo and Juliet*; 1936) ix, 43–4, 46, 48
Romeo (Seth Numrich; *Private Romeo*; 2011) ix–x, 76, 77, 78, 79, 80, 81, 82, 83
Romeo and Juliet (Film, dir. Franco Zeffirelli, 1968) ix, xx–xxi, xxiii, xxiv, 42, 53–7, 59, 61–2, 64, 66–8, 70, 72, 74, 86, 106–7, 109, 216, 231 nn.35, 37, 232 n.39, 249, 251, 256
Romeo and Juliet (Film, dir. George Cukor, 1936) ix, xxiii–xxiv, 42–53, 73–4, 85, 106–7, 211, 215, 219, 230 n.3, 256
Romeo and Juliet (Play) vii, xxii, xxiv, 41–2, 65, 68–9, 73–6, 78–85, 87, 106, 109, 115–16, 219, 229, 230 nn.5, 9, 233 n.72, 237 nn.28, 29, 40, 250, 253–5, 257
Room With a View, A (Film, dir. James Ivory, 1985) 119
Rooney, Mickey (Puck; *A Midsummer Night's Dream*, 1935) 2, 14, 222 n.2, 223 n.3

Rothwell, Kenneth S. 41–2, 52, 54, 90, 92, 96, 106–7, 113, 138, 167, 174, 182, 190, 221 n.2, 229 n.1, 231 n.36, 235 nn.2, 6, 236 n.12, 237 nn.23, 26, 239 n.5, 242 nn.27, 35, 243 n.5, 245 n.27, 256
royal favorite/s 98
Rude Mechanicals 119
Russo, Vito 246 n.1

sacrifice/s 68, 145, 157, 159, 162
sadistic/ally 21, 159
Salerio (John Sessions; *The Merchant of Venice*, 2004) 139, 141, 149, 153
Sam Singleton/Romeo (Seth Numrich; *Private Romeo*, 2011) ix–x, 76, 77, 78, 79, 80, 81, 82, 83
same-sex desire/s 62, 82, 84
same-sex friendship 140
same-sex intimacy 104
Saunders, Ben 186–8, 244 nn.12, 14, 15, 256
Scarlet Letter, The (Novel) 4
Schalkwyk, David 96–7, 105, 165, 236 n.13, 237 n.21, 242 n.26, 257
scopophilia 58, 224 n.13, 252
screwball comedy 37
Sebastian (character, *Twelfth Night*) xxv, 136–7, 163, 165–7, 171, 176–7, 242 n.29

Sebastian (Stephen Mackintosh; *Twelfth Night*, 1996) xi, xxv, xxvi, 92–3, 137, 160–77, 217–18, 242 n.29
Sedgwick, Eve Kosofsky xix, 74, 142, 234 n.85, 257
Seneca 225 n.30
serpent 4, 10
servant/s x, 90, 95–6, 100–4, 165
service 14, 76, 92, 96–7, 165, 169, 185, 190, 203, 206, 236 n.13, 237 n.21, 242 n.26, 257
Sessions, John (Philostrate; *William Shakespeare's A Midsummer Night's Dream*, 1999; Salerio; *William Shakespeare's The Merchant of Venice*, 2004) 123, 139
sex object/s 60, 64, 86
sex perversion 214
sex/es/iness/y xx–xxi, xxv, 3, 17–19, 24, 31, 35, 47, 52, 56, 68–9, 72, 74, 75, 81–2, 85–6, 89, 94, 106, 111–12, 115, 126, 132, 137, 171, 184, 188, 201, 209–10, 214, 217, 241 n.14
sexologist 36
sexual dissidence 53
sexual identity 51, 79, 87, 126, 192, 195
sexual intercourse 96, 101
sexual inversion 36
sexual liberation 55
sexual objectification 59

Sexual Revolution 55, 73, 216
sexual/ity/ized/ly xv, xix–xxii,
xxvi, 12–13, 15, 19,
21, 23–6, 28, 30, 36,
38, 52, 54–5, 57–8, 61,
63, 65–6, 72, 74, 81,
85, 103, 106, 109, 111,
113–14, 116, 126, 137,
142, 144, 148, 151, 153,
161, 166–7, 172, 182–8,
192, 194, 196–201,
203–5, 209–11, 215–16,
218, 221 n.7, 222 n.9,
223 n.10, 226 n.39,
227 n.56, 226 n.64,
231 n.34, 232 n.37,
233 n.73, 234 n.90, 236
nn.10, 16, 237 n.25,
239 nn.1, 3, 240 n.14,
241 n.20, 242 n.37, 243
nn.39, 41, 245 n.41,
250–8
Shakespeare film/s i, iii, vii–viii,
xv, xvii–xviii, xix–xxiii,
xxvii, 2, 64, 70, 84–7,
90–1, 119, 132–3, 137,
191, 211, 213, 217,
219–21, 222 n.2, 225
n.25, 226 n.36, 231
nn.24, 35, 241 n.41,
246, 252
Shakespeare in Love (Film, dir.
John Madden, 1998) xxi
Shakespeare, William vii, x–xi,
xv, xvii–xxv, 1–3, 8–12,
18–19, 21, 23, 25–31,
37–8, 41–3, 46–7, 51,
53–6, 65, 68, 71, 73,
75–83, 85, 87, 89–91,
95–7, 99, 101, 103,
106–8, 110, 114–15,
117–21, 125, 128, 131,
136–45, 148–50, 155,
160–1, 163, 165–6, 169,
171–2, 174–5, 177–9,
181–3, 190–1, 193–5,
198–9, 202–5, 207–9,
211, 215, 217–21, 221
nn.7, 8, 222 n.9, 223
nn.4, 9, 10, 225 n.31,
226 nn.36, 37, 44, 228
nn.64, 66, 68, 70, 229
nn.77, 78, 229, 230 n.5,
230 nn.8, 9, 231 nn.32,
35, 232 n.56, 233 n.70,
234 nn.79, 80, 235, 235
n.3, 236 nn.7, 10, 11,
13, 16, 18, 237 nn.20,
21, 25, 28, 29, 238
nn.42, 45, 54, 55, 239
n.1, 239 n.3, 239 n.4,
240 nn.7, 9, 10, 14, 241
nn.18, 19, 20, 21, 242
nn.24, 26, 27, 28, 32,
36, 243 nn.37, 39, 40,
41, 42, 245 nn.37, 45,
249–58
Shearer, Norma (Juliet; *Romeo
and Juliet*, 1936) 43, 85
Sheen, Michael (Lodovico;
Othello, 1995) 207
She's the Man (Film, dir. Andy
Fickman, 2006) 90
shipwreck 91, 170
shot/reverse shot technique
198–9, 206
Shylock (Al Pacino; *The
Merchant of Venice*,
2004) 146, 152, 154–7,
159

Shylock (character, *The Merchant of Venice*) 125
sick 81, 187, 211
simulacrum 58
sin/ner 78–81, 210
Sinfield, Alan 100, 154, 176–7, 188, 236 n.17, 241 n.20, 243 n.39, 257
Sir Andrew Aguecheek (Richard E. Grant; *Twelfth Night*, 1996) 172–3
Sir Toby Belch (Mel Smith; *Twelfth Night*, 1996) 172–3, 175
Sir Walter Raleigh 51
Skinner, Keith (Balthazar; *Romeo and Juliet*, 1968) 57
slavery 182
Smith, Beatrice-Welles 190
Smith, Bruce R. 104, 177, 206, 223 n.10, 227 n.51, 236 n.18, 237 n.20, 243 n.40, 245 n.45, 257
Smith, Mel (Sir Toby Belch; *Twelfth Night*, 1996) 172
snake ix, 4–6
Snout (Bill Irwin; *William Shakespeare's A Midsummer Night's Dream*, 1999) 120, 122, 123
Snug (Gregory Jbara; *William Shakespeare's A Midsummer Night's Dream*, 1999) 120
social customs 208
sodomite 23, 24
sodomy vii, xxii–xxiii, 1, 3, 24, 28, 116, 221 n.9, 222, 227 n.51, 234 n.90, 244 n.23, 254–5
Solanio (Gregor Fisher; *The Merchant of Venice*, 2004) 139, 141, 149
Sonnet 72 'O, lest the world should task you to recite' 153
spangled bra 107
spectatorial fantasmatic 63
Staunton, Imelda (Maria; *Twelfth Night*, 1996) 175
steamer 161–2
Steinbach, Ronald D. 50–1, 231 n.30, 257
Stephens, Toby (Duke Orsino; *Twelfth Night*, 1996) iv, x, 92–3, 102, 175
stereotype/s 36, 91, 113, 151, 178, 185, 196
sterility 192
Stewart, Patrick 240 n.5
Stonewall Riots 51, 73, 197, 216
straight 19, 30, 52, 54, 57, 59, 60, 62, 65, 69, 85–7, 109, 111–12, 114, 126, 151, 171, 187, 193, 197, 216
straight man 113
straight-acting 113
straighter-than-straight 194
straightest vii, 41, 82, 87, 229
straightgeist xix
straightjacket xx, 8
strangle 185
strikingly homosexual wish 185, 187
Stubbs, Imogen (Viola/Cesario;

Twelfth Night, 1996) iv, x, 91, 93–5, 102, 175
sublimated 185, 199, 244 n.14
sublimation 201, 211
subversion 62–3, 219, 236 n.9, 250
subversive/ly xx, 10, 62, 112
Summers, Joseph H. 29, 228 n.66, 258
suppressed 118
suppression 53
Sycamore Grove Theatre 117

Taming of the Shrew, The (Film, dir. Franco Zeffirelli, 1967) 53
Taming of the Shrew, The (Play) 125
Tate, Nahum 83
Taylor, A. B. 5, 21, 224 n.16, 226 n.46, 258
Taylor, Elizabeth 53
Taymor, Julie xviii
Tchaikovsky 42–3, 46, 85, 215
Teasdale, Verree (Hippolyta; *A Midsummer Night's Dream*; 1935) ix, 4–5
Tempest, The (Film, dir. Derek Jarman, 1979) xix–xxi
Tempest, The (Play) 125
testicles 61
textual criticism xxv, 14
Thalberg, Irving 43
Theilade, Nina (Fairy in Titania's Service; *A Midsummer Night's Dream*, 1935) 14
theological 23
Theseus (character, *A Midsummer Night's Dream*) 6, 9, 11, 19, 225 nn.28, 30, 252
Theseus (David Strathairn; *A Midsummer Night's Dream*, 1999) 120
Theseus (Ian Hunter; *A Midsummer Night's Dream*, 1935) xxiii, 3–11, 16, 19, 31–2, 39, 225 n.25, 227 n.59
Thisby 131–2
tights ix, 31, 48–9, 57, 61, 66, 193
Titania (Anita Louise; *A Midsummer Night's Dream*, 1935) xxiii, 12–17, 19–21, 23, 25–31, 37–9, 227 n.59
Titania (character, *A Midsummer Night's Dream*) 12–14, 17–18, 20–1, 23, 25–31, 38–9, 226 n.44, 228 n.61, 253
Titanic (Film, dir. James Cameron, 1997) 92
Titus Andronicus (Play) 243 n.1
To Wong Foo, Thanks For Everything, Julie Newmar (Film, dir. Beeban Kidron, 1995) 110
to-be-looked-at-ness 58–9
transgression/s 21, 29, 114, 188, 191
transgressive 4, 23, 49, 62, 130, 188
transvestite xxv, 110–13, 130
Traub, Valerie 136–7, 239 n.1, 258

traumatic experience 170
Tree, Herbert Beerbohm (King John; *King John,* 1899) xvii
Tucci, Stanley (Puck; *William Shakespeare's A Midsummer Night's Dream,* 1999) 119
Tulchin, Alan A. 207, 246 n.46
Turks 182
Tuscan/y 119, 131
Twelfth Night (Film, dir. Trevor Nunn, 1996) iv, vii–viii, x–xi, xxi, xxiv–xxvi, 89–91, 93–100, 102–5, 126, 132–3, 135, 137–8, 160, 162–4, 166–7, 169–72, 174–7, 217–18, 235, 235 n.5, 236 nn.7, 10, 239, 241 nn.21, 22, 23, 242 n.24, 243 n.37, 254–5, 258
Twelfth Night (Play) xxii, 90–1, 95, 97–8, 103, 125, 135–7, 160, 165–9, 171, 174–7, 217–18, 235 nn.1, 5, 236 n.7, 239 n.1, 241 n.23, 242 nn.24, 32, 251, 256–7
Two Antonios, The 135–7, 217–18, 239 nn.1, 2, 242 nn.25, 30, 243 n.39, 255
Tybalt (Basil Rathbone; *Romeo and Juliet*; 1936) ix, 43, 48–9, 215
Tybalt (John Leguizamo; *Romeo + Juliet,* 1996) 115–17

Tybalt (Michael York; *Romeo and Juliet*; 1968) ix, 57, 61–2, 64–7, 70–2, 86

ugly 174, 199
ultimate horror 194
unclimactic fumble 68–9
Ungerer, Gustave 171, 242 nn.31, 32
unrequited 75, 97, 101, 117, 199, 203
unsexing 4
usury 138, 160

vagina 36, 68
Van Sant, Gus xix–xxi
Van Watson, William xx, 55, 66, 216, 232 n.56, 233 n.70, 258
Varnado, Christine 68, 82, 233 n.73, 258
Venetian Senate 210
Venetians 182
Venice 146–7, 149, 152–5, 159, 178–9, 181, 191, 202
Verona ix, 48, 52, 61
Verona Beach 114, 116
vicious 174
Victorian xiv, 119, 131
Viola/Cesario (character, *Twelfth Night*) 93, 95, 103, 136
Viola/Cesario (Imogen Stubbs; *Twelfth Night,* 1996) iv, x, xxiv, xxvi, 91–6, 99, 102–3, 132, 162–3, 175, 217
visual grammar xxi, 198–200, 245 n.41, 252

visual pleasure 59, 232 n.48, 255
visual representation 14, 108, 203
visual rhetorical 109, 122
visual semiotics 106
Vitagraph 41, 90, 138, 182
voiceover/s 74, 161, 190–1
votaress 12, 15–16, 18, 25, 31
vulgarity 214

Warner Brothers 1, 37, 42, 214, 226 nn.36, 37, 229 n.78, 249
warrior queen 5
wedding ceremony 207
Wedding March 27
Weis, René 115–16, 233 n.72, 237 n.40, 257
Welles-Smith, Beatrice 190
West, Dominic (Lysander; *A Midsummer Night's Dream*, 1999) 127
Western xviii, 4, 17, 19, 25, 31, 73, 81, 110, 113, 122, 126, 182, 184, 202, 206, 219
Western Asia 49
white ewe 188
White, R. S. xv, 239 n.3, 255
Whiting, Leonard (Romeo; *Romeo and Juliet*, 1936) ix, xxiv, 53, 56, 57, 67, 216
Wilde, Oscar 84, 222 n.9, 231 n.34, 251, 255
William Shakespeare's A Midsummer Night's Dream (Film, dir. Michael Hoffman, 1999) vii, x, xxv, 89, 90, 118, 121, 128, 217, 235, 238 nn.45, 54, 252, 258
William Shakespeare's Romeo + Juliet (Film, dir. Baz Luhrmann, 1996) vii, x, xxiv, 89–90, 106–8, 110–11, 115–18, 126, 132–3, 217, 230 n.2, 235, 237 nn.22, 25, 238 n.42, 256
William Shakespeare's The Merchant of Venice (Film, dir. Michael Radford, 2004) x, xi, xxv, 138, 148, 150, 239 n.4, 241 n.18, 256, 258
willing suspension of disbelief 76, 234 n.89
Willson, Jr., Robert F. 38, 229 n.79, 258
witchcraft 173–4
wolves 21
woman warrior 10
Woo, John 106
wrestling 72
Wright, Max (Robin; *A Midsummer Night's Dream*, 1999) 120
Wyrick, Deborah 28, 29, 228 n.65, 258

York, Michael (Tybalt; *Romeo and Juliet*, 1936) ix, 57, 65
Young Hearts Run Free 107, 110
YouTube 73

Zabus, Chantal xix

Zeffirelli, Franco (dir. *Romeo and Juliet*, 1968) ix, xvii, xix–xxi, xxiii–xxiv, 42, 53–7, 59, 61–2, 64–74, 81, 86–7, 106–7, 109, 216, 219, 231 nn.35, 37, 232 nn.39, 46, 56, 233 n.70, 249, 251, 256, 258

www.ingramcontent.com/pod-product-compliance
Ingram Content Group UK Ltd.
Pitfield, Milton Keynes, MK11 3LW, UK
UKHW021829220426
470268UK00007B/67